FINDING
THE
LESBIANS

FINDING
THE
LESBIANS

———————•———————

Personal Accounts From Around The World

Edited by
Julia Penelope & Sarah Valentine

With a foreword by Alix Dobkin

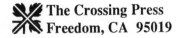 The Crossing Press
Freedom, CA 95019

We are grateful to the following authors and journals for permission to reprint previously published stories:

"Baby Fingers," © 1988 by Candis J. Graham. First published in *Breaking the Silence* 6, 2 (March 1988).

"From Kamp Girls to Political Dykes: Finding the Others through Thirty-Odd Years as a Lesbian from Aotearoa/New Zealand," © 1985 by Alison J. Laurie. First published in *Broadsheet*, issues 134 and 135, November and December, 1985.

"Birth Song," © 1988 by J.L. Williams. First published in *Common Lives/Lesbian Lives* 28 (Fall, 1988).

Cover illustration and design by Betsy Bayley
Typesetting by Claudia L'Amoreaux

Printed in the U.S.A.

Library of Congress Cataloging-in-Publication Data

Finding the lesbians : personal accounts from around the world /
    edited by Julia Penelope and Sarah Valentine.
        p.   cm.
    ISBN 0-89594-427-8 — ISBN 0-89594-426-X (pbk.)
    1. Lesbians.   I. Penelope, Julia, 1941-   . II. Valentine,
Sarah, 1959-
HQ75.5.F56   1990
306.76'63—dc20   89-78397
                                                                          CIP

Contents

Foreword

Finding the Lesbians is Good for Us and Good for Women

Most of the feelings and many of the experiences described in this collection are familiar. Well do I remember the longings, traumas and denials of teendom and pre-Lesbianhood. More than a few of the thoughts, questions and revelations of these stories have, at one time or another, been the subject of my attention and the object of my affection: This is familiar ground.

Reflecting back I remember moments when I consciously, if not actively, LOOKED for Lesbians, but mostly my consciousness was elsewhere: in my politics, my music and, in college, my art, intellectual life and the social circles and relationships they generated. I found Lesbians in college, but in some important ways I didn't want to. Too scary. Classic attraction-repulsion. The attraction was the idea of women sharing their full lives. I loved that for some women it was a reality and I secretly treasured the knowledge. I especially loved the Lesbian possibility because I met my first Lesbians while passionately and intensely enmeshed in my first truly Lesbian relationship. We were not "Lesbians," however, because we never spoke of ourselves as such and we never hung out with Lesbians.

Furthermore, we always dated boys (or men), manipulating and trading them between us with a mixture of amusement, indifference, fondness and contempt. But we were never cynical about love or emotional closeness, and NEVER about passion, which we reserved for each other. We loved each other as "people who just happen to be female." While in Lesbian company, I kept a distance, obnoxiously asserting my heterosexuality, clinging to my "visitor" status. Lesbians may have thrilled and excited me but I was not willing to put both feet in their outlaw, alcoholic world. I was not a Lesbian. I just happened to be head over heels in love with another woman who was not a Lesbian either. I felt smug in my ignorance. And safe. I did not look for Lesbians. I intended to stay safe.

The very act of looking for each other transforms us. It signs us on to adventures in strange territory. It obliges us to confront unknowns. Looking for Lesbians is demanding, propelling some of us in mighty bizarre directions and prompting others into some mighty peculiar behavior. Finding the Lesbians is a challenge and a dare. Finding Lesbians means finding our center and our voice. It means plugging into Universal Lesbian Power and the Exclusive Realm of Lesbian Possibility.

Our pursuit leads us across class and culture lines, race and religious lines, lines of all kinds, starting with personal boundaries: "Finding the Lesbians meant first finding myself" (Bev Jo, in "How I Found My Own Kind"). Because Lesbians and Lesbianism are truly everywhere all over the planet, we find ourselves violating traditional national and ethnic borderlines; borders indicating real difference, but drawn in ways to keep us separate, designed to isolate us, keep us in place outside of each other's awareness. Our need pushes us into places we would otherwise miss, introduces us to aspects of life and individuals we might otherwise decline to meet. It demands that we deal and therefore forces us to be strong.

Our search for Lesbians takes us through a variety of emotional as well as cultural landscapes. Our attitudes and approaches reflect a spectrum ranging from Cathy Avila's "I found the Lesbians quite by accident because, you see, I wasn't looking for them" ("NOW Is the Time, But Not the Place"), Sheila Anne's "Women related to men or ???—BLANK—there was nothingness. Nothingness was loaded with dread" ("Opening the Door"), to Janet Aalfs, whose mom is a Dyke, and Alison J. Laurie's "I began my unrelenting search for the 'others' when I was fifteen" ("From Kamp Girls to Political Dykes"), and "Well, ya know, I ran away from home when I was nine years old. I just had to find the Lesbians" (Catherine Odette, "New York, 1959").

2

Marilyn Murphy and her partner, Irene Weiss, "have honed our looking for Lesbians skills to a fine art, and to our delight have found us everywhere!" That " . . . unmistakable something about Lesbians" which Marilyn details becomes more recognizable the more of us we know, observe, think about. And so hidden worlds of experience become revealed. Some of it not entirely pleasant, which is one reason we are lucky to have collections like this. We don't have to survive these experiences personally to learn from them. We can read all about it in comfort, nodding our heads along with everything from terror to ecstasy.

I do go looking for Lesbians, but mostly I count on Lesbians finding me. I depend on it for my living as a Lesbian entertainer and educator. One way I accomplish this is by being visible. In that way I attract Lesbians, and those interested in Lesbians, and so many of them do manage to find me. Certainly I am not alone, as these stories testify. Lesbians attracting Lesbians is not uncommon, and our success rate probably corresponds directly to exactly how good we feel about being Dykes.

When I found Lesbian-Feminists it was Love at First Sight, because finding Lesbians meant finding a vast creative storehouse of pure treasure. The discovery of myself, the discovery of Lesbians, has proven invaluable for my art. It is a resource which allows for completely personal, original reflection upon universal Dyke experience. I had never heard of women as both object and subject of song in a conscious way, in a feminist way, and the creative possibility was and is—awesome.

These accounts take us from Alaska to Aotearoa, to Japan and Thailand, and into dance class with Donna Allegra and some intriguing women ("One Mirror, Three Reflections . . . "). Politically, finding Lesbians uncovered uncharted ground for practical experimentation and testing. Communication and interaction could now occur between peers without the unspoken limitations of heterosexualism. Finding Lesbians propelled my political savvy quantum leaps forward. Because the "personal," when it finally moved into synch with the "political," changed the universe for women. I, for one, have never been the same.

Lesbians of many cultures have educated me in the ways of the world because we reflect our geography. A German Dyke is a German. She is also a Dyke, a "Lesbian Possibility" available only to Lesbians.

A good-ole-girl from Dallas is a genuine Texan in every sense, but it's her Lesbian sensibility which allows me access to her life and makes it intelligible. Same language, different accent. We have a personal interest in each other because we are Lesbians and finding each other is important to us. For me finding Lesbians of all kinds has meant finding a wide world, a Lesbian world, of rich, remarkable, global proportions.

Finding Lesbians of unfamiliar and even fearsome cultures has widened my own vision considerably and deepened my comprehension. Who would have thought that this middle-aged Jew would be engaging in ongoing heart-to-heart discussions with German groups or individuals: passionately confronting, passionately connecting over the Holocaust, anti-Semitism, hostility towards Germans. We have brought out the best in each other, constructing comprehension and compassion from suspicion and defensiveness. These are powerful, personal instances of "Lesbian Possibility" realized.

Lesbians understand Alison J. Laurie's "unrelenting search." We share her desire for tangible, living proof of our being. Continually inventing ourselves we are extraordinary creatures becoming more extraordinary every day. Our fundamental creativity and contrariness place us considerably outside conventional images. We have only ourselves to refer to as models in heteropatriarchy because we are self-defined, uncontrollable. And we love women. So we need to find each other to see who we are and how we are together because we depend solely upon each other for Lesbian value, substance and meaning.[†] We do that for each other like no one else. No one else even comes close. And that's why we need to find the Lesbians. Through each other we learn what we look like, sound like, act like, think like, believe and feel like. And we discover how NOT like each other we are, too. We learn about our uniqueness from other Lesbians. With other Lesbians we are special rather than quirky.

When we find Lesbians, we find a difference: a hidden dimension. From one angle, the Lesbian universe we provide for each other may appear to be the same as the world most of us were born into, but it is not. A Lesbian dimension, imperceptible to the non-Lesbian, the

---

†"Lesbian meaning arises out of lesbian context as a result of lesbians interacting as lesbians. Without that there is no lesbian meaning." Sarah Lucia Hoagland, *Lesbian Ethics* (Palo Alto: Institute of Lesbian Studies, 1988), p. 300.

core and character of our world reveals the essential difference. Finding Lesbians constructs a universe in which we, for once, are central and crucial.

And the main reason we need to Find the Lesbians is because it feels so good when we do and so bad when we don't.

Finding the Lesbians is good for us and good for women.

Alix Dobkin

Introduction

RU12?

Are you a vagitarian, a "member of the tribe," or a "Future Dyke of America"? *Finding the Lesbians*—How do we do it in societies that pretend we don't exist? By accident and design. Whether we're looking or not. At work, in bars, at church, in elevators, at home, on busses and subways, in Greenwich Village and Vermillion, South Dakota, at family reunions and athletic events, at NOW meetings, in dance classes, at demonstrations, in school, in London and Aotearoa. Travel the world or check out your neighborhood: Lesbians *are* everywhere!

Before we realize we have to seek out Lesbians, however, each of us must "find her Lesbian self," a process described by Bev Jo in "How I Found My Own Kind" and Rosemary Reeves in "My Private Search." Finding Lesbians is a quest meaningful only to those of us who already know that we are Lesbians, undertaken only after we have found, identified and accepted the Lesbian we are. For many of us, it is a long and frustrating process we begin only after we've figured out that we *can't* be "The Only One in the World." It is a search made necessary by the context of our lives and the nature of our oppression: wherever we live, whatever our racial or ethnic backgrounds, whatever social or economic class we were born or worked our way into, we live in heteropatriarchal societies. Two assumptions determine the relationships perceived as "meaningful" and "valuable" in heteropatriarchies: men are the ruling class and everyone is, or should be, heterosexual.

Whether we are conscious or not of our oppression, however we choose to deal with it (or not), we know (or quickly find out) that, as biological females, heteropatriarchies restrict the possibilities of a woman's life and these restrictions are supported and enforced by laws, religious dogma, and social pressure to conform. A woman's existence in heteropatriarchies is justified only if she allows men sexual access to her on demand and then devotes her life to nurturing the results. These restrictions are socially enforced by rituals that bind women to men in the institution of marriage, and it takes some Lesbians *years* to find their way out of the heterosexual funhouse. Cathy Avila, Susan J. Wolfe, Jay Reed, and Linda M. Peterson describe different aspects of the experience of shedding one's assumed het identity and recomposing oneself as Lesbian.

At whatever point we acknowledge our Lesbian identity and decide to act on our desire, we violate patriarchal assumptions by existing. In general, heteropatriarchies deny our existence, suppressing evidence of our lives and struggles, making us invisible to each other. Or, because men want to believe all women's lives revolve around them, they caricature Lesbians, presenting us either as pathetic, desperate creatures too flawed to find a man or as their vile, presumptuous, swaggering imitators. Either way, prevailing descriptions insist that men must be at the center of our lives: we "really" want a man or "really" want to be one. The realities of our lives are more complex than such fabrications.

Still, what we are told or read about Lesbians exerts a malevolent influence in our lives until we name our desire and learn, by trial and error, the signs and codes that identify us to each other. Once we know we are Lesbians and turn our attention outward, seeking our other selves, our invisibility makes our search difficult and frustrating, even scary, as Sheila Anne describes it. Even now, two decades into the women's and gay liberation movements, Lesbians just coming out still have trouble finding their way into the submerged Lesbian culture we are creating, and many lifelong Lesbians still haven't heard that there's a Lesbian Movement, an international Lesbian network, lively and disputatious communities absorbed in the latest issues and controversies about who we are and what our lives mean.

How long it takes us to identify ourselves as Lesbians and our experiences along the way as we refuse the pretense to conformity (if only to ourselves) create vast differences in our understanding of what it *means* to be a Lesbian, differences evident in the stories collected here. Finding Lesbians has been my lifelong preoccupation, but it hasn't always been easy. From the age of nine on, I vainly looked for "others," ending up hopelessly (and painfully) "in love" with girls determined to live the heterosexually "normal" lives their mothers had planned for them. *I* may have been Obvious—for I certainly worked hard at looking and behaving the way the male-authored books assured me Lesbians looked and behaved—but my efforts to find other Lesbians were both frustrating and desperate. Jill Johnston once claimed that, in the 1950s, there were "no dykes in the land," but she was wrong. There were lots of "dykes," it's just that only a few of us claimed our identity: Bev Jo, Beth Karbe (in "Another Side of Things"), and Alison J. Laurie all describe experiences similar to mine in many ways, even though Alison's story began in Aotearoa, oceans away from Miami. In the 1950s, there were good reasons for fear and hiding for those who could: Joe McCarthy's self-hatred of his own homosexuality destroyed many lives and permanently damaged uncounted others.

Imagine a land inhabited by millions of Lesbians, many of whom can't find other Lesbians and believe, each of them, that they're "the only one." Imagine trying to develop a sense of one's Lesbian Self having only Stephen Gordon in *The Well of Loneliness* and Beebo Brinker in the Ann Bannon novels as role models. Yet millions of us did just that! I believed that, in order to find other Lesbians, I'd have to learn to ride a horse and wear jodhpurs or, as Catherine Odette did in "New York, 1959," get to Greenwich Village, the sooner the better.

I wasn't, as it turned out, a horsewoman, so I turned instead to plotting my escape from Miami, to the only alternative I knew of, New York City. *There,* I was sure, I would find the welcoming camaraderie of other Lesbians, living in the haunted world of the "twilight sex" for the rest of my days. I was twenty when I did make it to New York and Greenwich Village, but I'd already found other Lesbians. The rest was fantasy and despair.

Between the ages of eleven and fourteen, I searched the teams I played on and the school busses I rode for Lesbian faces, hoping to find one like myself. Unlike many Lesbians, however, I failed to develop "crushes" on my gym teachers. Not because some of them weren't Lesbians—they were—but because their insistence on discretion (in those days, symbolized by peter pan collars and straight (sic!) skirts) justified their abuse and ridicule of me. Yet, in spite of continued discouragement, Lesbians continue to find their way on high school athletic teams. In "Birth Song," J. L. Williams describes how two basketball players move toward each other on and off the court.

Like many other Lesbians, I "found" others because two "gay boys" in my high school *found me,* and they introduced me to "gay life" on the streets of Miami—teenagers from every high school roaming the night with pimps, prostitutes, con-men, addicts and pushers. Merril Mushroom describes meeting me at "Sex Manor" in "dykeling merril meets dykeling penny." We were all minors—"jail bait," looking for love and finding, instead, the dangers of marginal lives. I quickly learned to spot "the vice" in their suits and unmarked cars and to bluff my way into gay bars with my fake ID past the Mafia bouncers. Some of us survived. Some didn't. The Mafioso set my best butch "buddy" up on a stolen credit card rap and she did 15 years in a federal prison. Other friends ended up face down, dead on a sandy beach, executed Mafia-style: with a single bullet in the back of their heads. Others married gay men for "convenience."

Several of us were college-bound after high school, but I, at least, sensed no contradiction between my gay nightlife in the Miami bars and my aspiration to a Ph.D. in linguistics by the time I was 21. But the Investigating Committee on Communism and Homosexuality of the Florida state legislature, headed by Charlie Johns, didn't think "perverts" should attend college and I lost more friends to suicide and psychiatric "cures" as the Johns Committee hunted us down at every level of the Florida public school system. I was "asked to leave" Florida State University in the spring of 1959 during the purges carried out by that committee. (On the grapevine, Johns was rumored to have driven his Lesbian daughter out of the state so she couldn't threaten his political aspirations.) In "They Met through the Wall," T. Lynn describes how three Lesbians dealt with the queer-bashing frenzies instigated by Anita Bryant, Jerry Falwell, and their campus supporters in the 1980s.

I ended up back on the streets of Miami and Miami Beach where I put my street skills to good use surviving, not only there but in New Orleans, Hollywood, and, finally, New York, as a "kept butch." Kept by call-girls who taught me much of what I know about women's bodies and pleasure. At the time, I was content to have a roof over my head, food to eat, and pocket money for the bars where I waited for them to "get off work" at five a.m. In exchange, I sat up more than once holding my call-girl lover while she suffered through a Cuban abortion.

Since my days as a teenager on the streets, my life has changed, and changed, and changed again. In the three decades since "the gay boys" found me, I've found Lesbians everywhere. There was, for example, the Lesbian in an employment agency who took my phone number from a job application and called me. She wanted "to get to know me," she said. It turned out that her drag butch lover was "impotent" and the only thing that turned her on was watching her lover and another Lesbian make love. Was I interested, she wanted to know, in helping them? I wasn't. That particular situation didn't turn me on, but others have, like the Ft. Worth woman on a southbound train out of New York who decided I was "meant" for her.

Since my desperate search for other Lesbians ended in my early teens, my life has been filled with Lesbians. Lesbians who've helped me out of trouble, like the two from Dayton, Ohio who helped me change a flat outside of Valdosta, Georgia; helped me find my way, like the two Dykes in the TR-3 who waved to me as they sped by on the causeway between Biloxi, Mississippi and Louisiana. At a roadside tavern they told me where to find the gay bars in the French Quarter and which ones the Lesbians went to. Others have helped me from the cover of their closets. At The City College of New York, there was the head of Evening Student Personnel, who told me how to get student loans so I could stop working full-time and attend day school. The only form of payment any of them asked of me was something I did gladly: "Pass it on."

I've done my best to "pass it on." In 1976, a brilliant writer, frustrated by her inability to find other Lesbians, wrote me: "How," she asked, "do you manage to find other Lesbians, wherever you are, so quickly? How do you do it?" Her questions weren't unusual, but our very different contexts at the time were. I had just moved myself to the unlikely neighborhood of Vermillion, South Dakota, where I could stroll "across town" in a mere 7.5 minutes, while she lived in Colorado, in the midst of what I imagined to be a hotbed of out, radical Lesbians.

My writer friend had cause for amazement. After opening my Lesbian activist "shop" in Vermillion, only days had passed when Lesbians came knocking at my door in the Department of English, beginning with the two Lesbians who had successfully managed my hiring: the night after they had succeeded in offering the job to me, they unhesitatingly became lovers.

I've found The Lesbians all my life, whether I was looking for them or not: at work, on buses, in elevators, restaurants, bookstores. No.

More often, Lesbians have found me. There's no secret to my success. Lesbians tap me on the shoulder or wave or slow down to say "hi." I'm "findable." I look like thousands of other Dykes, and I'm frequently mistaken for someone else. Lesbians come up to me and say, "Don't I know you from Memphis (or Sacramento or Dallas or Boise)?" Usually, they don't, but we're soon talking and laughing as though I might be their long-lost friend.

Well, times *have* changed . . . some. Now Lesbians can find each other at political demonstrations, as in "Patti's Day Out," or through personal ads in magazines like *The Wishing Well*, as Terri de la Peña's happy ending assures us. Whatever the year, wherever we find ourselves, Lesbians continue to search for "others." In this international collection you'll meet remembered and new friends who share their experiences of looking for and finding The Lesbians. What is the Lesbian Look? Starting with Alix Dobkin's "Lesbian Code" learn the identifying signals of Lesbian connection from Marilyn Murphy and Candis J. Graham. Discover how Lesbians find each other from Alaska to Hong Kong in stories by Shelley Anderson, Janelle Lavelle, Beth Karbe, and Laura Davis, in English pubs and at Brigham Young University from Jill Flye and Linda M. Peterson. Does it pay to advertise? Merril Mushroom, Terri de la Peña, Alison J. Laurie and Berta Freistadt say YES! Play "Is She or Isn't She?—SHE IS!" with Donna Allegra, Adrienne Lauby, Anna Livia, and Susan J. Wolfe. The possibilities are endless!

Pass it on!

Julia Penelope

Introduction

Seek and Find

Like chameleons, Lesbians can blend into the scenery around us yet we maintain our uniqueness. Whether the location is the White House or a women's center, Lesbians can be found. Searching for and finding Lesbians is a process of learning to identify and recognize Lesbians. A Lesbian can be immediately obvious or blend in so well that you must look closely to notice her. As we become more certain of our own Lesbian identity, our perceptions sharpen and Lesbians come into focus in the unchanged scenery. The uniqueness of Lesbians is unmistakable. What changes is our perceptions, the things we look for when looking around us.

I started my search for Lesbians before I was a teenager, like some of the contributors to this anthology. Like them, I lacked a language or word to describe what I was trying to find. My earliest memories consist of wanting to be "close" to wimmin. What "close" meant I didn't know. I was drawn to wimmin who didn't fit into the conventional picture of the nuclear family. Like Bev Jo and Shelley Anderson, I found images and instances that have stayed with me after many years. Images preserved without fully understanding their meaning. We retained and cherished our images, knowing that they were a key to some core within us, something felt but as yet unarticulated. The richness of detail in stories like Beth Karbe's "They Came in a White Convertible" and Eleni Prineas's poem, "Pearly Bucket Moon," indicate both the significance of these images and to what extent we imprinted them in our minds.

When I became a teenager I found a language, a word. I was able to name the love *Lesbian*. My search began in earnest; I had a word. Yet, I was unable to see the Lesbians who moved within the scenery of my life. Instead, I grew close to wimmin who were not Lesbians. Like the characters in "Birth Song" and "Beginnings," I experienced the joy, intensity and pain of loving so strong and crashing so hard. My perception changed. *Lesbian* became a description of wimmin rather than a description of an activity. I began to search for wimmin who named themselves Lesbian. I looked at the wimmin around me from a new perspective.

I found the Lesbian community in my late teens. I drank in the stories and descriptions of Lesbians. Who we were, what we had accomplished as individuals and as a group, and what other Lesbians had experienced. "From Kamp Girls to Political Dykes: Finding Others through 30-odd Years as a Lesbian in Aotearoa/New Zealand," "dykeling merril meets dykeling penny," "New York, 1959," and "Happenstance" are the kinds of stories that guided me as I learned to identify and recognize the Lesbians in my surroundings. The more I listened to and shared with other Lesbians the less I was misled by the scenery.

Finding Lesbians has been, for me, a life-long challenge. At different points in my life, searching for Lesbians has varied in terms of critical need. What I have found is that I "need" Lesbians. Like water, Lesbians are a source of nourishment. I swim, dance, move sensuously, let go, fill myself, and love in fluid movement with other Lesbians. There have been times when the water was a trickle, when I had no idea how or where to find Lesbians. In hopes that the trickles become streams become rivers become lakes become oceans read on . . . and know that we are everywhere.

Sarah Valentine

Lesbian Code

Words and music by Alix Dobkin

She's a BD (baby Dyke)
She's a PD, possible, probable
She's a DD, she's a definite Dyke
She's a POU (positively one of us)
She's got hi-LP (good potential)
Suffering from PLT (pre-Lesbian tension)
Is she a wannabe, a DOT?
Maybe not a Dyke of Today, but she could be a Dyke of Tomorrow
Then she'll be a DIT (Dyke in training)
Or an FDA (future Dyke of America)
She'll be a Betty, a friend of Dorothy
She'll be our kind, that's OK . . .

Is she Lithuanian? (I don't know)
Is she Lebanese? Well, she's gifted!
She's Lebesian, Lesbonic and I happen to know
She's a vagitarian
She's a member of the club
She's a member of the team, of the family
She's a member of the lodge, of the church, the committee
And she sings in the choir
Is she a lima bean? (from Kentucky)
Is she a green new bean, or is she refried?
Is she a canned bean in the closet?

Or is she now with a man? Then she's a hasbean

REFRAIN:
She's a Fresbian from Fresno
In Lansing 48912
She lives in Dyke Heights
She's an Arkansas earth Dyke
Motor city Dykette
She goes to The Pagoda with the Chinese. You bet
She colors outside the lines in Charlotte

Is she an Aussie Dyke? Check it out, waddyareckon?
She's a likely one. Spot-o. Gottabe
She looks a bit sus. She must be of the faith
I'll put her on layby
She's a Leesbian from New Zealand
She's campas, a kiwi fruit from Aotearoa
You can spot the camp girl, spot the bus driver
She's on the bike. Camp as a row of tents
She's a "how's-your-mother?" over in Dublin
She's a "whatever-you're-havin' " in Belfast. In Cork
She's a quare girl, she's got a glad eye
She's got a kick in her. Drinks Tipperary water . . .

She's the Church of England. She's ginger
She's got Dutch boy fingers
She's an MOT: A member of the tribe
She's a gold star, got her ID card
She shops at Tescoes
A sister of the inclination
She's elite in Scotland. Auch eye. Zap!
She's all right. That's 100 points!
Is she a carpenter from Bristol?
Is she a bus driver from Nottingham?
Is she a motor Dyke? Is she a badgy Dyke?
Does she live in the Dykery? Ah, then she's

REFRAIN:
A Fresbian from Fresno . . .

Life on the Rock

Laura Davis

Ketchikan was a rough and tumble town, the bars open until five a.m. It was float planes roaring off the Tongass Channel, and seiners coming home, holds full of king salmon, Chinook to the natives. It was totem poles and canneries, a pulp mill that had been closed for years, unemployment a way of life. It was island fever, that peculiar disease known only to those whose life is bounded on all sides by water.

Ketchikan was everpresent rain, the grey lifeless color of ponchos, of wool shirts, of rain pants and flannels, the soft squishy damp of layers of wool, wrapping warmth in layers on the soft, sun-starved bodies beneath. The kind of skin underneath that was wrinkled, wet, and sticky to the touch, like over-ripe brie.

"Thirty-seven kinds of moss grow in this town," the waitress at the Arctic Bar told Jennifer and me our first day here. "Thirteen feet of rain a year, and we're proud of it!" She wore a hat with the Arctic Bar logo on it. It was a blue visor (for the rain, of course), with a relief picture of two grizzly bears fucking, and the logo:

ARCTIC BAR

KETCHIKAN ALASKA.

Ketchikan had honky tonks and strip joints. It was rumored that the Shamrock Bar and Supper Club, the sleaziest of all, lured underage girls from Washington and Arizona with promises of glamorous careers in dance. No one could prove it. I'm not sure anyone wanted to. The Shamrock was an institution. Empty-eyed girls in leopard drag, gyrating to the fantasies of the men jerking off in row one. Each girl did a set of three songs. The first one shirt on, the second one, shirt off, breasts exposed, the third, whatever her specialty was, really turning it on for her finale.

Then there were the churches. Thirty-seven on one island. God was here. There was no doubt about it. This was holy ground.

And wilds? There were wilds people in the lower forty-eight only dreamed of—raw, unharnessed power. This was one of the few places left where cement could not tame the earth below. Eagles still ruled here—bald, white-crowned eagles. There were thousands, majesty a fitting word, frontier still a reality, redneck a way of life. WE LOVE JAMES WATT roared the bumperstickers peeling wet off 4-wheel drive pick-ups. The average Alaskan family had at least three cars, all in some state of disrepair, all rusty.

Life here wasn't easy. You could wait six months for the goods you mail-ordered. The one daily plane in and the one daily plane out were regularly cancelled due to fog. You'd call the airport and ask when it was coming in. "The morning plane? Oh yeah. It got overheaded to Anchorage." That meant it flew right past us, sometimes all the way to Anchorage, a thousand miles away.

Weather here was a real factor to be reckoned with—a matter of life or death, not convenience. This was a harsh land. Accidents—in float planes, boats and wilderness—were the number one cause of death. And the average age in the state? Twenty-five.

And I was going to live here. I kept trying to say the words, to think them, even. I had a job. This is what I'd said I'd wanted for over a year now. A paid job in radio. I'd met these people at a conference. They said Alaska was a media wonderland. Working here could make a difference. What you did on the air meant something. Everything was new, untried. Anything was possible. And they were willing to pay me—well.

And so Ketchikan was something *I* had chosen. Jennifer and I had driven my little white Subaru and all my worldly belongings from Santa Cruz, California up through British Columbia to Prince Rupert. From there it was seven hours on the ferry, and then we docked in Ketchikan.

Jennifer had come along for the ride, my California dyke buddy longing for adventure, willing to help out a friend in need. This was just

18

two weeks out of her life. It was to be two years of mine.

I had enlisted Jennifer as my scout. She'd been my friend for years, and a loyal one too. Her job was to find the dykes in town—10% of any population, right?—and introduce me. I figured it would be easy for her. She wasn't shy. She loved women. And anyone who knew anything would spot Jennifer as a dyke. She liked to keep her wardrobe simple: flannel shirts, jeans, sneakers and a brown corduroy cap cocked on her head. I wore long dangling earrings, shifts with puffy sleeves, and passed more easily than she did. I meant to keep it that way. At least for a while. Coming out was a risk I couldn't afford to take. I had a new, highly visible job in a small town. News travels fast, and gossip even faster, when you're surrounded by water on all sides. That much was clear. But Jennifer? Well, she was just my friend who offered to help me move. She could get away with snooping around more than I could.

From the moment we crossed the Canadian border, there'd been something about the air. The sensation had gotten stronger and stronger every mile we drove. The air was cleaner, fresher, somehow, as if the air I'd breathed all my life in the lower 48 had been stale, recycled, never enough to really sustain life. Breathing was different here. The air was moist, tasty.

And once we boarded the Ferry Maluspina for the final ride to Ketchikan, the feeling of open space had increased. As the Maluspina rounded the curve of the Narrows, we saw Ketchikan for the first time. Deer Mountain sat triumphant with a cap of white, a breast with a protruding nipple. It was a lone peak, rising above an endless stretch of forest.

The town itself was dwarfed by wilderness. Life clearly hugged the edge of the island, and it buzzed right at the shoreline. Ketchikan was a waterfront town. Barges and ferries and tugs and trollers and trawlers and seiners a way of life. Water was what gave this town its life, and many of its inhabitants their death. Boating accidents were common—and severe. The water was icy, and hypothermia and cold water drowning had claimed many.

People lived on floathouses in the harbors, washing their kitchen floors down with sea water. Mostly everyone had a boat or at least a skiff. Travel by boat held infinite possibility. The only way to the airport, which was on the next island over, was a rinky-dink ferry that cost $1.50 a shot.

Travel by car was limited to fourteen miles of the main road in one direction, and sixteen miles in the other. That was all. We'd spent our first afternoon driving back and forth from one end of the road to the other. We had talked about waiting for a sunny day before we went out touristing, but the locals had laughed, saying we'd probably wait all year.

The first thing we noticed as we began to explore was that even the streets were strange. They were narrow wooden stairways winding up rock hillsides. There were street signs posted right on the steep slick steps where only human feet could tread. The streets here were covered with lichen, wet wood railings, soft and saturated to the touch.

Ketchikan was famous for its totem poles, and so we drove out to Totem Bight to see them. They were carved by the natives of the region—the Tlingit, the Tsimshian, and the Haida, and they were full of carved animal upon carved animal, each pole telling a story about life or the origin of life. They were near as tall as the tallest building in town, which boasted four stories.

To me, four stories meant this was a small town. But a fisherman we'd met at the dock that day told us that Ketchikan, with a population of 10,000, logged in as Alaska's fourth largest city, a virtual metropolis in the middle of the wilderness. When he told us that people came in on boats from miles around to do their big semi-annual shopping trips *here,* I laughed for a long time. And then I cried. If this was the hub of commerce and culture, then how was I to live?

Our second morning on The Rock, as the locals called it, Jennifer and I paid twenty dollars for breakfast and bought ourselves a newspaper. *The Ketchikan Daily News.* The best way to get your bearings in any new place was the daily paper.

It was a skinny thing—eight pages long. There was something strange about it that I couldn't place as we pored over page after page. And it wasn't until we reached the back page that I realized what it was. There had been no national or international news on the front page. Nor the one after that. Nor the one after that. Not till the back page.

"Jennifer," I said to her. "They don't seem to care about the rest of the world up here."

"Well," she replied, "this place is clearly the center of the universe, in their minds at least."

There might be more of a world vaguely out there somewhere, but when you came right down to it, who cared? And I had been hired to report the news?

That night we made another interesting discovery. We were watching *Dallas* on TV and it was the same one I had seen the week before, just before we left Santa Cruz.

"It's not the season for reruns," I said to Jennifer.

"No, it isn't," she replied, reaching for the TV section, page six of the newspaper. She studied it for a while, then said, "These shows are all old. The descriptions match all the shows that ran last week!"

It wasn't till the next morning, and another twenty dollar breakfast, that the waitress told us why—the local cable company got the signal cheaper if it was time-delayed a week. "Can't do nothing about it," she said. "They're a monopoly, like everything else in this town."

We'd been staying at Jim Webb's place. When I told the people at the station that I was going to take the job, they arranged for me to stay at Jim's house until I found a place of my own. Jim was the Program Director at the radio station. He'd been on vacation for a couple of months (Alaskans tend to take long vacations in southern places) and was going to be gone two more weeks. It seemed perfect. I was grateful to have something ready and waiting for me.

But when Jennifer and I found the place, we were in for a big surprise. No one had told me that Jim's teenage brother would be staying there too. "Slick," as he was called by his buddies, partied nightly with his friends in the living room, drinking beer and acting disgusting, as only teenage boys new to freedom can do. The apartment had one big open room. Jennifer and I, forced in by the rain, would lie trapped in bed together, above them in an open-air loft.

Clearly, I had to find another place to live. But rents were pressing $600 or $700 for a one-bedroom and vacancies were few and far between. This was worse than California. You had to know someone to get an apartment. And then what you got wasn't worth living in.

The nights of heavy metal and drunken teenagers continued.

As the days went by, my panic increased. Where was I going to live? How was I ever gonna make it here? A Jewish lesbian from New Jersey in a redneck island town? "But where are my people?" I wanted to scream at the end of the week, every woman looking like a dyke—

strong, capable, self-sufficient, husky, short hair, flannel shirts—yet every conversation I shyly tried to start had the same conclusion: husband, four kids, church on Sundays, oldest son still lost at sea. A yearly trip to the metropolis of Seattle was their biggest expedition: good for shopping sprees, secret abortions, medical specialists, and catching up on all the movies that didn't make it to the one Christian-owned theatre in town.

I had known my place in other worlds, known how to present myself. I was known, recognized, seen for what I was. But here? Here there was a blankness, a panic rising in me, my eyes hungry for a place to anchor.

It was the end of our sixth day in town. Jennifer was returning to California in three more days. In three days, I would be the only lesbian for miles. I would be alone. And Jennifer was more than ready to return to her life in California. I could tell, even though she tried to hide it.

The first few days off the ferry, Jennifer had summoned a lot of bravado, the beauty of a British Columbia fall still fresh and inspiring under her belt. She took her job seriously. She was going to set up her friend Laura with whatever queers existed in this town.

But as she'd run hopeful to "possible" after "possible," she'd come up short. And had grown quiet, wishing silently for home, island fever already close and hot around her. These things she did not say, of course, because I was the one who had to stay. But she looked at me, the mourner, big brown eyes, saucers, watching me.

End of day seven. We'd been in Ketchikan for a week. It seemed like forever. I was grumbling from beneath the blue plastic tarp I called a poncho, making yet another complaint to Jennifer about the endless rain, when I spied the ultimate T-shirt in the window of one of the tacky tourist shops downtown. You know, the kind filled with "authentic" Indian artifacts: ivory earrings, plastic miniature totem poles, green jade whale paperweights, paintings on velvet of salmon jumping up waterfalls. The shirt flew like a banner above it all. Stretched out, its glittered letters read: I SPENT A LIFETIME IN KETCHIKAN LAST WEEK. I couldn't have agreed more.

The cost? A mere $14.99. This was Alaska, after all.

I needed the validation. I bought it anyway.

We left the shop, back out into the slanting rain. We decided we were not only wet and depressed—but hungry. Bored with $8-dollar hamburgers and $3-dollar glasses of milk, we went to a new restaurant in the center of the one main street, Tongass Avenue. They featured pizza, Mexican food, and Chinese specialties. All on the same menu. "Jeez!" I said, "I can't believe this place!"

"Will you look at this?" Jennifer said, pointing to the menu. "Pineapple-ham pizza."

"Oh, you're kidding? That's disgusting!"

"It's worse than disgusting. It's vile."

"I can't believe I'm going to live in a town that serves ham and pineapple pizza! I can't believe they even have the nerve to call it pizza! That ought to be against the law. What possible relationship can ham and pineapple have to pizza?"

"One of the, let's say, quaint aspects of this town."

"Jennifer," I said, suddenly desperate. "What am I gonna do? What the hell am I gonna do?"

"I don't know what you're gonna do, honey. But I know what I'm gonna do. I'm gonna eat. What do you want?"

"I'm about to spill my guts out and you want to eat?"

"It'll help. I promise. A little beer, and we'll talk about it, okay?"

"Okay. Let's get a pitcher. Whatever they have on draft."

"A pitcher, Laura? That's not like you!"

"I'm an Alaskan now, remember? The highest rate of alcoholism in the country. I have to find some comfort, don't I?"

"Okay. If it helps you tonight." She smiled the best empathetic smile she could muster. "What else do you want?"

"Well, I guess we might as well try this stuff they call pizza. How about double cheese?"

"Coming right up. I'll go place the order."

Over dinner, which hardly deserved to be called pizza, Jennifer and I compiled the following list on several napkins:

TWENTY-THREE INEXPENSIVE THINGS TO DO WHEN YOU ARE LIVING IN A BORING ALASKAN TOWN

1. Complain.
2. Lose something valuable and find it later.
3. Call people long distance who you know will not be home.

23

4. Take the ferry to the airport and back.
5. Make travel reservations at the travel agent that you never intend to use. Cancel at the last minute.
6. Drive out and back on your town's one road.
7. Check your P.O. Box twice a day.
8. Pore over mail-order catalogues.
9. Write complaining letters to manufacturers and service establishments.
10. Boycott local politically correct cultural events of terrible quality.
11. Comparison shop.
12. Make numerous trips to the grocery store, always forgetting something so you have to go back.
13. Write long self-pitying letters to friends in other places.
14. Turn on the radio and TV at the same time, and pretend you are in a busy, distracting place.
15. Compulsively do anything healthy.
16. Sleep more.
17. Play solitaire. Often.
18. Plan for the future.
19. Floss your teeth or develop other new hygienic habits.
20. Mess up your room and clean it up slowly.
21. Study the HBO guide and plan your schedule around it.
22. Work a lot of overtime.
23. Consider taking up drinking as a new habit.

After our act of creative frenzy, we went back to drinking Budweiser. It was time to leave the restaurant, but we had nothing to do, nowhere but out in the rain to go. I suggested tic-tac-toe. Jennifer was considering my proposal when she suddenly looked up over her third glass of beer and brightened. "Laura," she hissed, motioning with her head to the two women sitting behind us. "I think there's two!"

"Cut it out. Don't torture me. I don't have much of a sense of humor about this anymore."

"No, no. I'm serious!"

"Yeah, sure. Just like all those others. Married, husband works for the Coast Guard, four kids, goes to Seattle once a year on a Christmas shopping spree, husband drinks a little too much, maybe hits her around a little . . . "

"No, Laura. This is different. I swear to you."

"Sure it is! I can tell you all about them without even turning around. One of them is married to a tugboat captain. The other is married to a fireman. This is the one night they're let out of the house, and only for two hours. From here they go to play bingo."

"Laura, you're not listening to me. The blond one winked at me!"

"The *who* did *what*?"

"She winked at me. The tall blond, two tables back."

I nonchalantly swiveled in my chair to steal a glance. And there on the table was a pineapple-ham pizza. "God Jennifer, they're eating it!"

"Eating what?"

"Ham-pineapple pizza! They can't be lesbians! What lesbian in her right mind would eat a ham-pineapple pizza?"

"We don't care what they eat, Laura. Take another look. Check out the *women* this time."

"All right. All right." I stole another glance. The two women were dressed in the latest in polyester sportswear. Definitely not a good sign. A little girl, about seven or so, sat beside the dark-haired one. Another bad sign, although, then again, you never know, what with artificial insemination and all. But in Alaska?

I looked again. The two women both had short hair. The blond by now had turned in her chair to face us. I stole a tiny glance directly at her out of the corner of my eye. She winked at me. Did it again!

I choked on my beer. "Jennifer," I whispered. "She did it to me too!"

"I told you!"

"Yeah, you were right, but now what do we do? We can't go over and talk to them! People might notice. And besides, what if we're wrong? What if they're just two friendly housewives on girls-night out? I can't risk it. What should we do? I can't alienate everyone in this town before I even start to work."

Jennifer was writing furiously on her napkin, ignoring my rising anxiety. I read her scrawl upside-down. "Hi. We're new in town and wondered if you knew of anything special going on for women around here?"

"You can't say that," I hushed. "What if we're wrong?"

"Then she'll just tell us about her church social."

"We can't!"

"Yes, we can. It's our only chance. Look, she winked at us. At both of us! Just fold this up in your hand, make your way to the bathroom, and while you're on your way, drop this on their table."

"I can't do that!" I said, panic locking my feet to the floor.

"Yes, you can."

"No, I can't!"

"Well, we have to do something. They're getting up to leave now."

Oh, fuck, I thought. Now what can we do? "Jennifer," I whispered, an urgent pleading.

The women and the little girl were loitering by the front counter, paying their check and making small talk with the cashier. I knew it was now or never, but I was about to choose never. The women headed out the door.

Jennifer grabbed my hand. "Not here," I hissed at her. "Let go!"

She didn't. "C'mon. I've been on good behavior all week. I'm not letting go, and I'm not going to let you blow the best opportunity we've had." She pulled me out of my chair, darted up to the front counter, threw down a twenty, and said, "Keep the change." Not that in Alaska there was too much change to keep. Then she pulled me out the front door.

The women and the little girl were getting into a brown Honda across the street. They seemed to be taking their sweet time about it, too. I took another look, faced into the rain, and started walking in the opposite direction. I just couldn't do anything else. Fear is a strong mistress. I felt full of glue inside.

Jennifer took one look at me and made her decision. She let me go with a frown, and ran across the street to their car. I followed, reluctant, hanging back behind her.

"We're new in town," Jennifer said to them, her voice moving fast. "At least Laura is. I'm not staying. I only came to help her move. I was wondering . . . I mean, we were wondering . . . "

"You two want some wine?" the blond asked. "My name's Jean."

I stared numbly at them.

"I'm Susan," said the dark-haired one. "Come on. Hop in. We only live a few blocks away." Jennifer and I looked at each other, incredulous. Susan continued. "Don't worry. We don't bite. We'll build up a fire and pour you some wine."

I hesitated. Just stood there rooted to the spot. "Don't stay out in the rain, dummy," the little girl said. I turned to Jennifer. She was already halfway in the car. I followed her lead, and we climbed in beside the little girl. "What's your name?" she asked me.

"Laura," I managed, as the car veered out onto the wet pavement.

"And what's your name?" she asked Jennifer.

"Jennifer. And what's your name?"

"Lisa. I'm seven-and-a-half years old. Welcome to Ketchikan."

Jean, Susan and Lisa lived in a big blue house just two blocks away. Unassuming in the front, once we got inside, it was huge, rambling, lots of open air. A big wood stove filled one whole wall of the living room. A wide door led into the kitchen, where wall-to-wall windows revealed a spectacular view of the channel and the islands beyond. They ate breakfast every morning looking at that?

Susan took our coats and whisked them away somewhere in the upper reaches of the house. Jean bustled around, efficiently building a fire, and offered us white wine out of a carton in the refrigerator. Susan made some popcorn, Lisa got ready for bed, and all of us settled in front of the fireplace.

Conversation was awkward, a ping pong game where neither side wanted to give their position away. We discussed why I'd come here. We talked about the radio station. We talked about the work the two of them did. We talked about the weather in California. We talked about Lisa's first-grade teacher. We talked about their dog who was thirteen years old and had arthritis. We talked about the end of the salmon run. In fact we talked about everything but the fact that we each knew what the others were. And we knew they knew. And they knew we knew. And no one could seem to break the ice.

It was an hour-and-a-half later, when Lisa had gone to bed and we were well into our fourth—or was it fifth?—glass of wine, that I finally decided to plunge ahead. "Well, where are the dykes in this town? I hate to think I'm going to be the only one."

Shocked silence. Jean and Susan looked like they'd been punched in the stomach. Jennifer's eyes opened wide with surprise. Did shy little Laura say that? I recoiled inside. How could I have been such a fool? They were really matrons, and this proved it! Their husbands were just away on a fishing trip and they were staying together so they'd have less meals to cook.

I wondered where our coats were. How could we get out of here

27

gracefully? Had I just ruined my career with my big mouth? "I'm sorry," I managed. "I just thought . . . well, I just . . . we've just been looking all week, and I was hoping . . . I mean . . . " Everything I said seemed to jam my foot deeper in my mouth.

"It's okay," said Susan. "It's just that we never hear that word up here. At least we never hope to."

"Word?" I asked, totally confused. "What word?"

She hesitated before answering. It was clearly hard for her to get it out. "Dyke."

"Oh," I said, getting it.

"Oh!" said Jennifer. "I guess we're not in California anymore, huh?"

"We use it as a friendly term in California," I explained, feeling lamer by the minute.

Jean and Susan looked even more puzzled. There was a long silence. I was afraid to say anything more. Finally Jean asked, "You mean being called a dyke is not considered an insult where you come from? Being called a dyke is about the worst thing I can think of."

This time Jennifer was the one who jumped right in. "Well you are, aren't you? I mean, we are."

Jean and Susan looked at each other. I guess they were deciding how much to tell. "Well, we are . . . gay," Susan said haltingly, "if that's what you mean."

"Are you the only ones? How long have you been together? What's it like living here?" The questions poured out, one on top of the other. I wanted to know everything all at once.

"Whoa! Hold on!" Jean cautioned. "We just talked about ourselves for the first time in the ten years we've been together! Give us a chance. This is new for us!"

I shut up, and I shut up fast. "Look," said Susan. "It's getting late. We have to go to work tomorrow. Why don't you both come back for dinner tomorrow night? We'll send Lisa to her grandmother's house. Then we'll tell you our whole story. Jean, is that all right with you?"

"Sure. Sure. You girls like prawns?"

"Love them," Jennifer said.

I groaned inside. Weren't they some kind of shrimp? I hated shrimp. Those tiny little pink things that tasted like iodine and were served on the edge of cocktail glasses at Bar Mitzvahs? "Sounds great," I said, figuring I'd get them down somehow.

"What's the matter? You don't like prawns?" Jean asked. I must have been unconvincing. "That's okay. Don't worry. We'll cook up the King we caught last week out by the cabin. Come by at six."

Jennifer and I arrived at six on the button, bearing flowers under my poncho, a new box of wine under hers. It was storming outside. We were soaked, as usual. Ponchos without tight sleeves did little to protect one from the horizontal rain Ketchikan was famous for. Susan offered us dry clothes, which we gratefully accepted. Then she tossed ours in the dryer. "They'll be done by the time we finish eating," she said.

I will never say another bad word for the rest of my life about shrimp, any kind of shrimp. They'd come fresh off the boat that day, and Jean cooked them whole for three minutes in wine with pickling spice thrown in. Drained minutes later, they were on the table, in a huge bowl, enough prawns for us to gorge to our hearts' content. She'd whipped up a big bowl of fresh hollandaise sauce for dipping. We had two big bowls, one at either end of the table, for the shells.

Then we got a prawn peeling lesson. If it was a female, you pulled off the red eggs attached to the underbelly. Then you did what you did to the males—crack the shell from underneath and peel back on each side up to the top. Then grab the fat end of the meat as it emerges, hold onto the tail with the other hand, and give a sharp jerk until the whole prawn pops out. Then toss the shell, dip and eat.

I hesitated with my first bite, which was really more of a very small nibble, but after that lovely surprise, there was no stopping me. And then there was the salmon. That night I became a salmon connoisseur. Never again would I eat anything they call salmon in the lower forty-eight. I learned the difference between a King and a Coho, between Humpies and Sockeye. Kings were the best, and that's what we were having. Fresh.

"We caught this one last weekend out by my folks' cabin. It was about four in the afternoon. All we'd caught all day were rock cods and a couple of dog sharks. I'd lost three perfectly good hooks to those damn sharks. We were about to call it a day, when Susan got a tug on her line," Jean told us.

I watched Jean as she finished preparing the filets. She cooked them on a charcoal grill in a protected alleyway just outside the kitchen door. She applied a thick sauce made of brown sugar, butter, and lemon which she'd melted together on the stove. She flipped the fish, brushed them again and again. The smell actually took my attention away from the prawns, it was so sweet and alluring.

Susan picked up the thread of the story. "It was no tug! I thought I was about to be jerked overboard. That thing took the hook and started running so fast . . . "

"We decided to follow it. I started up the motor, and we took off after that fish, making sure the line stayed taut."

Susan jumped back in, "We followed that fish for ten minutes before we even got a glimpse of him. Then he leaped out of the water, and was he a beauty! Flashing silver . . . and big!"

"We knew right then he was at least a thirty-pounder."

"He went down deep then. Dove right down to the bottom, or as near as he could get. My line was going out so fast, I was sure I'd come to the end of the reel. Then just as the last yards of line were shooting out, he stopped, dead in the water."

" 'Reel it in!' I screamed at her," Jean said, flipping the filets once more.

"And I did, using every bit of strength to pull that sucker in. I got about 20 yards of line in, and then he took off again. But he wasn't as strong this time, and he only went half as far. We were tiring him out. So I reeled him in again. This time I got him up to the surface, just 15 feet from the boat, but he was not ready to give up!"

" 'Give him some slack,' I told her," Jean added, " 'or he'll snap the line!' "

"So I let him go for a third time. This time he stayed near the surface, flopping and carrying on. I was afraid of losing him. I was getting tired, just like he was."

"So I took the pole," Jean said, stabbing the filets and laying them steaming on a plate, "and had Susan get the motor. He came up so easy. All I had to do was reel him in again. This time I got him all the way on to the floor of the boat!" She looked at Susan with affection. "Of course, she'd done all the work!"

"That fish did flop. We had to stay out of his way. He was violent! Wanted back in that water more than anything! Here," she said, serving us each a piece. "Taste this!"

I wasn't sure about eating someone I'd come to know so intimately. But hell, this was Alaska. This is how people lived up here. My first bite: the sauce had permeated the tender pink flesh. Each piece flaked easily from the bite before. There was a sweet, tangy crust on the top, yet the flavor of the salmon wasn't masked at all. There was nothing fishy tasting about this fish. It was subtle, clean-tasting, truly a gift from the sea.

"So," I said, sipping on more boxed wine. "Do we get to hear your story or not?" I was being coy, flirting with them. The wine had loosened my tongue.

Jean and Susan looked at each other. "Jean, you want to start?"

"May as well." There was a long pause. The storm had come up, with increased vigor, battering the porch outside the kitchen windows. It was grey, not just grey, but 20 shades of grey outside that window. I'd never seen anything like it. It was good to be inside.

"I was born and raised in this town," Jean began. "My parents still live right by the high school. I knew I was, well . . . different . . . when I was an early teenager. I had a best friend named Deedee, and we started fooling around. One day my mother caught us in bed together."

"Oh, shit," Jennifer said. "What happened?"

"Well, Mom made a big scene and said I couldn't ever see Deedee again. After that, she pretended like it had never happened. I think she hoped if she turned her head like that, it would just go away. I wanted it to go away myself. I hadn't really thought we were doing anything wrong until Mom caught us and made such a fuss. So I spent the next bunch of years trying to make it work with guys. The sex was okay, but I just never really cared about any of them."

"When I was twenty I went to college in Washington state. It was a big move for an Alaskan like me. I met Jackie and we started spending time together. I initiated her. I've brought out all the women I've been with. Fact is," she paused, "you two are the first real lesbians I ever met."

Jennifer looked at me and I looked at Jennifer. "Then what happened?" Jennifer asked. "With Jackie?"

"Well," Jean explained, "The dean caught wind of it and we both were kicked out of school."

"I managed to get a job working for the probation department in Bellingham. I did real well there, but after a couple of years, my past caught up with me, and somebody told the chief what I was. He called me into his office and told me to have my desk cleaned out by five p.m."

I looked out the window. This was no simple story. Here I was, a politically active, socially conscious lesbian, just up from the south. I thought I knew what discrimination was about? I, who'd lived in Northern California dyke heaven?

Jean continued. "I came back up here. It's such a small state that I knew everybody back then. I had friends, and they got me a job working for the state in Juneau. That's where I met Susan."

"That was ten years ago," Susan chimed in. "I was married with three kids." I did some fast figuring in my head. Lisa wasn't ten. So where had she come from?

"My kids live with their dad in Seattle now," Susan went on. "They just left a month-and-a-half ago. They didn't like the idea of having a couple of," and she hesitated before she said the word, "dykes for parents. They'd become full-fledged teenagers and they didn't want their friends to know."

"But how did you two get together?" I asked.

"We were friends for a long time first," Jean replied. "But I knew I wanted Susan from the beginning. She was a housewife. It was obvious she wasn't happy with her husband, so I worked on her. I clearly offered the better alternative."

"We moved into a trailer together," Susan continued. "The kids were two, four, and five. So we had two adults, three kids and the dog, of course. It was a little tight."

"And nobody knew about you?" Jennifer asked, still incredulous.

"Who was there to tell?" Jean answered. "Why would I risk losing another job? I thought it was a miracle I had one at all."

"But didn't people know anyway? You two lived together for God's sake," I said. "People aren't that stupid."

"It's not a question of stupidity, Laura," Susan explained. "People only see what they want to see. You know, out of sight, out of mind."

I was having a hard time getting it. It was a life so different from mine. "What about Lisa?" I asked. "If that's okay to ask."

"Might as well," Jean said. "You're the first ones ever getting the whole story. I took Susan on a camping trip in Washington once. We met up with an old boyfriend of mine, and the three of us ended up having dinner together. Well, one thing led to another, and we ended up in the sack together, the three of us. Just once, but it was enough. I got pregnant."

"For a long time I couldn't decide what to do. Lisa kind of happened by default. The kids wanted a baby brother or sister, and I couldn't seem to make up my mind. You can't get an abortion in this town anyway. You have to fly down to Seattle, and I didn't want to go through that. So we had Lisa."

"But what did people think, you having a baby with no husband?" Jennifer asked.

"I guess they just thought I made a mistake," Jean answered. "No one ever talked to me about it. And they wouldn't let Susan in the hospital. I had to be there all by myself."

"I'll never forget it," Susan continued. "This big sign on the door of the pediatric ward, IMMEDIATE FAMILY ONLY. It wasn't till she was a week old that I even got to see her."

"That's awful," I said. "Couldn't you have done something?"

Jean smiled. She was getting used to our questions. "You have to understand, Laura, we never even thought things could be different. We were just happy to have each other."

"But how did you end up here?" Jennifer asked.

"I got transferred to the Ketchikan office," Jean said. "That was five years ago. We bought this house, and then two years ago, I had to fire one of my employees. He just wasn't working out. Anyway, to make a long, bloody story short, he filed a discrimination suit against me in Ketchikan District Court and said I'd fired him because I was a lesbian and I hated men. That was the gist of it."

"There were eighteen months of depositions. Character witnesses. People swearing I was normal. Susan and I both had to go in separately and make depositions."

"What did you say?" I asked.

"We lied," Susan said. "I swore that we'd never been lovers."

There was a long silence. Lightning filled the window now, lighting up the entire grey-black sky.

"Never again will I do something like that," Jean continued. "It wasn't worth it. That lie broke the back of our relationship. Susan's leaving here in two months to go to graduate school in Oregon. But that's not the only reason she's leaving."

"I just couldn't look her in the eye anymore after I signed that piece of paper," Susan explained. "What had our ten years been about if I had to be ashamed and lie about it? I decided I couldn't live in Alaska anymore if that's what it required." Susan paused, looked out the window. "So I applied to graduate school, and now I'm going." She looked at Jean. It was clear these two still loved each other.

"So I lost Susan and the kids," Jean said. "And I swear I'll never lie like that again." She paused, running her fork over the scraps left on her plate. "That's why we picked you two up. We spotted you right away. If it had been six months ago, we would have fled that restaurant so we wouldn't be seen anywhere near you. But now . . . hey, what did we have to lose? I've lost everything I care about already."

"We talked it over when we saw you sitting there," added Susan, "and we decided that no one else should have to go through what we went through up here, all by themselves. So we decided to take you in."

There was another long silence. Jean looked across the table at me. "You sure you want to live here?" she asked me.

The rain was coming down in horizontal sheets now, pelting the porch and smearing the windows. I stared out at the dark, wet night, wondering what I'd gotten myself into now. "Yeah, I'm sure," I replied softly.

The faces around me looked unconvinced.

Turning the Glass Corner:

Southern Sensibilities & Dykely Connectedness

Janelle M. Lavelle

In North Carolina, a self-respecting lesbian is *not* going to meet other dykes at a Mary Kay convention or a gathering of the Cotton Wives of America.

Just about any other locale, however, should be fair pickings. I myself, or some other friend whose word I trust, have managed to find other dykes in such alien places as:

a Liberty Bible College rally (the campus Jerry Falwell calls home);

a Jesse Helms-owned radio station;

a Garden Club meeting (admittedly, this was the big statewide one and not the one in the lesbian's town of Waxhaw, but . . .);

co-teaching the Free Will Baptist Youth Bible Study Class;

Lamaze classes at the YWCA; and

working in the ladies' wear section of a K-mart store (the lesbian turned out to be the only one who always wore a skirt).

It is not the finding of lesbians, but rather the connecting there-with, that can become rather byzantine in our culture here. In every Carolina town except Durham, where even the straight women act like lesbians, there are none of the wimmin's cultural centers and wimmin-only spaces that Yankee lesbians are so fond of. Even when we're out of the closet, in a Letters-to-the-Editor, playing-Meg-Christian-music-outside-where-the-neighbors-can-hear kind of way, most of us favor some level of blending into the scenery. When one abides in a place where riding a horse while wearing a Confederate soldier outfit is usually considered to be a perfectly acceptable pastime during half-time ceremonies of a football game, it behooves one to be a bit selective about where one chooses to be conspicuous.

It is considered quite impolitic to scream, "hey, lezzie!" when one spots a potential sister across a crowded room. There are specific ritual behaviors required when one observes a potential "Enchanted One" on the horizon.

In Greensboro, North Carolina, a middling-size city where I've spent the last 20 years, dyke-connecting was once quite simple. If one noticed a Potential Dyke at, say, a Presby House Forum on The Crisis of Contemporary Mainstream Religion, one could maneuver one's charming self into the same approximate location, strike up a conversation and mention casually, "I'm a friend of Diana McGuire. Do you know her?"

For many years, that sentence was as blatant as tattooing a scarlet "L" on one's chest. Diana McGuire was a drop-dead gorgeous, totally "out" lesbian who had the second most sexy voice I have ever heard (the #1 voice belonged to a Guilford College switchboard operator who disappeared into the ivy at Amherst with her girlfriend years ago).

Diana's name was the dyke secret handshake: everyone with an ounce of lesbianism in them knew her, or at least *of* her, and had watched her soap-opera life over the years with a kind of morbid fascination. If the potential Dyke replied with a cautious confirmation of a nodding acquaintance with Diana, one was automatically halfway home toward a life-long friendship.

But times change, and relationships get more complicated. Under the influence of an exceptionally security-minded partner, Diana eventually became a financial consultant, developed a mind-boggling amnesia about her past, and disappeared from sight (except for those fortunate enough to have a spare $10,000 with which to play the stock market). Connecting with potential Dykes did not disappear with Diana; it simply became a bit more complicated, and developed a complex set of ritualistic cues.

There are, of course, traditional ways to meet Carolina lesbians: softball teams, social groups like TALF (Triad Area Lesbian Feminists), LUNA (Lesbians Up for New Adventures), the various gay/ lesbian political alliances, self-help groups like Gay Alcoholics Anonymous, religious groups like Integrity or Metropolitan Community Church, YWCAs in Durham or Winston-Salem (all other towns' YWCAs are fairly homophobic, but those two are safe).

Unfortunately, independent research has determined that the same

25 women belong to all of these groups: one keeps tripping over the same bodies whatever the city with which one is dealing. To meet any of the other dykes in the state—the 90% who seem to be permanently submerged into the mainstream—then one is required, probably by some law somewhere, to creatively implement other, more creative connecting behaviors.

This is actually much less of a closet-busting procedure than it suggests. Unless one badly misreads the clues, one seldom ends up standing buck-naked queer before god and everyone. Unless they are hopelessly fundamentalist in outlook, true Southerners allow gay people the dignity of assuming they are tolerated. As long as one acts as if it is no more odd to seek out fellow lesbians than to seek out those with a shared fascination for African violets or tole painting, one seldom encounters overt hostility. But there are unspoken, unwritten conventions to the process, mysterious to the novice and often tricky for even the most experienced.

My most recent experience with the required conventions occurred when I launched a part-time career as a general flunky at the local office of a statewide trade publication. Six other people were working there, including the man who was considerate enough to hire me despite all the openly-gay credentials on my resume, one open-minded straight woman (we talked about AIDS and Gay Alcoholics Anonymous a lot), another pleasant soul who wouldn't know a lesbian if she encountered two making love on the production room floor, one alluring-but-prickly editor who engaged my lesbo-radar the first time I passed her office door, and one charming black single mother named Denise for whom I could get no reading at all.

I attempted to connect with the alluring-but-prickly editor immediately; but either she knows some still-hostile ex-lover of mine, or her recognition of my own sexual calling seemed too threatening to her (although I tend toward dresses and low heels, and her idea of dressing up seemed to be pulling the sleeves of her sweatshirt down to her wrists). Whatever the reason, we never did progress to the point of civilized conversation; she responded to everything I said as if I had some subliminal insult in mind.

The initial contact between Denise and me occurred on a day when we spent eight boring hours cutting advertisements out of the latest issue of our publication. Our conversation went thusly:

Me (yawning): Sorry, but I was up all night finishing an article that was due today.

Denise: Who was the article for?

Me (said with a slight vocal hesitation): I write mostly for a, uh, feminist liberal, uh, newspaper.

Denise: Oh? Which one?

Me: It's called Bugle Publications in Raleigh. They publish a, uh, bi-weekly, uh, newspaper.

[Fifteen minutes of scissors snipping ensues.]

Denise: That's interesting. I used to work for two feminist presses. One was in Oregon.

Me (pulse quickening hopefully): Oh? I've never been to Oregon.

[She rhapsodizes poetically about the beauties of the Oregon coast, and is as positive, if not gushy, about the "group of feminist women" she knew there. More snipping.]

Me (hopes now are high): Have you got any plans this weekend?

Denise: A friend and I are going up to camp at ————— (woman-only land in Virginia).

Me (Hooray! Hooray!): I've never been there, but I've heard it's great. I *love* to camp. . . .

The key word here was "feminist." To most women the term may conjure images of Gloria Steinem, Germaine Greer, and other "straight looking and acting" types. But it is probably the most popular code word for dykes over 30. Straight feminists are so rare in these parts that the word is a dead giveaway.

The above conversation, with slight adjustments for occupation and season, has occurred scores of times in my dealings with Carolina women.

As Denise continued talking that day, I learned she had visited half the women-only habitats in about seven states. Not only was she probably a dyke, I realized; she was a better plugged-in, more sub-culturally aware dyke than I can ever hope to be!

I have decided since then that the twice-daily (minimum) phone calls she receives from a gentle-sounding lady probably amount to more than simply a friend calling to say hey.

Denise and I turned some glass corner of direct acknowledgement about a month later when a coming-out story I wrote was published in *The Front Page,* my home-base Carolina gay and lesbian newspaper. She came into my workroom one day, when everyone else was deeply occupied elsewhere, and said, "I read a story you wrote recently, and I liked it a whole lot. I thought it had a lot to say about my own life, too."

I smiled politely and acknowledged her compliment as quietly as she had expressed it. But inside I was yelling like a banshee, going "thank you, thank you!"

In subsequent weeks I think there was a bit of change in the external behavior of the alluring-but-prickly editor. She wore discreet gay-event T-shirts several times; I think the photograph on her desk of another attractive woman in hiking boots was a new development, too. And I am certain I saw her chortle when our absentee Editor-in-Chief (the type of guy who makes one sorry that the phrase "male chauvinist pig" is no longer in vogue) ran around asking everyone except me what they knew about *The Front Page* when I listed it as a publication credit in a non-gay newspaper. He thought it might be a new outlet for his own writing, and no one liked him enough to explain that it's the kind of paper which pays for itself with ads for drag show contests and lesbian luaus.

One ritual for dyke connecting is this kind of indirect, gradual establishment of "guilt"-by-association. Names, places and activities of an increasingly obvious nature are offered by each party, tit-for-tat, as trust builds: a carefully-danced step, individual to individual, touching ever-so gently on shared connectors.

Such skills are especially important to develop because many traditional avenues of conjunction like organizations and liberal social groups seldom work for meeting people here. The last Social Movement that successfully developed here was the formation of the Confederacy; it didn't work, the participants got burned, and southerners haven't trusted *any* idea that involves assembling more than ten people since.

The few groups that have struggled here are seldom fertile lesbian ground. Our National Organization for Women (NOW) chapter, for instance, was hopelessly homophobic for most of its existence (that seems, thank heavens, to have finally changed). They knew who I was; but they were profoundly uncomfortable when I appeared as an open lesbian, particularly with other open lesbians, at any of their events.

Such dyke-fearing groups seldom function as a bridge. But on one occasion even NOW pulled through. The group's president called me one day, circling like a dog looking for a place to sleep as she told me about a woman, a recent transplant from Indiana, who had contacted her the night before. The woman was having "trouble with her roommate," the NOW lady said, "and you seem to know a lot of people with roommates . . . " Her voice trailed off into a panic. I feigned ignorance for a few minutes to see how awkward a place she would work herself into. Her embarrassment seemed so bottomless, however, that guilt got the better of me and I helped her out by explaining that the answer was yes, I am a lesbian, and that she could give the Indiana lady my phone number if she wanted to.

She hung up in a grateful rush. The Indiana woman, accustomed to NOW chapters that were melting pots of lesbian sensibility, was indeed having "roommate trouble": her middle-aged lover of twelve years had taken up with a 19-year-old rugby player. She turned out to be quite pleasant despite the angst of the break-up, eventually accustomed herself to southern life quite well and is still a friend.

Other unlikely means for beaming across the Carolina distances for contact with friendly women exist. Accepting a southern identity as a lesbian means many things, not the least of which is a respect for other people's limitations. We are graced with an easily intertwining life here that women in other parts of the country struggle daily to achieve. Sometimes such complex associations seem like a gift; other times it feels, as one friend says, more like living with bees in one's head—too tight, too confining, too hard to escape the stupidities of one's past because reminders (both human and non) constantly surround us. Everyone really does know everyone else around here.

This interconnectedness does have one important advantage: non-lesbian people, male and female, are a primary source for finding new and exciting dykes. Gay men, for instance, have been invaluable: my male *Front Page* editor has connected me to at least 30 wonderful new women of every imaginable lesbian description in the last year, often with me kicking and screaming about how I'm just "too shy" to call a total stranger on the phone about some lesbian news story. "CALL HER," he finally insists, demanding some woman's deathless comments on a pending story. It works every time.

Gay men are essential for snagging invitations to the most interesting parties; for supplying useful gossip about which female flower-shop patrons send flowers to other women with "love" and "forever" in the note; and for escorting lost lady lab technicians, whose sexual identity is in the formative stages, to post-theater restaurant dinners. Patricia, my Significant Other, often inspires a unique protectiveness and love in otherwise shallow fey young men. They reward her by taking her under wing and introducing her to other shy women who will benefit from a totally non-threatening lesbian presence (we call this her "lost puppy" ministry).

A fact of life in the Carolinas is that most gay organizations involved in useful, as opposed to merely social, activities are sexually integrated. This is always a horrific shock to women who come here from Smith College demanding female-only groups. We natives have learned to explain patiently, as often as necessary, that the transplants are going to have to learn to appreciate gay men's peculiar virtues on some level, or their lives will be sadly limited.

Gay men love to matchmake, are often better at spotting dykes than dykes themselves (conversely, I myself have yet to err in a suspicion about a potentially gay man; maybe one sex can smell that the other ain't the least interested), and will feed a person when she's broke if she will exert herself to be moderately entertaining. In the south, at least, gay men are an all-around useful concept.

Another important factor in forming lesbian associations here is non-gay women. Soon after I left my husband, a straight woman friend named Lola met me at the only predominantly-female bar in town. She likes to dance without getting hit on by leeches, so she periodically visits the gay nightspots.

Having only recently been cured of my bout with the heterosexual virus, I did not know a soul there, so Lola introduced me around the place. The female bartender, in a state of passive lust for Lola's motherly body and bedroom eyes, was eager to believe that any friend of Lola's was *de facto* a friend of hers. She presented me to the other regulars, thus vouching for my acceptability, and the group of us eventually formed a loose confederation we called Phi Nu Delta (Friday Night Dykes) to support us through the early 1980s when Reagan took over and life as we know it seemed in increasing jeopardy.

Another straight friend of mine, Liz, has been creating a home for her dyke friends for fifteen years. She has a huge unruly house full of male children and a writer husband who has learned to disappear into his study when the anti-male rhetoric starts to fly fiercely in the living room.

Liz's home has been our tactical base for presidential debates, New Year's parties, and elaborate planning sessions for removal of the world's male hierarchy. Occasionally a dyke who has become a bit too flush with rejection, alcoholic spirits or emotion declares to Liz her undying love. Liz always responds with gratitude, appreciating the affection but hopelessly het in her tastes.

I have formed some of my strongest friendships with the dykes in Liz's circle. She fulfills our occasional longings for a family that looks and sounds like the families of our childhood when they were chugging on all cylinders. She has built her chosen family around and within her biological one; we borrow her kids when we want to see *Bambi,* and she encourages the dykes to build independent relationships with her boys and husband.

She also owns the only typesetting shop in town which will willingly print the word "lesbian" (most of the other printers blanch and say they are just too busy for the next ten years or so). She functions as the token heterosexual on the boards of gay groups, does the ads for *The Front Page,* and writes to city council members on gay issues— supporting the community with the serenity possible for a person unconcerned about any opponents' attempts to call her own sexuality into question.

None of these approaches rates high on the Political Correctness scoreboard. But there is a special radicalism involved in treating dyke-finding like any other social interaction. By insisting through our behavior that lesbianism falls within the wide realm of southern eccentricity, dykedom becomes part of the unique southern dailiness that allows life here to flow more mellowly than in colder climes.

A basic fact of life in the Carolinas (except, again in Durham, where Yankee-style ruthlessness is politically mandated) is that, no matter what the social class, color, sexual orientation, or professional calling of the people involved, nothing is as important to most true southerners as ascertaining that everyone "saves face" in a socially acceptable fashion. People who elect stock car drivers and gospel singers to public office know, deep in their hearts, that they dare not criticize anyone else too freely.

In my younger years, I found such civility stifling. But now, as 40 rears its inarguable head and most of my revolutionary activity has moved from the streets to the keyboard, I am grateful for the southern rituals that make it possible for me to challenge stereotypes through the simple fact of my existence. I can embarrass myself at will in the local newspaper columns, and gather with any manner of bell-curve deviants at public places, as long as I respect the fact that one does not directly mention personal peculiarities in any but the most intimate of settings.

The reward? If one values the life of the surface as well as the life of the soul, southern-style dykes are blessed with a long, rich and tradition-laden history. Life is more than what one old friend calls HDRs: Heavy, Deep and Real conversations, storms and trauma, pain and gut-kicking distress. Life is also day-to-day relationships with one's own, and other more-or-less peaceful tribes, participating in whatever simple pleasures and duties tribal life demands.

Some gifted and caring people here are currently involved in attempting to energize the local gay and lesbian community into political action. My friends in the group often seem puzzled about why there has been no sudden rush of support from the gay masses—why so many here seem content to drift along in the grey area where their lives are neither overtly forbidden nor supported. It is difficult to explain, this grey comfort zone, and even more difficult for those who know no other place to conceive of a life lived any other way. It is most comparable to being wrapped in cotton batting: never bruised, but never able to feel the full warmth of a loving embrace, either.

Compared to what lesbian life here once was, and what we who came out here expected it to be, the reality of this cotton batting is an immense improvement. And many are loathe to give it up for an uncertain future of politicization.

I know of no other place in the known universe where an "out" dyke can do charitable civic work with a woman named Muffi one week, and write an anti-sodomy law polemic the next. One lesbian I know swears that, if we can conquer the misimpressions of the Junior League, and attain access to all that money, power, and influence, we can conquer the world.

The Junior League is a bit further into southern acceptability than I care to embark. But I find the theory behind the approach to be sound: if one can work out the whys and wherefores, a southern lesbian really can be both in the world but not of it. She can partake of its women and gay-centered institutions without being sucked into the fan. Many women I know either mistrust all non-dykes to such a degree that they refuse to participate in the life around them, or they are so compromised by fear that they will not reach out to their own lesbian people.

I believe a middle course, and a potpourri of lesbians hewing to that middle, are out there. Those of us who see life's excitement from both sides are obligated to educate these middle women, helping them become safe and free enough to touch their lesbian sisters.

How I Found My Own Kind

Bev Jo

Finding other Lesbians meant first finding myself. From my earliest memories, I felt intense love for other girls. I was a Lesbian in the depths of my heart—Lesbians are my blood. But that didn't mean I was aware of feeling sexual. I just knew that I wanted to be with other little girls like myself, in a community of our own, away from boys, men, and families, where we could love and protect each other. That intensity of feeling kept me alive and hopeful, and was more important than anything—even though my parents and the Catholicism I was subjected to at school declared that girls shouldn't love other girls.

In 1953, when I was three years old, I loved my girlfriend who lived on the corner, in an apartment over a liquor store. In that same year, my family moved across the river to Cincinnati, from our poor neighborhood into a working-class one. I was fearful of the new changes in my life, but was also brave. I remember my mother hitting me because I dared to climb up over the bars of my crib to go exploring instead of quietly taking a nap. She kept trying to constrain me. She curled my hair and forced me to wear short dresses and painful shoes, but I fought back in every way I could, hating the artificiality and posing that meant being a "real" girl. I persisted in being myself.

I knew I was different because of the strength of my feelings. Other girls weren't yet committing themselves to boys, but they practiced for their future role as wife and mother by playing house, dressing up, and looking after dolls. I always searched for my own kind, and when I started grade school at five, I found Rosemary. She was ten years old, fat, with dark hair and green eyes, and she was different, like me. She also fought against the rules of male-defined femininity. Our school, parents, and culture demanded that we act "ladylike" and never defend ourselves when boys taunted and attacked us. We refused to learn phony feminine mannerisms, and so we were branded "tomboys." But we were *nothing* like boys in our very female courage.

Rosemary had that clearly Lesbian feeling to her that is now so familiar to me. She felt alive in that way that the het world only knows how to define as "queer." I was friends with other girls, but I was drawn to Rosemary. I was madly in love with her and wanted to look at her, hear her voice, kiss her, hug her, and be with her every moment. I knew these were forbidden, "terrible" feelings. But I didn't care because it felt so good and true, like nothing else did in my life. As painful as it was to feel overpoweringly a way that was considered so wrong, I still felt I was being my own, true self.

Rosemary wasn't considered "pretty" by the other girls and their parents, but to me she was gorgeous. She was an outcast and became more so as she grew older. We played together sometimes, but didn't become friends until I was 12 and she was 16. She was much more in touch with her anger than I was, and that scared me. But we talked and walked the streets of our neighborhood at night, in the snow and the spring rains. The heterosexual families were all in their lighted homes with the façade of togetherness covering the reality of family rape and violence. I felt safe outside in the darkness with Rosemary. I'd never felt such a magical time. At twilight, we watched the bats flying out from the spruce trees in her backyard.

When I was thirteen, I started high school. Later that year, Rosemary moved out of her parents' house into an apartment across town, and into a new life. I rarely saw her after that. One day I visited her, and she told me she was a Lesbian. I had always suspected I was too, but what she now said terrified me. Her new friends taught her what it meant to be "gay." From what she told me, and from what I saw of two of them that day, they were both male-identified and het-identified— very feminine and recently heterosexual. Her roommate was an ex-wife and mother, and her lover was actually a bisexual, with bleached hair and make-up. Rosemary knew she was Butch, because she'd always been true to her female self by rejecting femininity. Beyond the fact that she didn't wear make-up and the uncomfortable, restricting clothes that men designate as "women's" clothes, Rosemary simply looked like a Lesbian: She spoke and moved with directness, without any game-playing pretense. Her two friends told her that meant she was "masculine" and could be lovers only with Fems, and should use a dildo.

This made Rosemary tormented and self-hating. Knowing she was a Lesbian was freeing for her, but what her friends told her felt wrong. Yet they had the experience and power of being treated more as "real" women in a world controlled by men than Rosemary did. After all, they had both been het—one was still fucking men, and the other was a mother (male society's true sign of "womanhood"). They still passed as het, while Rosemary was hated and reviled as a blatant Lesbian by strangers, acquaintances, family and even her "gay" friends. Rosemary's roommate and lover therefore knew what sexual apparatus was needed to satisfy "normal" women—as far as they were concerned, she was just a young, inexperienced queer, so what did she know?

Rosemary had always fought with her pride and strength against the lies of her family, culture, and society. Now that she had found what she believed were her own kind at last, she was particularly vulnerable. Already an outcast in the "real" world, she was determined to be accepted in the "gay world." The saddest part was that she was in love with a Butch friend, but that was as forbidden to her as loving another girl was among heterosexuals.

The idea of a dildo revolted me. The "gay life" Rosemary described was nothing like how I felt or what I wanted, and that confused me about if I really was a Lesbian. I knew I wanted nothing to do with dildos, whether artificial or real. How I wish I could go back and tell Rosemary clearly what I was feeling then. I didn't have the words for what I now know. I knew only that there had to be another way, that being a Lesbian couldn't mean we were imitation heterosexuals. I tried to find out everything I could about Lesbians, but in 1963, the only books I found described us as "sick." In films like *The Children's Hour* and novels like *The Well of Loneliness,* we killed ourselves or abandoned those we loved so they could find "true love and happiness" with pricks. Yet there was no other word for "girls who wanted only to be with girls."

That was the last time I saw Rosemary for four years. She moved with her family to Arizona and seldom wrote. When we finally did meet again, she was celibate and had rejected Lesbianism as "wrong."[1]

High school was a new world for me. I made friends with a group of girls who were very female-loving. They weren't Lesbians, but they weren't (yet) actively heterosexual. I fell in love with one of them, Ann, who had intense dark brown eyes and a cutting, sarcastic wit that she used to question the religious dogma we were taught. We stayed friends for years, but eventually she got married.

When I was fifteen, my family moved to California and it was a very painful change for me. I desperately missed my friends, and my new high school was more class-privileged and snobbish than my old working-class school. I continued searching for others like myself. I made new friends and sometimes dared to say I thought I was a Lesbian. I was assured that I couldn't be, since I didn't "want to be a man." One friend completely snubbed me after I talked with her, and when I asked her why, she would only say that our families were "too different" for us to stay friends. That was true—mine was working-class and hers was upper-middle class. But I also suspected that she wanted nothing to do with Lesbians.

Then I found Marg. What drew me to her was that she looked and felt like a Lesbian. She had very short hair, wore no skirts or dresses (except the required school uniform), no frills or make-up, was solid in herself, and passionate in her feelings and ideas. She loved her girl-friends deeply and had nothing to do with boys. I was afraid of being discovered as a queer, but Marg didn't seem to care what people thought, and she was openly, physically affectionate with her friends.

As our other friends grew more heterosexual, Marg and I grew closer. We began to realize we loved each other; we touched, and gradually became lovers. My world was transformed. I had never felt so awake and alive. Life came into sharp focus, the air was clearer, the scent and taste of wind, ocean, and rain were exhilarating, music touched me more deeply, and I was filled with feelings I'd never dreamed possible.

We didn't have advice or one piece of writing to encourage or support us, or tell us what it meant to be a Lesbian. We were surrounded by Lesbian-hatred, yet we simply followed our feelings past the lies and discovered how to love each other and how to make love with each other. We never thought of using "sex toys," dildos, pornography, or sado-masochism. Why should we? Neither of us had been near pricks or was interested in one. We already had more than enough pain and restriction, because we were underage and legally owned by our parents. Our religion, school, families, society, and most of our friends denied or forbade our existence.

Marg and I kept our love secret for as long as we could, which was hard, considering we were radiant in our ecstasy. We were rarely able to be alone together, and *nothing* could be more exciting than just being together, finally, filling ourselves with the sight, scent, sound, and feel of each other. We never had enough time or were able to get enough of the feel of each other's face, mouth, skin, hands, vulva . . .

I was seventeen and Marg was sixteen. Before we became lovers, I moved to a dormitory at college to escape my parents, but came back every chance I had, to be with Marg. We couldn't see each other for weeks at a time, since Marg was often forbidden to see friends and was almost never allowed to sleep away from home. She'd always been restricted by her mother, but now, as she grew happier, her parents grew more suspicious. I stayed overnight at her house as often as I could, because that was the only way we had time alone together. Her parents questioned me relentlessly. Why would a college student want to come back and visit with a high school girl? They watched the way we looked into each other's eyes.

We wrote to each other every day, and eventually Marg's mother searched her room and found my letters. She told my father, and Marg and I were ordered to never see each other again. We met secretly when we could, and continued writing through friends, but we were discovered again. Her parents copied my letters and sent them and Marg to a psychiatrist. Marg seemed to lose heart.

This was such a painful time. All I could think about was being able to be with Marg. I transferred to go to the school that she planned to go to, so that we could finally be together, but her parents found out and refused to let her go. She was kept a virtual prisoner, and it became impossible for us to see each other or even to write. Slowly, we lost each other. I didn't know when I'd ever see Marg again. She finally stopped writing to me and became heterosexual. A couple of years ago I found Marg and talked with her. She became a fundamentalist christian and believes that "it's morally wrong to be a Lesbian."

I still feel the loss even now, of who Marg was, of the potential and unbelievable intensity of love and passion that we felt. I was worn down over and over by what was done to us, and the worst part was the lack of support and information. I was in torment, fearing that my love for Marg meant I was hurting her, because it was "sick" to be a Lesbian.

Still, I continued searching, through the pain and isolation, for others of my kind. I went to a meeting of the Daughters of Bilitis, but they had a 21-year-old age limit, for their legal protection. Through that one meeting, I met Jane. She was twenty and had been lovers with her best friend in high school. They too were discovered, but stayed lovers. What made it easier for Jane was that she also had a boyfriend who she made a commitment to marry. Jane pressured me to become lovers with her, even though she still had her girlfriend and boyfriend. It seemed to be a cold decision on her part, without intensity or love. I refused at first, but then, out of loneliness, did become lovers with her and she was the first woman I lived with. Whenever her boyfriend came to stay with her, I had to give up my place in her bed so they could fuck. It was horrible. I found that it wasn't enough to find someone who wanted to make love with her own kind, but that she also had to love and be committed to her own kind.

I continued searching and finally found a Lesbian community in Berkeley, California. I went to "Gay Women's Liberation" meetings, and over the next year (1971) there were dances, parties, concerts, and readings. They were for "women-only," but were mostly Lesbian-sponsored and attended by Lesbians. With the growth of Lesbian feminism, there was a blossoming of Lesbian-identified publications. I read every pro-Lesbian article and book I found, and my life was transformed. There are more of us than I had ever dreamed was possible. At first it seemed as if everyone was coming out, and we were so happy to find each other. Then, as time passed, it became clear that only a few were committed enough to loving our own kind to go through all the pain and oppression Lesbians suffer.

No matter what hardship exists in my life, I feel deeply ecstatic and proud to be a Lesbian. It's worth all the hate-filled stares, threats, harassment, and violence that I, as an out Lesbian, experience from men and het women. No amount of acceptance or praise I would get for behaving the way females are supposed to behave in patriarchy is worth giving up my love for my own kind. But for many Lesbians, passing as het and being treated as het didn't give them enough. They want to be accepted by their families and het society, and to get all the privilege that only het women are allowed. Many of the Lesbians I've known had been het and were still very male-identified, and so they eventually went back to men.

But, no matter how hard things become, my life will never be what it was like before. I know that there *are* other Dykes, and why any

49

female would choose to be with men when she could be with Lesbians is incomprehensible to me. It now isn't enough for me to find women who *seem* to be Lesbians—I choose to be close only to Lesbians who truly love Lesbians, who are committed to *staying* Lesbians, who are proudly, visibly Dykes, and who are close only with other Dykes.

So I've found my own kind at last, the most Lesbian of all—Dyke Separatists. I became a Separatist in 1972 and discovered that just as non-Lesbians fear and hate Lesbians and lie about us, so also do non-Lesbians and non-Separatist Lesbians fear and hate Separatists and lie about us. We dare to say we truly love ourselves and other Dykes. That love and commitment means we also dare to name the crimes that men and boys continually commit against all females and our earth. We are courageous enough to say clearly that we want only to be with our own kind, other Dykes. To non-Separatists, just as to men and het women, that's unforgivable, because all females are meant to live for and through men and are meant to breed and care for boys. But Dyke Separatists persist—we survive the hatred and abuse that's thrown at us. We love and care for each other. We are everywhere, across the earth, from all backgrounds and nations. We recognize each other because we look like Dykes, feel like Dykes, and are creating truly Dyke cultures. So my dream is just beginning, but it's also come true.

Notes

1. I've tried to find Rosemary for the last 20 years. If you think that you recognize her from my story, please ask her to write me at: Battleaxe, P.O. Box 9806, Oakland, CA 94613.

Looking for Lesbians

Marilyn Murphy

Looking for Lesbians is a hobby I share with my companion lover, Irene. It is an amusing pastime when we are at home, surrounded by women we know are Lesbians; but when we go traveling the back roads of North America in our motor home, looking for Lesbians becomes serious business. We usually stay in campgrounds in national, state, provincial, and county parks far from urban centers. As a result, we are not able to consult a phone book and then casually drop in at a local women's bookstore, bar or center whenever we need the sight of other Lesbians. We started our RV expedition firm in the belief that "We Are Everywhere!" Over the past four years, we have honed our looking-for-Lesbians skills to a fine art, and to our delight have found us everywhere.

So, what does a Lesbian look like? Well, speaking very generally, a Lesbian, when not at work or in costume, looks like a woman for whom bodily comfort when wearing clothes is more important than appearing "attractive," that is, of drawing to one's self the sexual attention of men. Lesbians, generally, seem less elaborately dressed, made-up, coiffed, than other women. In fashion magazines this Lesbian look is called "understated."

So, what does a Lesbian look like? I smiled and smiled at a stunning, short-haired woman standing alone at a scenic view pull-off on a Vermont highway. She was wearing highly polished, flat-heeled shoes, a blazer, a tailored silk blouse and sharply-creased pants. She slipped her hands, fingernails short and manicured, into her pockets and smiled back at me. We saw her again when she passed us on the road in a white Cadillac convertible with the top down. I honked and she smiled and waved as she sped by. Irene agreed the woman was a Lesbian and called me a flirt. She knows my fondness for the "blazer dyke" look.

The Lesbian clues here were more subtle than clothing. The fact that this Lesbian did not "soften" the severity of her clothes with a "feminine frill" was encouraging. For us, the clincher was the way she flipped that jacket behind her hip bones in an unmistakable dykely way as she put her hands in her pants pocket.

Checking out shoes when looking for Lesbians is an elimination device, a negative marker. Lesbians wear sensible shoes whenever possible. Irene and I have learned to pass right by a woman who looks like a Lesbian from head to ankle, but wears flimsy shoes with pointed toes and heels. She is sure to mention a husband by her second sentence.

So, what does a Lesbian look like? Well, we saw two old women drive into a campground in a large motorhome. One dog and no men accompanied them. These are Lesbian-positive clues. We seldom see old women in campgrounds unless they are accompanied by old men. They walked the dog, each wearing a long "ladies" winter coat and lipstick. We casually intercepted them.

"Nice dog," says Irene. The dog growled. We mentioned the movie about nuclear war on TV the evening before.

"They should go to Russia. Show it to the Communists," they angrily replied. We walked on. If they were Lesbians, I did not want to know.

"Not Lesbians," pronounced my expert. "There are Lesbians who wear 'ladies' coats and Lesbians who wear lipstick. There are even Lesbians who prefer nuclear war to 'Godless Communism'; but Lesbians would not let their dog growl at women without correcting it."

We had better luck with two old women in a pick-up truck pulling a thirty-foot trailer. The dyke driving backed the rig into the campsite next to us in three moves! We walked over to check them out. They were wearing identical jackets adorned with patches from every state park in South Carolina. We admired their trailer; they admired our motor home. We talked about favorite parks. Then one woman asked, "You two sisters?"

I answered, "No, are you?"

"Nope!" they smiled and invited us for dinner in their thirty-footer. It wasn't more than three sentences later that we were using the "L" word.

In our travels, we frequently see pairs of women who pique our interest. They wear either look-alike backpacks or look-alike boots or shoes, windbreakers or parkas, or all of the above, in the same color, style, or brand. We call it the Lesbian Bobbsey Twins look. We love it. We've met lots of great Lesbians because of it.

At a campground in Maine, we were in the laundry room staring at the dryer when a blue van pulled up. It contained two women and one large dog. The woman nearest us was wearing three tiny earrings in one ear and no make-up. I started to get excited, but Irene advised caution. She reminded me that the line between Dyke attire and non-Lesbian casual is fuzzy nowadays. The stranger hauled herself out of the van in one large motion. She stood there, in hiking boots and blue jeans, smoothing out the wrinkles in her plaid flannel shirt. When she smiled in that certain way at her similarly clothed companion, Irene admitted we had struck gold. She ambled out of the laundry room wearing her WOMEN TAKE BACK THE NIGHT T-shirt and struck up a conversation with the women. Soon, we were enjoying our first four-Lesbian conversation in a month and loving it.

Lesbians can usually be found in the company of other women. Non-Lesbians frequently spend most of their time with women too, so this is not a clue in and of itself. Refinements are needed.

One warm November day, walking along the path through the sand dunes at Huntington Beach State Park in South Carolina, we saw two women seated on a blanket on the deserted beach. We stood and watched them a minute and knew they were Lesbians. How did we know they were Lesbians? Well, I thought they were Lesbians because they were two women over thirty, seated together while flying a kite. They were not amusing a child. They were not holding the kite for a husband. They were sitting on a beach and flying a kite for their own pleasure, an unlikely activity for non-Lesbians.

"John dear, I am going camping with Mary for a few days so we can bask on the beach and fly kites," she says.

"What a great idea," he says. "Have a good time."

No way!

Irene was sure they were Lesbians when the woman with the kite, wanting to stand up, handed the kite-string holder to the other woman without asking AND without looking to see if she was taking it. They knew we were Lesbians, not because we were two middle-aged women on the beach at a park unaccompanied by children or men. They said they knew because of the intimacy they perceived in our gestures, movements, conversation and activity as we set up our beach space.

Another time we set up camp in a park in Manitoba in sight of a motor home with Florida plates. We watched a woman emerge with a dog on a leash. She was wearing a green and white striped rugby shirt tucked into very tailored cotton pants which were closed with a narrow belt. Her hair was short and her face was make-up free. Irene went out to make conversation using the dog as a pretense. Pretty soon she called me over "to see the dog." Juanita was talkative and kept saying "we" this and "we" that. She did not mention a husband; and her conversation was remarkably free of sex-specific pronouns. We were encouraged. It wasn't long before Ginny stuck her head out the RV door, saw us and came over. She was dressed much like her partner, the Bobbsey Twins again. We had a fine time with them. Like us, they were retired and living full-time on the road.

Of course, all of our Lesbian clues are only partly true, or sometimes true, or for some Lesbians, never true. Irene has been looking for Lesbians for forty years and she still gets fooled—not in thinking a woman is a Lesbian when she is not; but in thinking a woman is not a Lesbian when she is. I err in the other direction, assuming women are Lesbians only to have them stroll away, hanging onto the arm of a non-woman.

Still, there is an unmistakable something about Lesbians. Perhaps it is the walk; and I do not mean the Lesbian stomp. The Lesbian walk is a solid placing of the feet on the ground, not a tentative, tippy-toed sway, but the assertively nonchalant stride of a woman who belongs to herself. I have seen Lesbians costumed for work in dresses and high-heels, walking Lesbian. The sight is awe-inspiring.

Along with the walk is a certain stance, a way of moving the body that is Lesbian. Lesbians, generally, move as if the various parts of our bodies, in use at the moment, belong to us, not as if the parts were borrowed from their owners and heaven help us if we bruise anything.

Standing with one's feet apart, rather than with one foot slightly forward, or with one foot carrying most of the weight, is a Lesbian stance. One or both hands in the pockets of pants, especially when wearing a blazer, is a Lesbian stance. More than eight inches of space between the knees when sitting in slacks in public is suspect; crossing one's legs by putting the ankle of one leg on the knee of the other is a dead giveaway!

However, the most telling clue when looking for Lesbians is eye contact. I learned about the eye contact theory from Rita Mae Brown when we first met back in 1975. She said she can tell a woman is a Lesbian when she makes eye contact with her. If the woman looks back, holding contact instead of letting her gaze slide quickly away, she is probably a Lesbian.

"That's not true," I argued. "I usually make eye contact with women; and I am not a Lesbian."

"Hmmmmmmm!" said Rita Mae as she began to laugh.

NOW Is the Time, But Not the Place

Cathy Avila

I found the Lesbians quite by accident because, you see, I wasn't looking for them. And quite honestly, I wasn't looking for them because I didn't know they existed. No "real" Lesbians were visible to me or existed for me until I was well into my thirties. How could I be so naïve? I had always been a curious person, wanting to know as much as I could about the world around me. So how could I, a seemingly smart and aware female, not be cognizant of the fact that there was something out there other than the boy-loves-girl-loves-boy model? It was easy. I was a perfect example of successful social conditioning into hetero-sexuality. Through my strong catholic childhood and into my leftist-liberal twenties, I was given no other script than "woman as appendage to man." None of the images I was supplied with, of possible scenarios for how I might live my life, depicted women loving other women. I didn't know what Lesbianism was all about. Incredible, isn't it? Yet, I believe my lack of awareness of the existence of Lesbians to be the experience of most women on this planet.

So when did the Lesbians finally come into my life and how did I find them? It's a story that begins at a national NOW convention in Los Angeles in October of 1979. A friend from work convinced me to attend the convention with her from Friday night through Sunday. Never having attended a NOW meeting, I had no idea what I was going to see, hear, or do there, but was excited about getting away to something "new and unknown." What I experienced that weekend was so different from what I had experienced in my association with the male left (a political alignment I had made during my college days in the late sixties and which had remained my political identification through the seventies). At the NOW convention I saw women—hundreds of them—running the show, setting priorities, defining issues, making decisions. I had never before been in the presence of so many women, let alone women doing something for themselves and not for men. I saw and heard things I had never encountered before. The women I talked with over the course of that weekend awakened me to a politics beyond the male liberal left—the Women's Liberation Movement. I went away from the convention transformed and promising myself to commit time and energy to my new-found politics.

But that commitment took a few years to implement. Working full-time and going to school nights left me with little time and energy to give to the WLM. Over the next two years I did occasionally attend a NOW meeting of the local chapter in a nearby town. I did not become an active member, however, but went now and then to hear a guest speaker or to be in the company of women. They were a lot like me—immigrants from the liberal politics of the left, married or involved with men. Several of them had "exceptional" men who came to the meetings with them, helped them sell raffle tickets or allowed themselves to be pushed into doing childcare for the evening. These women were friendly enough, but being with them did not give me the "charge" I had felt at that national convention. I felt I was looking for more than these women, who were so similar to myself, had to offer.

That "more" came my way one August when four women I had met through the NOW chapter approached me about starting a NOW chapter in the town I lived in. They were disillusioned with the other chapter, feeling it was too conservative and cliquish. I was pleased to be asked to join them on the convening committee and happy to finally give that time and energy I had promised myself to commit to the Women's Movement. The five of us, all het women, vowed to make this a chapter that truly valued diversity and that took an active and visible role in the community.

I quickly became passionately involved in the work needed to get the chapter functioning: planning a kick-off program for September, printing and distributing flyers, arranging for childcare and refreshments, and putting together a survey to be given out at our first meeting, a survey which was intended to give us an idea of the issues women in our community were interested in.

Seeing it listed in material we had received from the state chapter, we included the category "Lesbian Rights" in our interest inventory (next to the bottom of a long list of issues). At that time I had no awareness of the rights that Lesbians would want or need to fight for. But just the mention of that word, *Lesbian,* sparked an interest. Yes I was interested, yes I wanted to know who and what these Lesbians were all about and what their issues were. Except for the rare Lesbian character in a novel, I had only met, briefly, two women in my life who had openly identified themselves as Lesbian. The women I had worked with in leftist politics had all been so "male-aligned" that I assumed by their lack of stating or acting otherwise, that they, too, were heterosexual. When I filled out my survey, I checked the category "Lesbian Rights." (Only myself and one other woman that night felt this issue important enough to check.) I was anxious to know about these women who were a mystery to me.

My involvement in the fledgling chapter began to consume all my free time. Virtually every night of the week and weekends, I was involved with women. One weekend in November several of us attended the NOW state board meeting in Los Angeles. Once again I was euphoric from being with so many women. I listened with rapt attention to the general discussions on proposed pay equity and childcare legislation and a report on discriminatory insurance practices in the state. I was learning the issues the organization prioritized and fought for in the public arena. All weekend long, my mind was continually being filled with ideas that, like seeds, had been planted, were germinating, and would soon burst into my life as new growth. Yet, not once that weekend did Lesbian Rights or issues affecting the lives of Lesbians come under discussion. There, among that large group of women, the Lesbians were invisible.

Time passed, and although there was still much to be done, our new chapter was off the ground. At our monthly meeting in February we showed the movie *Pink Triangle* and followed it up with a panel (two women and two men) representing the local Gay and Lesbian Service Center. I was fascinated that the two Lesbians sitting in front of a large audience in the YWCA in a very conservative community were declaring by their presence that they were unafraid to say that they loved women. I wanted them to open my eyes, to tell me everything about themselves and their Lesbianism, how they got there, what it meant in their lives, how different it was to be woman-identified. I wanted to know because I really had no idea. But since the men talked more openly and freely, I had to tuck my questions away. The mystery would not be solved for me that night.

But new questions, rather than answers, kept emerging, many because of a short article on homophobia that we printed on the front page of our February newsletter. I remember having to look up the word *homophobia* in the dictionary when I did the paste-up for the newsletter, as I had never before encountered the word in my readings or discussions. The questions in the article created in me a stronger desire and need to know about Lesbianism.

QUESTION: "Have you ever thought you could spot one?"

"No, someone please give me some clues as to what to look for!"

QUESTION: "Not asked about a woman's female lover, although you regularly ask about someone's husband/boyfriend when you run into het friends?"

"No. No woman has ever told me about her relationship with another woman. I wish someone would tell me what it's like!"

QUESTION: "Felt that gay people are too outspoken about gay rights?"

"No, what are the things that Lesbians are concerned about and fighting for?"

By March, three Dykes who had joined the chapter had formed the Lesbian Rights Task Force. But since our encounters had been brief, I did not yet know any of them well enough to take one aside and describe to her my intense need to know about Lesbianism. For by then, I had the beginning of a realization that I had been lied to and brainwashed all my life and that when I penetrated this unknown, I might find myself.

I finally "met" The Lesbian at my house one night in March. Only six months into the chapter's existence, profound political differences had arisen over what issues the chapter should give priority to working on and how visible the chapter should be in the community. A large group of women wanted the time, energy, and money of chapter members to be spent on setting up the organizational structure of the chapter. They opposed those of us whose priority was working on issues out in the community. That night in March, several of us had met to discuss what we felt could be done about this "bureaucracy" versus "activism" split.

Sitting at the far end of the couch, across the room from me, was a woman I had met a couple of times at general meetings. Many things about her aroused my curiosity and I found myself, throughout the course of the evening, watching and listening to her at the expense of my attention to the group. She did not talk a lot, but when she spoke, she displayed a quick intelligence and a clear and concise manner of explaining her ideas. I urgently wanted to get to know her!

As usual, after the meeting women hung around talking, not wanting to leave each other's company. I was very glad that Terri stayed on. I managed, finally, to engage in a casual conversation with her. And then we were the only ones standing in my living-room and we were asking question upon question of each other. Both of us were zealous in our desire to get to know the other. Terri told me that she lived with another woman, and until recently they had been lovers. My heart leaped, for I knew I had finally found, in my new friend, the woman I could ask, without fear or shame, to tell me what it meant to be a Lesbian, the woman who would help me to open that hidden door into the world I had come to believe I might belong in.

Terri and I began to see a lot of each other. I would deluge her with questions about why, when, and how she had identified her own Lesbianism. She never laughed at my naïveté and patiently answered my inquiries.

Things in my life began to change rapidly. In April, only seven months after its inception, several of us left the local NOW chapter, but still intended to participate at the state level. Instead of spending our time in pro-woman activism, we had become consumed with fighting the bureaucrats who by then had taken over the chapter. At the last general meeting we attended, several of us wore lavender armbands as a symbol of protest against the homophobia that had emerged in recent months. In May, not yet having embraced my Lesbian self, I had to deal with a het friend's fear (this was a woman who up to this point had not appeared to have any problems with Terri's Lesbianism) of having to sleep in the same bed with Terri at a weekend state board meeting. Homophobia was no longer an intellectual concept, but had begun to have personal meaning in my life.

In June, along with Terri and several refugee friends from NOW, I attended a Meg Christian and Cris Williamson concert and finally and overwhelmingly found the Lesbians. And in July, after attending the NOW state convention and realizing that for both of us the organization was not the place for what had by then become our need for more radical activism, Terri and I took a short trip up the coast of California. It was on this trip that I came out. I had found the Lesbian in myself!

As I look back on my experience of finding the Lesbians, I am glad for the short time I spent in NOW. I doubt that my political radicalization would have been as swift without that mainstream involvement in women's liberation. Through the experience, I discovered my own Lesbianism. But I feel lucky to have found the Lesbians behind the cover-up that was done of them. At first I was bewildered that the largest women's rights organization would allow Lesbian existence to be hidden. But the reasons for this became obvious to me after I came out as a Lesbian and continued for a short time to work politically with het women.

It is the heterosexual women in NOW who need and maintain the invisibility of Lesbians. Heterosexual women do not want to see or understand Lesbian Lives. To do so puts them face to face with the contradictions in their own lives, the lies they have accepted from men, and the privileges they have for being heterosexual. They fear and cover up Lesbians so they don't have to take responsibility for the choice they have made to align themselves with men. And the Lesbians in NOW share responsibility for their invisibility because they comply with the limits that het women set.

My hope is that each Lesbian who is presently working in NOW will one day come to prioritize Lesbians and realize that mainstream women's organizations do not work for us.

I feel fortunate that something in me sparked a curiosity that resulted in my intense desire to know about Lesbianism. Finding the Lesbians was like discovering a buried treasure of untold riches after sorting through the clues and pieces of an unknown puzzle. And the greatest treasure of all was finding the Lesbian in me!

Breaking
the Mormon Mold

Linda M. Peterson

Have you ever met or read writing by a lesbian mormon or a lesbian ex-mormon? Would you know it if you had? Ever since I came out of the mormon church and into the lesbian world, I have looked for clues that would identify lesbians as being from the same background as me, as I imagine women from other religious or otherwise specialized backgrounds have. When I saw the call for material about finding lesbians, I saw it as an opportunity to investigate the connections among lesbians with mormon backgrounds. I sent out a questionnaire to the few women I knew, and got it published in *An Affinity for Women*, a newsletter for lesbians with mormon backgrounds.[1]

There are two women who have each met hundreds of lesbian mormons (LMs) and lesbian ex-mormons (LEMs). One of them is Sonia Johnson, undoubtedly the most famous mormon woman, I should say ex-mormon lesbian, of our time. The story of her struggles with, and eventual excommunication from, the mormon church is told in her book *From Housewife to Heretic* (1981) and her coming out story is included in her second book *Going Out of Our Minds: The Metaphysics of Liberation* (1987). You can run across Sonia on public television; she has made hundreds of public appearances including her campaign for president as the Citizen's Party candidate in 1984. She gets calls all the time. Everywhere she goes, the LMs and LEMs go up to talk to her. I did it myself. You don't even have to be looking for Sonia to find her; she is publicly visible.

The other woman who knows hundreds of LMs and LEMs is Ina Mae Murri, who lives in Fremont, California. Ina Mae grew up mormon in Idaho, was discharged from the Air Force for lesbianism and, after a retreat into marriage, came out again in the late '60s. In 1978 she met two other LEMs after putting a note in a Bay Area women's newspaper. In 1979 she found out about Affirmation, an organization for gay and lesbian mormons, similar to the Catholic organization Dignity, and became the women's contact, which she still is. About the same time she put an ad in *Lesbian Connection,* in the first of several attempts, not all by Ina Mae, to start a LEMs newsletter. This project, which represents perhaps the third time identifiable lesbian mormon writing has actually been published, got off to what seems to be a really solid start in 1988. *An Affinity for Women,* with some financial support from Affirmation but completely under Ina Mae's editorial control, is formally described as a newsletter and "a support group for, by and about lesbians who have been or are presently associated with the mormon church." The mailing list has over a hundred names on it. Ina Mae also gets referrals from Sonia Johnson and Affirmation, organizes gatherings at her home and at the West Coast Women's Music and Comedy Festival, and puts up ads in bars when she travels. If you know where to look, it's not hard to find Ina Mae. Over the years she has met, counseled, and/or corresponded with several hundred LEMs.

Including me. I responded to one of the attempts to start a newsletter, and ended up going to meet Ina Mae and her lover on my next trip back to the States. When I met her I felt like I was visiting one of my mormon aunts. It was wonderfully warm in her home. I relaxed into mormon hospitality, but without all of the customary restrictions on what could be drunk, smoked, or talked about.

About the same time I met Ina Mae, I also went to a couple of workshops for LEMs at the Michigan Womyn's Music Festival. The first time I sat in a circle of twenty lesbians with mormon connections, I was overwhelmed. These women had gone through at least parts of the incredibly well-correlated mormon education system. They had given two-and-a-half-minute talks in church from the time they were three. They had been overseen by the double network of family and priesthood that kept track of what you ate and drank, what meetings you attended, whether you paid your ten percent tithing. They had been taught that wickedness never was happiness, and that lesbianism most assuredly was wickedness. And yet, there we all were, sitting together as lesbians. I drove my lover Amanda crazy afterwards, trying to tell her all about every one of them and how they'd got from mormonism to Michigan.

For the last few years I have been organizing workshops there myself. It is typical for first-timers at Michigan to be impressed by the number and diversity of workshops offered, but more than once I've been told of women's true amazement when they find one that really is just for them, for LEMs. Besides doing workshops, I have put up notices at lesbian or women's events, including WomanGathering and Flight of the Mind Writing Workshop for Women, where I met Treth, the playwright. Through these efforts and through the questionnaire in *An Affinity for Women* to gather information for this article, in other words, by making myself visible, I have met or corresponded with more than 50 LEMs. Some of them I have contact with only once a year at Michigan, but they still feel like my sisters, or some kind of mormon relatives.

I did not start out with the intention of making myself visible as a lesbian ex-mormon. When I arrived in Japan in 1979, in the spirit of an adventurous search for a new lifestyle, the last thing on my mind was seeking out mormons of any persuasion. I was trying to undo twenty-seven years of mormon training by experimenting with anything that mormons were against. I thought I could just throw away those twenty-seven years of being soaked in mormonism: nearly all of my family experiences—holidays, reunions, and vacations; most of my education, including the infamous "seminary," religious classes I attended at six in the morning five days a week before going to public high school, and two degrees at mormon Brigham Young University. Even my first lesbian lover—all of my life was inextricably connected with mormonism.

However, at the same time that I was consciously trying to forget or deny my past, I was also unconsciously broadcasting it. When you are an American living in Japan, everyone wants to know why. Students ask you. Other expatriates ask you. Back home or on airplanes, anywhere you go, people ask, "Why did you go to Japan?" I found that in nearly every situation I told people that I was running away from the mormon church. This was not a consciously chosen strategy, but a result of compulsive honesty. One unexpected result of this was that I started meeting other LEMs before I was conscious of wanting to, in fact before it had occurred to me that knowing them might be a good idea. One lesbian friend in Japan was so fascinated by my story that it was she who brought me that clipping about the LEMs newsletter. She also introduced me to two other LEMs who were living in another part of Japan.

I asked one of my LEM correspondents if she had ever been introduced to another LEM specifically because the introducer knew they were both LEMs. Treth, being a playwright, responded with a facetious bit of dialogue in which the friend says, "Treth, I'd like you to meet so-and-so, she's an ex-mormon like you," and then Treth says, "Oh, hello. I'm glad to meet you. So, you're an ex-mormon?" Treth thought this was highly unlikely because her experience is that someone tells her about another LEM and maybe sometime they happen to meet. In fact, her facetious scenario is exactly what happened to me at one of our lesbian weekends. My friend came running up wanting me to meet two new arrivals. She was excited because they were ex-mormons. I was excited too. I started toward them and had to laugh; they were both dressed in white. To a mormon, white clothes mean baptism, the temple, and heaven. I thought for a moment that I had died and gone to the celestial kingdom, just like the scene when the old man dies in the mormon classic film, *Man's Search for Happiness*.

We began the standard mormon gambit of finding out if we were related and who we knew in common. It turned out that I had been in graduate school at BYU with K's roommate. I had heard K's name dozens of times, and had in fact been jealous of her because I had had a crush on the roommate, who was obviously deeply attached to K. I had been shown pictures of K, but we had never met. Together we moaned and commiserated about the roommate's marriage to a man we both knew, who we were both sure was really gay. The roommate, we agreed, should have been a dyke. From there we went on with plentiful laughter, and not a little hysteria, to discuss other aspects of BYU during the late '60s and early '70s, and other things, like how we were dealing with our families. A few weeks later I flew to a small town in another part of Japan where K and her lover lived. We spent an entire weekend talking, laughing and crying about mormon experiences.

That initial meeting was typical for me of the times when I have met lesbian mormons or ex-mormons. Always there is a sense of familiarity, a common language, an understanding of doctrinal twists and emotional patterns, the ability to push the right buttons, and lots of shared laughter. I always go back to Amanda full of excitement; she has learned to recognize the signs of the emotional release it gives me to meet other LEMs.

That's why I go on seeking out other LEMS. It's fun. It's energizing. It's great to laugh with women who understand my clever use of mormon language. Also, it seems to be important for me to tell my mormon stories. Because of living in Japan and having so many conversational openings given to me, I got the chance to tell my escape-from-the-mormon-church story dozens of times. I told it laughing, I told it crying, I told it angry and I told it sad. Now I think I've finished telling it; it's almost to the boredom stage; it's just a fact. But I have a lot of other mormon stories that I haven't finished with. And it's often better to tell them without having to stop to explain a bit of doctrine or language. When you stop, you lose your emotional flow; you pull out of the feelings that may need to be expressed.

I've been lucky, and I've also had the freedom and the inclination to put myself in the right place to meet other LEMs. When I sent out my questionnaire about "Lesbian Ex-Mormons: How Did/Do We Find Each Other," I was full of hope and assumptions. I thought I would collect heartwarming and inspiring stories about how lesbian ex-mormons had found each other and helped each other sort out and overcome the patriarchal training of mormonism. I imagined that lots of LEMs had been connecting and I just hadn't heard about it. I was assuming that other LEMs' experiences were like mine and we all just needed to get some of it into print. However, when the responses started coming in, I found out just how connected we aren't. More than one woman said that she thought it would be great to actually meet another LEM, to know concretely that she wasn't the only one. Anne in Pittsburgh wrote of searching in vain for a story of a mormon in books like *Different Daughters* and anthologies of coming out stories. Some women wrote of not having met or heard about anyone other than Ina Mae or Sonia. As a kind of control I asked a straight ex-mormon acquaintance of mine if she knew any other straight ex-mormons, and she said no, but if I ran across any would I please put them in touch with her. After all, there are only six or seven million mormons in the whole world, and no one's keeping track of the exes.

I got responses from all across the United States. As mormons are concentrated in Utah, Idaho, and California, LEMs in those places tend to know other LEMs. Mormons are scarce in other places, as I know well from growing up mormon in Texas, and LEMs in places like

Tennessee tend never to have met another one.

Even women who live in Utah or California don't necessarily know other LEMs unless they have somehow made themselves visible. One Utah lesbian sought others by placing personal ads in the local gay paper. Others find LEMs at gay and lesbian organization meetings. There are many difficulties with public strategies in places with a high concentration of mormons; one woman reported that when she tried to distribute my questionnaire in Utah, she was met with fear and suspicion. How did they know that I wasn't some kind of undercover agent for the church, planning to collect names and addresses and then turn them in for excommunication? In fact this is not just a theological matter in situations where closeted lesbians work in church, or even public organizations, under mormon bosses who would happily fire a known lesbian.

Connecting, finding other LEMs, is the first step, and maintaining and strengthening the connections is the challenge after that. Every lesbian reacts to being a lesbian and a mormon in her own way, and goes through her own process of adjusting. Between LEMs and LMs (lesbian mormons), women who claim their lesbian identity but still consider themselves mormons, or believe in mormon doctrine and try to live by mormon standards, there is sometimes tension, and often disbelief.

Casey, a Utah woman who is active in Affirmation and the Gay and Lesbian Alliance (GLA), has met most of the LEMs and LMs she knows at GLA meetings when the matter of religion was brought up. "It was usually dropped like a hot potato, though," she says. "I haven't had the opportunity to talk with any of them in great detail about the mormon church and it seems almost taboo to some of them to bring it up. I do have a lot of questions I would like to ask the ones who are still practicing mormons, but I haven't had the courage to step beyond those bounds (of silence) yet. My general reaction is to watch them closely to see if the church is something painful for them, or if it is something they love or hate. The painful people are impossible to talk to. The love people just don't think about their differences with the church, and the hate people are just plain bitter and that is something I don't like, because the church will always have a special place in my heart, though we differ on some points."

Although we have always spent part of the time laughing and enjoying ourselves at LEMs workshops I have attended or facilitated at the Michigan Womyn's Music Festival, differences in attitudes to mormonism are usually clear. I found out from doing the questionnaire that a lesbian who attended a workshop I facilitated didn't come back the next year because she felt that others were trying to tell her how she should feel. Perhaps there was an unbalanced mixture of love-and-hate lesbians that year, but in any case the tendency to say things like, "But how can you . . . ?" or "But don't you know about . . . ?" is strong. Lesbians who are most clearly separated from the mormon church tend to be more outspoken than those whose ties remain closer.

I hate the thought that these differences keep us from finding each other and exploring our pasts together. I think it only fair that women state their feelings about the church as clearly as they can, but I see no reason why that should be the end of the discussion. I guess I feel that, especially for lesbians who have spent all or most of their lives in mormon culture, what we have in common may be more relevant to our personal process and progress than how we happen to feel about the church at a given time.

I feel there are many things about the mormon church and its policies that all members do not know. Also, like all women raised in patriarchy, it's difficult for women trained in the particular mormon brand of "the patriarchal order" to change our interpretation of behavior we know about but have been carefully taught to interpret in a particular way. It's been really useful for me to hear other lesbians talk about experiences I haven't had, like going on a mission, or going through the temple to be married, or having missionaries appear at a time of vulnerability after a death, birth, move or divorce. It helps me deal with my relatives more effectively, for one thing. Treth says she keeps talking about the church with other LEMs just in case she comes across something she missed. Maybe within the stories of other LEMs we can all find some answers to our own questions.

Notes

1. You can write to *An Affinity for Women* c/o Ina Mae Murri, 16089 Carolyn St., San Leandro, CA 94578.

From Kamp Girls to Political Dykes:

Finding the Others Through Thirty-odd Years as a Lesbian from Aotearoa/New Zealand.[†]

Alison J. Laurie

I began my unrelenting search for the "others" when I was fifteen. It was 1956, and I had heard the word *lesbian* and identified with it. I had been having kisses, cuddles and crushes on other girls since I was ten.

The first word I had found was *homosexual*. In the typical ignorance about sex of the fifties, I had been trying to get a sex education at the Wellington Public Library. I discovered Freud in the Reference Section, and learned that the "others" who were attracted to their own sex were all either in prisons or in mental institutions. This was not hopeful.

There were of course "others" at my all-girls' school, among both the teachers and students. But we were all afraid, and there was no way to discuss this subject.

Coffee bars began in Wellington. They were daring and new, bohemian. The first one was the Man Friday, followed by the Sorrento, the Picasso and the Casa Fontana. Writers, artists, unusual people went to them. I went every night. But there were no "others" there. At every opportunity I asked if anyone had ever met someone "like that." I did not say that I thought I was one.

---

†A slightly different version was published in issues 134 and 135 of the New Zealand Feminist magazine *Broadsheet* (November and December 1985) and is reprinted here with their permission and that of the author.

It was now 1957 and I was a sixth-former. I played hockey every Saturday. In the morning I played for school and in the afternoon for Old Girls. I was sure that some of the Old Girls were "like that," but I was only sixteen and they were cool, distant, guarded.

One day someone at the coffee bar talked about a "dreadful woman" who had made a pass at her. I found out the woman's name and where she worked.

She worked on the pattern counter of the D.I.C. store in Wellington. I went to see her and wore a tie so that she would realize that I was "one." She invited me home. We made love. She lent me a copy of *The Well of Loneliness*. I thought it was a wonderful book. It meant that there were indeed "others" and that they were not in prisons or mental institutions. They wore tweed suits and lived in London. Since they lived in London, perhaps some might live in Auckland? It was a much bigger city than Wellington . . .

My new friend didn't know. She wasn't much use at all really. She didn't know any "others" and said that she wasn't "like that." She said she only made love to women sometimes.

School finished. I went to Auckland. I stayed with writers and artists—friends of the bohemian coffee bar crowd in Wellington. I asked them about lesbians and grew bolder. I now said that "I thought I might be one."

At last I met a man who took me to the Ca d'Oro. It was early 1958. The Ca d'Oro was full of fluffy young men in chiffon scarves and make-up. I felt that I had come home. The young men and I went everywhere together. I wore a tie. The streets were dark and dangerous. People often chased us and tried to beat us up. "Queers!" they would shout. I was a fast runner. I had gone in full drag to a Trades Hall dance, passed as a boy and danced with girls. Afterwards I had to run ten blocks to safety pursued by a gang of milk-bar cowboys.

The young men did not know any other lesbians—except for two who had gone to Sydney. "That's where all the kamp girls are," they said. I liked being a kamp girl. I learnt a new vocabulary that was called "the palare."

PALARE—used by kamp boys and girls until the late sixties.
homi—man
polone—woman
homi-polone—homosexual
kamp—homosexual (possibly derived from police records, an

abbreviation for "known as male prostitute." Used in the scene for both sexes.)

bona—good

naff—bad

on jon wa—over there

square—heterosexual

trade—sex

rough trade—sex with squares (used by men)

butch—sexually "active"

bitch—sexually "passive"

British queens off the Home Boats had brought the palare to Aotearoa/New Zealand. Port cities like Auckland and Wellington had regular influxes of foreign queens who brought news of "others" in every port in the world. They influenced the Aotearoa/New Zealand scene profoundly in those days before general air travel.

But they brought no news of other kamp girls in Aotearoa/New Zealand. Still, I was able to return to Wellington with contacts for the kamp scene and to mix with kamp boys and go to parties. This was a great relief.

I looked everywhere for kamp girls. Anyone I thought might be, I put on my tie and went to visit. I went to Christchurch, made an appointment to see Ngaio Marsh. She was polite and we discussed theatre—my stated reason for seeking her out. I was too nervous to bring up my hidden agenda directly.

At last I heard about another kamp girl. We were introduced at a party. She was from Christchurch, newly arrived in Wellington. She knew no one else either. We became lovers. One afternoon we were making love at my parents' home while they were out at work. They returned unexpectedly and my lover hid in the wardrobe. My father moved forward, exclaiming "I know you've got a man in here." He flung open the wardrobe door and out stepped a naked woman. He retreated and my mother advanced. I immediately left home and we began to live together as lovers in a small flat in the inner city. I was seventeen.

One day we were out driving by Central Park. We saw two young women walking. They looked "different." We stopped the car and asked them for the time. We all had dinner together. We moved into a flat in Watson Street together. This flat became a centre for the "funny" parties. Kamp boys came, and bohemians. Some women came sometimes who said they "might be like that." The police raided our parties. We kept on having them.

We heard about two others in Auckland. We immediately jumped in the car and drove there to meet them. Now we were six.

It was November, 1958. We Wellington four decided to go to Sydney, where all those others were. We sailed on the "Monowai," our friends holding streamers as the boat hooted away with the entire known Wellington lesbian community. We went straight to Kings Cross. The beer-garden behind the Rex Hotel was full of lesbians. Some wore ties and suits and others frilly dresses.

"Are you butch or bitch?" asked Young Jerry, tall and tough. It seemed more prestigious to be butch, so I opted for this role socially and remained largely bitch in bed with my older lovers. I kept this a secret. It was frowned upon—called "turning." There were a lot of rules in the subculture. Breaking any of them meant you got beaten up. I learned to fight—the instruction was very similar to a modern women's self-defense course, except that it was free, informal and for real.

As squares were always trying to bash up kamps, it was vitally necessary, too. Some of the Sydney butches were amazingly good fighters. Dutch Kerry, Motorbike Bobby, Young Jerry were especially good. Tramtracks, Big Jan, Kiwi Jean, French Jackie and Flake were useful but not as outstanding. Everyone had butch names just as the kamp boys had their kamp names. The kamp boys were called things like The Countess, Gigi, Scotch Annie. My butch name was New Zealand Bobby.

The police raided the Rex often. I became an expert at eluding them—leave through the front bars before they locked the glass doors at quarter to ten (closing time at ten) or climb the iron fence, run like hell. They charged lesbians usually with consorting—which meant "habitually consorting with *known* (not convicted) criminals." Nine "consorting bookings" and you could go up for two years. I only ever got four (in South Australia). Otherwise there was always vagrancy (few out kamps could get or hold regular jobs); drunkenness, obscene language, resisting arrest, or even "being in possession of a stolen hotel glass"—after they'd pushed you out the gate with it. They were the Sydney Vice Squad, and they ruled the Cross, hunting homosexuals and prostitutes. Lesbians were seen as prostitutes—some were—and as *sexual outlaws,* who had broken all the rules and should be able to be arrested for

72

something. They treated us like hunted animals; our visibility angered them, and they wanted us to disappear.

As for us, we saw the police as a natural catastrophe—like floods, fires, earthquakes. There was nothing you could do about these things except to try and escape them. We had no analysis, no understanding that society could be changed. We simply tried to survive, as ourselves, as kamp girls, natural rebels. We did not feel that the police might not be entitled to hunt us, but accepted them as inevitable.

I was beaten up for suggesting that a woman ask for a lawyer. It was seen as a stupid—even dangerous—suggestion. Fighting back with threats of lawyers would only make the police even angrier at us. But part of me felt that what was happening was unfair and unjust, though I had no idea how things could ever be different.

Melbourne and Adelaide were exactly the same. The public lesbian scene was dangerous and difficult. There were many other New Zealand lesbians around, too. In spite of everything I loved it. The "mateship" was amazing and close, important enough for any risk. And the freedom to be ourselves, to be real, to be queer, affirmed us.

There were private, closeted scenes too, but they were hard to find and cliquey. They were fearful of being "sprung" by kamps who were too obvious. They were mainly older middle-class women. I knew some of them, learnt many things from them—like how to behave in a nice restaurant if you are taken to dinner. But they too had no sense of anything being able to change—except for the one strange woman who danced naked to Beethoven and lent me de Beauvoir's *The Second Sex.* She sowed some wild ideas, more than a decade too early for them to make any sense.

I returned to Aotearoa/New Zealand. There were a few more lesbians around. I had an affair with Anna Hoffman. Anna was a woman constantly harassed by the police. She had hit New Zealand headlines as early as 1956 when, as a sixteen-year-old, she had been deported home from Australia as a social menace. She'd had a lesbian affair with artist Rosaleen Norton, billed as "the witch of Kings Cross," sensationalized in the Sydney press. After this both the New Zealand police and press hounded her—including the police actually holding up the Lyttelton train when we were on it, in order to take us off and find out what the notorious Anna was doing in their Lyttelton.

As for me, I broke up with Anna and went to work for broadcasting, trying to be more closety by now. The police still raided our parties, so we tried to establish a pub for lesbians. Very important, because drinking was vital—women weren't supposed to, so it was a rebellion and an affirmation of our denial of conventional femininity. We did not identify with square women. There were us kamps—both boys and girls—and them, all those heterosexuals. If anything, we had more contact with heterosexual men, some of whom were quite friendly to lesbians. Most heterosexual women were uptight and nasty to us— especially the "fruit-flies," the square girls who hung around kamp boys.

Women couldn't drink in public bars in those days of six o'clock closing—in fact, some hotels did not admit women at all. This meant we couldn't drink at the Royal Oak Hotel, where the kamp boys went, unless we managed to sneak in wearing drag. Finally we found the Western Park, a scungy unpopular pub then, which agreed to allow kamp girls to drink there.

It was 1961 and the kamp girls' scene had grown larger. Many Maori had begun moving to the cities and among them were not only many more Maori drag-queens but also Maori kamp girls. They formed the basis of our first lesbian communities, some of them ex-services with additional knowledge of closet networks there. By now there were about fifteen of us in Wellington who were prepared to "mix" in the kamp life. There were maybe a few more in Auckland, which we visited frequently, driving all Friday night in ancient Fords or Morrises at 40 mph top speed, to socialize together for a Saturday. We also knew kamp girls in Christchurch—about five of them and we would take the overnight boat to Lyttelton on Friday night, returning Saturday night as it didn't sail on Sundays. Inter-city relationships were the rage, given our small numbers in each place, and most of our weekly wages were spent on travel.

Some Australian kamp girls visited here too, inspired by the large numbers of kamps from Aotearoa/New Zealand living over there. Motorbike Bobby and Little Hank made a great impression as they toured in full drag down Queen Street, Lambton Quay and in Cathedral Square. These were great events in our lives.

There were by now quite a lot of rules in our Aotearoa/New Zealand subculture.

- Don't spring your mates at work or with their families and square friends.
- Always be loyal to all other kamps.

- Tell the police nothing.
- Be butch or bitch and if you do turn, don't admit it.
- Maintain that you were "born this way" if you want to be accepted as a real kamp.
- Never have sex with men unless you do it for money.
- Know how to fight and don't ever be a coward.
- Drink lots, take your shout at the bar and be drunk often.
- Dress with kamp style, always press your pants and iron your shirt, never be sloppy.
- Be very clean, shower a lot and keep your fingernails very short or you'll hurt someone—and wear short hair.
- Learn to dance the latest. (It was the Twist.)
- Don't get off with your mates' girlfriends.
- Don't break up couples.
- Most importantly, learn to lead a double life if you want to hold down a job. Dresses at work—pants were totally unacceptable in any job then—and high heels. Learn to tell lies, to monitor yourself constantly, to always hold back. Kamp girls get fired, kicked out of flats—always, if "they" find out.

And so we lived. But I was also a socialist and involved with the Campaign for Nuclear Disarmament (CND). The socialists kicked me out, afraid that I was a "security risk"—queers can be pressured you know. CND didn't seem to mind as much—but they were mostly fringe people themselves then. I read a lot, and began to believe in social change.

I read a book, *The Homosexual in America,* by Donald Webster Cory. A kamp boy had smuggled it in—no such books were available on open sale in Aotearoa/New Zealand then. This book spoke of social acceptance. It also listed the addresses of some American homosexual organizations—One Incorporated and Mattachine. I was very excited. I wrote away immediately for their magazines. Through these I discovered the Daughters of Bilitis—the American lesbian organization started in 1958.

It was hard to get foreign exchange in 1963 but I was able to change some pounds on the street with a U.S. sailor for American dollars and to get a few issues of DOB's publication, *The Ladder.* (One and Mattachine had luckily sent their sample magazines free.)

Through *The Ladder* I found out about the Minorities Research

Group (MRG), Britain's first lesbian organization started in 1962. I wrote to them, and subscribed to *Arena Three,* their magazine. I passed it round the crowd, but very few others were interested. They thought subscribing to such a magazine was really risky, and what was the point anyway?

By now the crowd was much larger. The Royal Oak had opened the Bistro Bar and women could drink there. With the increasing urban shift more Maori kamps had come to Wellington. I had an important relationship with a Maori kamp girl from Nelson, whose Mormon family, though initially welcoming, finally tried to break the relationship up. But Wellington seemed safer than it had been just three years earlier—there were more of us, and now we had a better place to meet.

But I thought it was important that we organize, as they were doing overseas. I put ads in *The Evening Post* for the "Radclyffe Hall Memorial Society." I did get replies and met a few more lesbians—but no-one wanted to start a branch of the MRG in Aotearoa/New Zealand.

The kamp boys were quite numerous by now. They started the Dorian Society. We held a meeting with them but they refused to let kamp girls join. We were very disappointed.

I decided that I must go away, to where there was an organization that I could join, and be part of something that might work for some kind of change. So in late 1964 I left for London—and the MRG.

I sailed from Auckland on the "Castel Felice," and the entire known Auckland lesbian community came to farewell me—all 25 of them by this time—holding the streamers and singing the songs in what was once an important leave-taking ritual for all those kamps from Aotearoa/New Zealand who went permanently into exile "overseas." I was sure, then, that I would never return.

I was pleased to find six other kamps onboard the Castel Felice, and the five-week trip was interesting. We tried to find the "others" at Naples, but ended up at a brothel full of drag-queens.

On arriving in London I went straight to the Gateways, already an herstoric place in 1964, and also found the Robin Hood. To me it seemed like a multitude of lesbians, but the best was yet to come. Within a week I was able to go to an MRG meeting—the first known lesbian organization in Britain, which I had left Aotearoa/New Zealand to find.

MRG had members all over Britain, ran advertisements in newspapers and held monthly meetings in London as well as special interest group meetings. Many of the women who had started it were "colonials" as we were called at that time, from Australia, "South Africa," "Rhodesia" and Aotearoa/New Zealand. Some of the "South African" women—whites—had tried in small ways to oppose apartheid and felt that they had more than one reason to reject their country and live in London.

My first political work as a homosexual girl—for in London we were not kamp, and we were not yet women—was to help mail out *Arena Three,* the monthly magazine, and to start getting up and talking at meetings. There were often a hundred or so homosexual girls at meetings so this was quite intimidating at first. Then I volunteered to run a group. The weekly Literary Group met at my flat and a dozen of us read Dylan Thomas and other male authors very seriously.

It did not occur to us to read many women authors. We knew of few lesbian books except *The Well of Loneliness,* which we'd all read and re-read, and with no women's bookshops, or movement, or politics, why should it have? We were lesbians, not women, so why read women authors particularly?

Bryan Magee from the BBC wanted to make a TV programme about female homosexuals—he had just made one about male homosexuals. We were all very pleased at his interest. I was assigned the task of showing him around the clubs. I took him to the Robin Hood and the Gateways and introduced him to the girls. Everyone was thrilled that the BBC would do a documentary on sex variants like us, pleased that people like him were "sympathetic."

Other people came and wanted to do research, MRG cooperated enthusiastically. We went along and filled out questionnaires, did inkblot tests. It was so nice that the experts were willing to study us, perhaps prove that we were mentally normal. This would help us to win acceptance. We looked forward to a time when we might be tolerated, might be allowed to live in peace, might be granted a few crumbs from the table.

This was a very radical view. Most London lesbians, who did not belong to MRG, thought that nothing could change, and that the less the outside world knew about us the better. Then no-one would suspect that we existed. That was much safer.

Then, in Easter 1965, I went as part of the MRG delegation to a lesbian conference in Holland. We became aware of this conference when an American lesbian living in Amsterdam visited London. Otherwise there had been few international links that we knew about.

That conference changed my life. There were 300 lesbians there, mainly from the Dutch mixed homophile organization, the COC. Holland had no laws against homosexuality; their society was quite tolerant of variants apparently. At the conference many lesbians talked about social change—although no-one except the British delegation was wearing slacks—and they all looked very serious and conservative. I was very impressed. My expectations began to expand. If not quite equal to heterosexuals, perhaps almost so . . . ?

I left London, and with lesbian friends explored Europe on the thumb. My decision to live in Copenhagen was based on a tall, Danish lesbian that I met in a piano bar, Lille Rosenberg, one romantic night, so it was hardly political at first. But I soon became involved with the Forbund of 1948, which was another of the European mixed homophile post-war organizations. I helped with mailings, until one day I found that I could speak Danish well enough to say a few things at meetings. As time went by I could say more and more, and I began to think and feel like a Dane.

I visited the United States, but returned to Denmark. The States seemed so apolitical, so disorganized apart from the Daughters of Bilitis, which I thought wasn't as effective as the Danish F48.

The Americans might be more free-wheeling and have lots more bars, but the Danes were getting articles into the newspapers about homophiles. And anyway, the bars in New York were all mafia-controlled, with thugs wearing guns guarding the doors, and everywhere in the States it seemed you could be arrested for wearing more than three items of male clothing. I had put away my tie and butch identity when I left Aotearoa/New Zealand, and was now trying out that new word "femme" as an identity, but I still wore pants and shirts.

And I liked being a homophile. *Homophile* was such a wonderful word, so much less sexual, somehow, than being plain old *homosexual*. More dignified too, very Greek and everything. I liked the Danish beer, and the piano-bars where you danced waltzes, and the discos which were just beginning with wilder, louder music, and the Danish lesbians who made jokes in bed and laughed a lot.

My new lover was Norwegian though, and as we moved in together on New Year's Eve in 1969 neither of us knew that within a year our whole world would have changed.

When we read about New York's Stonewall riots (the first large scale lesbian and gay rebellion against police harassment) that June, we were amazed. Homophile men and women rioting in the streets! We held weekend seminars to discuss it. Something called gay liberation had happened. What was it all about?

The new ideas were mind-blowing. You could be lesbian, gay or however you wanted to be. You didn't have to integrate into society, or beg for tolerance and acceptance. You could do your own thing. You could be free to be yourself. You could—and should—come out of the closet.

We held our first public demonstration in the Faelled Park in the middle of Copenhagen. There were hippies all around, with long hair and beads, smoking hashish. People talked about civil rights, made comparisons with the Black civil rights movement in the States. People talked about the anti-Vietnam war movement. The sun was shining. At that moment everything seemed possible. We were going to be free at last, we were gay people, liberating ourselves and the world.

Then more things happened. A small group of heterosexual women calling themselves Redstockings who said they were feminist, whatever that was (something to do with that old suffrage movement, perhaps), invited the gay women from F48 to meet with them at a weekend seminar. We went, dubiously, and they talked about something called women's liberation. They said that they thought that we were oppressed by the gay men in F48, and that we should do something about it. And they said that we were oppressed by society in general as women!

We went away and started our own consciousness-raising groups to talk about all this. It was an amazing discovery, that we shared an oppression with 51% of the population, instead of our gay 10%. And what was even more amazing was that these women said that we were their sisters. They said they felt solidarity with us.

Soon we started a group called the Q-Activists—Q for queer and for *qvinde*, an old Danish word for women. We met at the newly-seized women's house, an empty building we had helped our sisters liberate from the Copenhagen municipality. The top floor was lesbian space, and we began to refer to ourselves as lesbians, that frightening word we had always avoided.

We used the Q-Activists as a pressure group within the F48, to get more women onto the committee, and to get a women-only night at the Pan Club, owned by the organization. We held a Scandinavian lesbian conference at the women's house in 1972, and though not many came it was a start.

I went to the States again that year, too, because that was where it was all happening now. I worked on an issue of *The Lesbian Tide*, met lesbians who were starting groups and magazines everywhere. I started to call myself a lesbian-feminist.

"All women are lesbian except those who don't know it yet," and "feminism the theory, lesbianism the practice," and "in a society where men oppress women, to be lesbian is a sign of mental health" were the slogans. Butch and femme were laid to rest. We were roleless, liberated—and any woman could choose to be lesbian—should choose to be lesbian. Few did, as yet.

We read Elizabeth Gould Davis's *The First Sex* and became excited about the matriarchy. Men were mutants, we said, women were actually superior to them!

The ideas were all developing. They were new, stimulating. I felt I was part of a movement which was forming them, finding them, exploring them. There were no limits any more. I felt a strong urge to return to Aotearoa/New Zealand. Letters from friends implied that the revolution might actually reach there, too.

I packed a VW combi van with supplies and American lesbian magazines like *The Lesbian Tide* and *The Furies* and with my Norwegian lover and an escaped American headmistress set off from Denmark to drive overland to Aotearoa/New Zealand, shipping the vehicle across intervening oceans. We arrived in early 1973, to a blazing January. Gay liberation and women's liberation had already started in Auckland and in Wellington.

We were mainly in Wellington at first, where I was asked to speak at some early abortion meetings, and here and there about gay liberation overseas. About six of us went to a gay liberation party in Auckland, following a meeting where men had said they really wanted more lesbian involvement. We were all bashed up at the party by drunken gay misogynists and everyone ended up feeling that it was quite impossible to work with any of the men. As for me, I went back to Wellington and worked in the mixed gay liberation group until we split after a dance with half the takings and announced that we were going to organize separately as lesbians.

We met with Christchurch lesbians and Sisters for Homophile Equality (SHE) was formed in both Christchurch and in Wellington.

We might call ourselves lesbians but you couldn't have an organization with that in the title . . . SHE was New Zealand's first and only national lesbian organization. We started *Circle* magazine in December 1973, and reprinted articles from my American lesbian magazines, which I was busily distributing around the country. Lesbian feminism hit Aotearoa/New Zealand as a fully formed blast from abroad, but fell on fertile ground, among many of the lesbians from gay liberation for starters.

Lesbians wrote to *Circle* from all over Aotearoa/New Zealand, and issues were put out from Christchurch and Auckland as well as Wellington. We held a national lesbain conference at Victoria University in Wellington at Easter 1974, and got media coverage although we held out for women journalists only. We were on radio talk-backs, were mentioned in the news. And we held a lesbian demo outside parliament. We often sang "I Am Woman" and did ring dances. We believed in the sisterhood and the matriarchy-to-come.

I returned to Denmark in 1975 and was part of a group trying to set up an international lesbian front. To my surprise all kinds of new lesbians were "coming out" of the women's movement. Although we had wanted this to happen it was surprising when it did, and difficult to adjust to. I had known some of the women as heterosexual feminists and it was hard to accept them as the new experts on lesbian political theory. They seemed in some way to lack what I felt was a lesbian identity, though I was unable to analyse quite why.

I went to a lesbian conference in Amsterdam, with women who didn't know and couldn't have cared that there had been one there ten years before, and how important it had been. I sought out some of those 1965 lesbians and found them now quite anti-political. "We can't stand all these new lesbians," they said, "they're so negative." I disagreed of course, on principle, but somehow there was less joy in the air. Unemployment was starting to happen in Europe, political discussions seemed different, we talked more about rape and violence, about men and what they were doing to the world. We talked less and less about sisterhood until finally we didn't talk about it at all, because none of us could really believe in it quite the way we had when the sun shone and it was always summer, and the whole world was poised on the brink of change.

I asked one of the new lesbians to dance at a social after a meeting. Then I tried to kiss her, gently, as we had been doing for the previous five years. She pushed me away roughly and said I was behaving like a man. I felt hurt and didn't understand. I got drunk in a corner with some twenty-year-olds, crying into the schnapps bottle and trying to explain to them that there was something happening now that wasn't what I thought I'd fought to achieve. Something uptight, critical, rejecting. Something not quite—lesbian.

I was only 35, but I was beginning to feel like an old woman of the movement. Most of the lesbians my age were not to be found in the lesbian movement. Many were back working in the mixed homophile organizations, now changing their names to associations of gay men and women. Or they were branching out to start women's refuges, getting involved in the peace movement, active in the political women's movement.

I had moved to Norway and found that the only lesbian group I wanted to work in was one called The Panthers, involved in social and cultural activities of lesbian poetry, discussions and sing-alongs.

I got involved with the Norwegian F48 and a huge split over Marxist-Leninist politics, which resulted in the formation of the Workers' Homophile Association (AHF)—which turned out to be not at all marxist anyway. It all made for interesting political intrigues, but I grew tired and began working very hard so that I could spend part of each year back in Aotearoa/New Zealand.

My work as a tour guide made saving money easy, especially doing lots of trips through the U.S.S.R., where there were few consumer temptations. I did, of course, and dangerously, search for Soviet lesbians whenever I could.

Back in Aotearoa/New Zealand, by 1977 SHE was dying, though *Circle* still continued. Many lesbians had come out through the women's movement here too, and certain conflicts were beginning to emerge. The sisterhood had turned out to be far more complicated than we had imagined.

We were becoming conscious of other oppressions like race and class which created differences between lesbians. As yet we had little analysis of any of this and few lesbians attempted to really do anything about it. In 1978 a lesbian centre started in Wellington and political work included forays into the Human Rights Commission where chief commissioner Downey had concluded that "some kinds of discrimination cannot be outlawed." Newsletters were published, women's bookshops began providing regular access to the flood of books coming off the international women's presses, and women's music was strumming and beating its discs into every lesbian home. There were crafts, too, and poetry, and women's art in the Women's Gallery.

Overseas again, there was now the International Lesbian Information Service (ILIS) and the International Association of Lesbians, Gay Women and Gay Men (IGA) providing regular international networking and holding annual conferences for delegates from as many as 30 countries.

Many lesbians were beginning to work with gay men again, though tentatively, and only on specific issues. Others continued to develop a strong separatist politics, and some women were moving to the land. Pornography became an important issue, though as yet no lesbian analysis had been made.

As for me, I returned to Aotearoa/New Zealand permanently. It was 1982, and I worked on a couple of issues of *Circle* for old times' sake, and then got into lesbian broadcasting on our first lesbian radio programme which still runs weekly here in Wellington. We performed some lesbian plays, saw the first lesbian centre die and another begin, to vanish in its turn. We saw several lesbian clubs come and go in Wellington and other places too, and lesbian phone-in services develop around the country. There were regular but informal links with lesbians everywhere.

But when the homosexual law reform campaign came, we had no lesbian political organization to tackle it and had to develop strategies on the run. We battled against a U.S.-inspired moral majority (so-called) which petitioned against us door-to-door and whose hatred thundered at us from public platforms throughout the country. They gathered a claimed 800,000 signatures from our population of three million, from children, old people in nursing homes, frightened lesbians and gay men, and with many multiple signatures. They presented their petition to parliament in a Nuremburg-style rally with god, the family and our colonial flags waving while anthems were sung. We fought them and some of us were arrested; we disrupted their meetings and we ripped up their petitions when we could. We won some and lost some; male homosexuality was decriminalized but human rights were ruled out for the time being. It was 1986 and many of us were exhausted by that campaign but we have survived it.

What do the political dykes of the eighties have in common with the kamp girls of the fifties? Our ability to survive is the single most important thing.

Not all of the kamp girls did survive. Some are dead, lost to suicide, or the slow deaths of stress diseases. Others married, to live a daily lie, a double life made tolerable by tranquilizers or booze, and perhaps an affair with the woman down the road. Some married gay men to provide a double disguise for two frightened people. Others lost their minds into alcoholism, living half-lives in the shadows, while other good women were attacked by the shock treatments and drugs of psychiatric institutions. And every single one of us carries scars.

And I know how easy it would be to put us all right back into the fifties, with the no-communication and the no-visibility and a relentless search that finds you only four others.

Close the bookshops and ban or burn the magazines and the books; prohibit the phone-lines and the public advertising; close the clubs and the centres. Only now do I know that there was a world-wide movement once before—the first wave of lesbian and gay liberation smashed at its German centre by the Nazis in 1933 and throughout the rest of occupied Europe from 1938 onwards. It vanished with few traces; the first great Nazi book-burning in Berlin was of the lesbian and gay books, manuscripts and records from an institute founded in the 1890s. I have heard lesbian and gay historians say that what was remarkable about the surviving copies of the last issues of the lesbian and gay magazines of the time is that they were so unsuspecting. Their last issues wrote of next month's dance, next issue's feature. They were all closed down without warning. I look at Clause 28 in Britain and I wonder what new state treachery is in store for us.

My own search for the others began in the fifties, long after the Homocaust of Europe. As yet we know very little about the lives of earlier lesbians in Aotearoa/New Zealand, either in the pre-war period or during the past thousand years since the migrations or after the white invasion of the nineteenth century.

My search for the others continues—back into our lesbian past, in our present and on into our future. Sometimes I find them, and when I do I am convinced more and more of our ability to survive against all odds, and to re-emerge from our hiding-places in even the worst of societies. To find the others we may need to re-define what we mean by lesbian, what we mean by sex, and how we understand love. But the others are always there somewhere if you just keep on looking.

Happenstance

Susan J. Wolfe

For me, finding lesbians has been a matter of happenstance: I stand around, and I happen to find them.

I found two of the significant lesbians in my life because I got a job as an English professor at the University of South Dakota in Vermillion. Now, perhaps a Midwestern town with a population of under 10,000 doesn't seem like a logical lesbian hot-spot and I'm sure that if I'd willfully sought out a likely site for dyke-hunting, I wouldn't have picked this one. But, as it happened, I was finishing up a Ph.D. in English, jobs in the field were scarce, and USD offered me an interview. Encouraged by my advisor's husband and my own, but personally reluctant even to interview at a university in this setting, I booked a flight from New York to Sioux Falls anyway.

I hated the whole interview and nearly all the circumstances surrounding it. If I'd read Del Martin, I'd have known this wasn't the place to find lesbians. I'd have stayed in, or near, a big city. But then, I wasn't looking for lesbians. At least, not consciously. I was interviewing, hoping I wouldn't be offered a job in this wasteland. If I blew the interview, I wouldn't have to take the job. Otherwise, I'd wind up taking it, because my husband wanted me to, because I didn't think I really had a choice.

There was a John Deere tractor in the Sioux Falls airport. To me, the presence of that green behemoth said it all. Born and raised in New York City, my idea of rural was the suburbs of Long Island. In New

York airports, dealers feature the new Pontiac models; no one browses for farm equipment. And, as we drove the 60-plus miles to the university, we passed only one car, a beat-up white station wagon traveling North, across the meridian—which my driver, the chairman of the department, identified as one belonging to someone from the Art Department.

I was horrified; I'd grown up in New York City, where there were so many people per square block that most of my "neighbors" were total strangers to me. Here, though, a person could drive for hours without passing another car, without seeing a lighted window in what I would learn to think of as "homesteads." As we drove the interstate from the largest city in the state, there was nothing to look at but endless fields of dead cornstalks. It would be years until I'd appreciate these enough to comment "minimum tillage."

I was told that the chairman would be in his office from 7:45 a.m. on the day I was to interview. I assumed it was a tacit instruction to appear at that barbaric hour. So I did, and was put on display in the coffee room for hours, while interested parties wandered in to look me over. I sat there, waiting for the interview to start, but it never seemed to. (It was only much later in the day that I discovered my only formal interview was to be with the dean—the department committee had made up its mind that I was the right candidate for the job, sight unseen.)

Those who know me now find this hard to picture, but I went to that interview in a charcoal-grey, silk and wool blend, size eight designer dress. Then as now, I hated the kinds of clothes men want women to dress up in. I looked the part ("hopeful job candidate"), but felt unnatural, as if there were no way to arrange my body on the hard wooden chair. Nonetheless I sat on, exchanging pleasantries, fielding questions that seemed only occasionally pertinent.

And in she walked, in bib overalls covered with designs, embroidered slogans, looking tough. I can't remember what I said. I think it was, "Thank god! You're wearing jeans." I think I supposed that what I felt was relief. I have a vague memory of carrying on what was on my part an inane, brief conversation about how much I enjoyed wearing jeans. She had been introduced to me as the head of the department student advisory committee, so why I thought her attire constituted appropriate daywear for junior faculty is beyond me. Maybe discussing my preference in attire served to obscure my other "preference"—an attraction to women obvious (in retrospect) from the fact that I was staring stupidly at the body of this stranger, instead of concentrating on my job interview. This tactic—"When confused about your lesbianism, babble irrelevantly about *anything* else"—must have worked. Even I wasn't aware of what I was imagining.

For her part, she says what drew her to me was the fact that I kicked my shoes off at the reception the chairman threw for me. I guess I didn't think about it: I've never been good at maintaining a consistent impression when I'm trying to pretend I'm someone I'm not, the off-white deep pile of the carpet looked lush, and my feet seemed to respond to it of their own accord, wriggling out of my high heels and into the carpet. When I sensed her staring at me, I became so confused I threatened her. To be specific, I asked her if she was staring at me, and when she laughingly declared she had been, I offered to hand her "a knuckle sandwich on Jewish rye."

Remember me saying I hated the whole interview process? Well, I hated the way I acted when I realized Cathy—a woman!—was staring at my legs, but I didn't know how else to act. It would've helped if I could've sorted out what I was feeling.

It took another lesbian to bring us together. She happened into my life, too. To be exact, she happened to apply for the position replacing me so that I could write my dissertation. I don't know what the odds of a lesbian's applying were, since we had, I think, only a dozen or so applicants.

I was the only person teaching linguistics. Remember, I was and am in a small department at a small university. So I was the person in the department best qualified to screen the credentials for my replacement. And that was how I found my first "real lesbian"—a woman who knew she was one, and said so.

Cathy was on the screening committee, probably because she was still on that student advisory committee. And we felt we had to stand up for Julia, whose credentials were the best we had, but whose lesbianism made some committee members very uncomfortable.

Some karma, huh? Here's this lesbian looking for a job, and two of the five people on the screening committee are latent lesbians looking to come out. Conversely, here are these two lesbians, from the D.C. and N.Y.C. areas, who wind up on the same screening committee in Vermillion, looking at this dyke's vita.

Not that light dawned on me right away. I didn't know anything was happening to me while I was self-righteously defending the right of a "gay person" to equal employment opportunities. Luckily, my unconscious is a lot more intelligent than my rational mind. It has a healthy, stubborn assertiveness once it has figured out what I need. It had already decided that I needed to be a lesbian, that I needed to know that I was a lesbian and to live like one . . . openly, "out."

The committee met in November. The chairman was tolerant enough to hire Julia, or maybe he was professional enough to hire the person best qualified for the job. So, anyway, she was coming in January. I had talked to her on the phone. She sounded nice enough, my first bona fide lesbian. And she was a linguist. I had a piece of data to file in my unconscious: it was possible to have a Ph.D., to be a linguist, and to be a lesbian.

Like I said, my unconscious is intelligent. It managed to block from consciousness the likely consequences of what I was about to do in December, 1975—that is, get Cathy and me roaring drunk so that we could have enough pseudo-courage to be honest. This time-honored technique worked. (I probably should say that using alcohol as an excuse for coming out is a custom which is more honored in the breach than in the observance. I wish I hadn't felt we needed liquid courage then. We don't now, and I hope new dykes don't have to feel that they do.)

We've been living together for twelve years now, in Vermillion, South Dakota, so I guess you could say it all worked out. Not that changing my entire personal life was simple. It took me a couple of years to get Cathy's attention. I invited her to go to a conference with me, she went hunting with a male colleague; I offered to give her a lift home, she preferred to hitch. I gave her a rose and a bottle of champagne for her birthday, she offered to share it, and I panicked and backed off.

Looking back, I guess I was doing a courtship dance as elaborate as those performed by great African birds. But if that's what I was doing, I never really told myself, let alone Cathy.

I started to work with Julia in 1976. Then, since I had both a lover and a dyke friend, divorcing and coming out publicly seemed like the next step, so I did.

I don't mean to sound flip about having lesbians "happen" to me. Strictly speaking, I suppose I had a lot to do with bringing lesbians into my life. But, in the beginning at least, I wasn't necessarily thinking about finding lesbians . . . just about hiring Julia, or having Cathy in my life.

I have a friend named Sylvia. She once told me I was "a risk-taker." I said I didn't think of myself as taking risks; I simply act on the only logical choice at the time. She replied, "That's what I mean." I'm still not sure I know what she meant. I do know that sometimes I find what (and who) I'm looking for, before I'm even conscious that I'm looking for something.

They Met
Through the Wall

T. Lynn

In 1982, Anita Bryant's excruciating gay discrimination crusade was finally coming to an end. It was two years into President Reagan's pro-American, anti-left anything administration, and the campus of the Ohio State University was swept with Reagan's conservative ideals—intensified by a surging number of student Christian groups that led daily preaching sessions on the campus grounds calling for gays to repent their ways. It was a time when lesbians and gays were quiet.

Feeling a need to respond, but lacking an outlet, one woman quietly screamed her protests on the bathroom wall of the Main Library. She vehemently scorned Bryant and Reagan's discriminatory words and actions against gay men and lesbians in delicate handwriting, scrolled with a fine-point lavender pen. She signed each message Simone.

Simone's graffiti attracted a lot of attention. Her messages were often flanked by angry threats and zealous pro-Reagan diatribes. Support, however, came from a young lesbian who called herself Bruce. These two were soon joined by a third graffitist named Heidi. After arguing politics with the other anonymous wall-writers, three against who knows how many, Simone, Bruce and Heidi began a dialogue of their own.

A daily ritual of corresponding soon evolved and quickly developed into a unique support network for each of them. Upon this public slate, Simone, Bruce and Heidi wrote long letters discussing their private lives: coming out, meeting other lesbians, and first love/sexual relationships with women. A year after they began writing to each other, Simone, Bruce and Heidi would finally meet. A few years later, they talked with me about their experiences of writing on the wall.

Going through a divorce and a custody battle over her two young children, Simone was just recognizing her lesbianism when she began writing. Because of her family situation, Simone's emotions and her ability to express them were restricted, so she vented her thoughts in the safety of anonymity.

"I was really shy," said Simone a few years later. "I didn't talk in class and I didn't talk to people. Writing on the walls was like stopping insecurities because I was so afraid that people would not like me and yet I had all these things inside of me that I needed to get out and nobody to say it to—so it was like—write."

The four of us drank a beer together in Bruce's living room miles and years away from the wall. We laughed when Bruce told us about her first time in a lesbian bar, and we were quiet when the loneliness of that time in 1982 was shared.

That year was Bruce's first year on campus. Although she had been out for a while, she had been unable to find even the frays of the small lesbian knots on campus. Lacking the stability of a lesbian community, a network or support system of any sort, Bruce wrote to Simone.

"I was only a freshman and I'd been there two quarters without talking to a soul," said Bruce. "So I started writing to Simone on the wall—that's when I started writing, because I had no one else to talk to and here's somebody I wanted to say something to—just to say something."

Heidi, having recently returned from Europe, was also trying to understand her lesbian self in a conservative environment. Fairly limited in her understanding and knowledge of the lesbian clusters on campus, she tapped into Bruce and Simone's new support group.

Regardless of her reasons, the need for each woman to communicate with someone, anyone, was great, no matter how faceless and anonymous that communication might have been—as in writing on the bathroom walls—this need for trust and expression was asked for and returned by all three.

Amid the neatly written notes of the triad, death threats against gays in general and Simone in particular stabbed through their letters.

New threats appeared frequently, often in bold, black letters, covering the writing left by Simone, Bruce and Heidi. "That's what scared me," said Simone, "because I was comin' out on the wall and I was writin' that stuff and then I'm thinkin' they're not playin' when they say all fags oughta be killed. This is not a game. This is not something you say to let out your frustrations like when you say 'nuke the Iranians,' you know, 'cause there's nothing left to say. They really mean it—those aren't empty threats."

People don't just call for murdering gays and lesbians because they are powerless to do anything about their frustration. Straight society can and does kill lesbians and gay men. Simone said that she often felt she was risking her personal safety by being openly, albeit anonymously, lesbian amongst people who could harm her if they knew who she was.

In spite of the threats, Simone, Bruce and Heidi continued writing, thereby strengthening their friendship through their dependence on each other. Even though they each only knew the other by a pseudonym on the wall, these women became friends without faces, names, or even true identities.

Simone laughed, " . . . everybody I think that wrote on the wall thought that the other people that were writing really had it all together."

"She has this neat handwriting," said Heidi pointing to Simone. "And then she was so confident on the wall and it's like . . . " Heidi shrugged. "That's why I was so embarrassed to meet her."

" . . . on the wall you could be whoever you wanted 'cause I know that person was nothing like I am," said Bruce. "I'm making this sort of tough-sounding person."

But they were there for each other in that time and that place, expressing otherwise confined thoughts and feelings in a way that was open, yet safe in its anonymity, and that's all that mattered for this friendship to become strong. Like all good friendships, especially those that form between lesbians, each woman would look back on her experience of writing on the wall and know she had gained something more than a friend. She had learned something about herself and discovered a way to put the woman on the wall, and the woman she was, together.

With her new empowerment, Simone concluded her disguise as Simone. "I can't afford to hide," she said. "I might lose something I want." She stopped hiding by writing on the wall, "Simone loves Sarah. Simone's Mary's name. Simone's name is Mary."

". . . growing up," said Bruce. "We grew up enough to get out of writing on the walls. We met somebody. We met ourselves. We knew what to do with it and it all started just because we wrote and found each other . . . Everything goes through stages and that was a stage in our lives that we needed to go through and get out and meet people and once it ended we just drifted away from it. It wasn't even anything we needed to say goodbye to."

The graffiti is gone now. During the summer of '83, the walls were washed down and painted red. Simone, Bruce and Heidi are gone too, scrubbed away and painted over. The three women who were once Simone, Bruce and Heidi, however, have kept a part of what began as anonymous writing on the wall and developed into the women they really are, and the friendship they have together.

Baby Fingers[†]

Candis J. Graham

I've been thinking about telling Karen a secret. It's not exactly a secret. Among some women it's common knowledge. For the rest, it's information that needs to be shared. But you must be careful about who you tell, that's all. It's not the sort of secret you blurt out to just anyone.

I've been thinking about it for days and days, waiting for the right moment to tell Karen. She isn't one of those women you need to be careful around. It's amazing, really, the way women confide in her and tell her anything. I think it's because she listens carefully and always has something thoughtful to say. She has an aura of warmth and caring.

At least she used to, until she lost her job five months ago. Since then she's become a different woman. She's depressed and irritable almost all the time. I know she's worried about money and that can drive a woman to despair. She says job-hunting is the most demeaning experience on this earth. It certainly is getting to her.

That's why I've been wondering if I should tell her the secret. Lately she has a negative response to everything. But I've been thinking that this secret might change her mood. You see, I'm going to tell her how to tell if a woman is a dyke.

I haven't handed out questionnaires or done any scholarly studies or anything like that. My research is based on personal experience, that's all. Some things you just know. It's like wisdom. You can learn an awful lot from your own experiences and from paying attention to others.

---

† This revised version of "Baby Fingers" is reprinted here with the permission of the author and the journal *Breaking the Silence*, where it was first published (vol. 6, no. 2 [March 1988]).

I don't need a government committee to study the matter for two years. The government's always doing that, have you noticed? They avoid doing anything by studying it. Then, when they're finished, they're liable to make things worse than they were before they started. Governments can be pretty stupid.

Karen says the government spent a small fortune to send two different committees across Canada to study child care. Such a waste of good money. I mean, if you have to look after a small child or three, and if you have a job outside your home or want to get a job, or even if you want to work at home in peace and quiet, you don't need a study to tell you about the lack of good child care in your neighbourhood. Do you need a bunch of politicians to help you figure out that the child care centre down the road has a waiting list? If there is a child care centre down the road.

Life is strange. I never used to think about child care at all. It comes of getting involved with a feminist. I swore I'd never get involved with one. Everyone knows you're asking for trouble. Me, living with a feminist. I can hardly believe it.

My life sure has changed since I got involved with Karen. For one thing, I know more about child care than I ever wanted to know. No self-respecting dyke wants to know about child care. That's for the hets.

Don't get me wrong. Some dykes have kids. I know that. Some had kids before they realized they were dykes. That, I can understand. But some had kids after knowing they were dykes. That amazes me. I mean, it's just copying the hets. And who wants to do that?

I have some sympathy for them. Life's not easy for hets, anyone can see that. Which is a good reason, if you happen to need one, for not copying their ways.

Anyway, if dykes have kids, that's their problem. They had the kids, not me.

Karen disagrees. She says child care is one of the basic issues for all women, like food and shelter and being safe on the street. And, she says, if it affects one woman it affects all of us. That's the feminist way of thinking. Have you noticed?

Yeah, I got myself involved with a feminist and my life's just not the same. I knew, from the moment I set eyes on Karen, I knew she was a feminist. I should have known better. I couldn't help myself, that's all. I liked her smile. Karen's got a smile that makes me melt, like banana nut ice cream on a hot July day. That's me, whenever she smiles, a puddle of banana nut ice cream.

But do you know what scares me? I'm starting to think like them. It sort of happened gradually at first and I didn't notice. Then one day, just a few weeks ago, it hit me. I'm starting to think the way they do. I'm still in shock, let me tell you.

Like me caring about child care. You give me one good reason why I should care about child care. And don't say it's because what affects one woman affects all of us!

I'll never forget the day I realized I was starting to think like a feminist. Once a week, every Friday, all of us that work in the office go out for lunch. A few weeks ago, as we were waiting for the food to arrive, Jill starting talking about child care. She's the typist. She's twenty or so, and she's got her life all figured out. Well, she started on about how mothers should stay home with their children.

I don't care what mothers do with their children, but I figure they should have a choice. I don't like to hear anyone saying what women should do and shouldn't do. So I jumped in with my two cents worth and said women should have a choice. Seemed like a reasonable thing to say.

Well! Jill looked at me and said, "Are you one of those *feminists*?" She made it sound like a four-letter word.

I didn't like it one bit. How could she ask such a thing? I was so mad I wanted to spit. Does it make me a feminist if I think women should have some choices?

What bothered me more than anything was the way she said it, *feminist*. It made me so mad, the way her voice abused that word. They have some good ideas, feminists, when you look right at it. And that's just what I said to Jill. But before we could get into a humdinger of a fight, the food arrived and everyone started talking about the weather.

When I told Karen about it that evening, she laughed and laughed. "Poor misguided soul. She thinks you're a feminist!"

Karen has been frowning for months, so I was glad to see her laughing. But I didn't appreciate what she was laughing at.

"I'm glad you're amused."

That made her laugh even more.

But, as I told Karen, I'm getting really pissed off at Jill. She's always mouthing off about something and she's against everything. I'd never tell her the secret. It would be dangerous. Jill's the kind that thinks dykes are perverts and if she had her way we'd all be locked up in mental institutions.

That made Karen start laughing all over again. "They'd have to build a lot of institutions!"

"Quit laughing. It isn't funny."

Karen was holding her stomach as she slid off the chair. "Ho ho ho ho. You. A feminist. Ho ho ho ho ho."

At least my best friend, Maureen, agrees with me about this feminist stuff. She's a dyke too, and we go back a long ways. She has two kids, had 'em before she figured out that she was a dyke. They're in school, and after school they go to a program at the community centre until she gets home from work. Maureen doesn't make enough money to have to pay for the program. She's fully subsidized. Which is a relief for her. She says if she was making enough money to pay for the after-school program, she couldn't afford it. That doesn't make any sense to me.

Maureen's all for child care. She agrees with the feminists about that. She says she could have used good child care when the kids were younger, after her ex left and she had to go out and earn some money to pay the rent and so forth. She got by, but she had to live on welfare for quite a while, which is no picnic.

I've been worrying about Maureen lately. She's so excited about child care that she joined one of those women's groups that's trying to get the government to give more funding to non-profit centres. They want to create more subsidized places for children and increase the salaries of caregivers and that sort of thing. That's how it starts. Next thing you know, she'll be thinking like a feminist too.

It's one thing to set up a government committee to look at child care. But honestly, can you imagine the Prime Minister setting up a government committee to figure out which of us are dykes? He'd appoint all his old friends as members, men, of course, with maybe a token woman, and they'd fly first class all over the country and stay in nice hotels while they interviewed people.

I bet it would pay good money, but they'd never ask someone like me to be on the committee. I could tell them a thing or two. And they'd never ask Karen, though she sure needs a job and she knows a lot about dykes, having been one her whole life. But Karen doesn't know everything, which is why I'm tempted to tell her this secret.

Come to think of it, maybe that committee on how to tell if a woman is a dyke isn't such a bizarre idea. Something like that happened in the '50s, didn't it, in the States with McCarthyism, when they hunted for communists and homosexuals and accused them of unAmerican activity? I remember that from high school history. It was spooky. That committee sure didn't know much. I mean, as if there's a connection between communists and us. Look at how the communist countries like the U.S.S.R. and China and Cuba treat lesbians and gay men. Bad news.

But that was all a long time ago. It could never happen now. Though sometimes I wonder. I mean, some of the countries with powerful resources have frightening leaders. They're about as right-wing as you can get and they're liable to do anything. And now there's AIDS. Some people are being real jerks about it. The way I see it, they're using AIDS as an excuse to be mean through and through. There are people like that, have you noticed? Some people are evil. They're out to get the gay men. Next, they'll go after dykes. No one is safe.

I'm getting off track here. I'm supposed to be telling Karen how to tell if a woman is a dyke.

First, Karen needs to know another secret. All women are dykes. So you see, the trick is, how to tell the ones that *know* they are dykes.

Karen was not impressed. She got that annoyed look on her face. "All women are not dykes!"

"Ssh! The neighbours might hear you. It's a secret."

She lowered her voice, but she said each word slowly and clearly, as if I'd have trouble understanding. "Elizabeth, many women are not dykes."

I had to smile. For all their high ideals and funny way of thinking, feminists can overlook some basic realities.

But now I didn't know if I should tell her how to tell the women who know they are dykes. I mean, feminists think they know everything. She might be offended and think she should have known. But I've never heard one talk about how to tell a dyke. And let me tell you, lately I've been spending a lot of time with feminists. Karen and her friends.

And there's my Aunt Susan. She's a feminist too, and she approves of Karen. They stick together, those feminists. Aunt Susan was all smiles when I introduced her to Karen, and she was awfully pleased when she saw we were getting friendly. I think she figured Karen would be a good influence on me.

I've never told Aunt Susan this secret. Although she's a feminist, one of those militant ones, always raving about some injustice to women, she's not a dyke. At least, she doesn't think she's a dyke. Such a shame, I think. She's my favourite aunt. We're very close. She's been like a mother to me and nothing would give me more pleasure than to see her with a good woman.

But I'm off track again.

Karen. She's full of surprises. I thought she'd agree that we're all dykes. Feminists can be unpredictable. That's another thing I've learned lately.

I like to live dangerously, so I decided to go ahead and tell her how to tell if a woman's a dyke. It was bound to be interesting, whatever her response. These feminists have an opinion on everything. I just knew she'd have something to say. And this secret is a handy thing to know, how to tell the dykes from the hets. From the women who *think* they're hets, I should say. It's the sort of information a dyke needs to have in the world. And it's my way of being a good influence on Karen.

"Do you know how to tell if a woman is a dyke?"

She shook her head. "Is this a joke?"

"No, it's not a joke. This is serious. And don't you yell it out, either, for the neighbours to hear. It's a secret."

"Okay. Tell me. How do you know if a woman is a dyke?"

"You can tell if she's a dyke, I mean you can tell if she knows she's a dyke, by her pinkie ring." I wiggled my baby finger at Karen. I bought the pinkie ring for myself shortly after I came out, when I was nineteen. It's yellow gold and has my initial engraved on it, a fancy "E" with loops and swirls.

Karen stopped staring at the shopping list and looked at me. "A pinkie ring? I've never heard anything so ridiculous in my life!"

Well, this is not the way to talk to your girl-friend. But I knew she didn't really mean it. She's just defensive 'cause she's a feminist and here's something she didn't know. And, as I said, she's a little irritable lately about not having a job or any money.

"It's not ridiculous. It works. Try it sometime. You'll see."

And then I told her what happened to me last year, when I started working for Findley's Furniture Store downtown. I'm the bookkeeper. I'm good with figures, if you know what I mean. The owner's daughter is the buyer for the store. My first day on the job we were introduced and I knew right off that she was a dyke. It wasn't just the way she looked me right in the eye and said, "I'm pleased to meet you and I'm looking forward to working with you. Let me know if you need anything." She had this aura of confidence and self-assurance that you rarely see in het women.

So the next day, I wore my pinkie ring on my baby finger. When she came to my office to check through the file of invoices to be paid, which we call accounts payable in the business, she looked at my ring and then she grinned at me. An ear-to-ear grin. She knew and she knew I knew and I knew she knew I knew.

"And that's how you can tell if a woman is a dyke."

Karen stood up and shoved the shopping list in her back pocket. "Elizabeth, you live in a world of your own." And she left to get the groceries. She didn't even kiss me goodbye.

That's what I mean about her being irritable lately. Some girlfriends might be offended, but not me. I understand. It won't last. She'll find a job soon and go back to being her lovable self.

I don't know why they're called pinkie rings. I've wondered about that. Pink is not a dyke kind of colour. If any colour is, it's lavender. Especially if you believe in that lesbian liberation stuff. Lavender is popular with some dykes, have you noticed? Perhaps we should call it a lavender ring.

I must remember to tell Karen this doesn't always work. Some dykes don't wear pinkie rings. Some don't wear any jewelry at all. I've even noticed that some dykes wear pink. There aren't any hard and fast rules about this. We're a diverse group of women, that's for sure.

And, occasionally, I've seen a non-dyke wearing a pinkie ring. I haven't figured that out yet, but I think it may be a subconscious gesture. You know, a cry for help.

I've decided, sitting here waiting for her to come home with the groceries, to get Karen a pinkie ring for her birthday. So she can try it out for herself. There's no better way to test something than to try it out for yourself, don't you think?

I can't wait for her to try it out. Maybe I'll buy the ring next week. Why wait until her birthday? I mean, it might work as a good-luck charm in her search for a job. And won't she be thrilled, to have a dyke ring to wear.

I just hope when Karen is out and about, with that pinkie ring flashing on her baby finger, that all the dykes who know the secret will give her a wink and a nudge to let her know they know. As the feminists say, sisterhood is powerful.

The Promised Land Recedes Into A Grey Horizon

Anna Livia

The prospect of one, possibly two, months in Western Australia looking after her mother failed to thrill the pants off Theda Kyrannidis.

But it would put useful distance between her and Ranier. Ranier was Theda's guilty secret. Her guilty, gorgeous, cunt-melting secret. At first content to be where Ranier was, to talk to Ranier about the free radicals in the carbon chain, Rita Hayworth in *Gilda*, magic realism in the modern lesbian novel, whatever she could think of to keep Ranier interested, Theda felt things had come to a head the day she called Ranier's ansaphone three times during the day, when she knew Ranier would be out, just to have Ranier's voice to herself for three times thirty-two seconds. Theda had blushed the last time she had seen Ranier. Ranier, quite reasonably, had asked why. It was impossible to explain that she had been gazing at Ranier, because Ranier was god-damn gorgeous, everyone said that, and even Ranier described herself as charming; that she, Theda, had been gazing when Ranier caught her eye and looked back at her, and that there had been an annoyed, or annoyable, something in Ranier's look which made Theda think that maybe Ranier thought that she, Theda, was only staring at Ranier's fat, for it was true that Ranier was magnificently fat, as well as magnificent. So Theda had blushed and been quite unable to explain. Utterly aware that good lesbians do not fall in love, that falling is selfish, takes no account of the other save as involuntary catcher, Theda had proceeded, against all the messages her brain could feed her, to fall in love with Ranier.

Next time Theda ventured to ring at an hour when Ranier might be home. Ranier said it was nice to hear Theda's voice. Theda asked how Ranier was and Ranier said she'd just had a root canal and Theda asked was that teeth. Then Theda said it, what was on her mind; 'love,' she had said, and 'fallen,' and there was an 'I' which referred to herself, and a 'you' which referred to Ranier. Ranier said, kindly, that all this was very interesting but did not have anything to do with her and anyway she had two lovers already. Maybe she and Theda could see each other once Theda had fallen out of love again; Ranier made it a policy never to sleep with anyone in the grip of an infatuation. In the meantime if Theda came across any good lesbian novels in the magic realist mode, maybe she could leave the details on Ranier's ansaphone. Theda, accustomed to a more intimate relationship with Ranier's ansaphone, declined. And fled.

Arranging leave of absence from work, and someone to feed the plants and water the goldfish, Theda set about the more difficult, but ultimately more rewarding task of finding lesbians in Perth. Her mother would suggest she join the Women's Cricket Club. Her mother had been promoting the Cricket Club as a cure for every female malady of the last twenty-five years, from menstrual cramps and adolescent spots to hot flashes and single blessedness. As lesbians, like God, are everywhere, they are most certainly at the local cricket game. Theda had, however, only a month or two to find them and thought it swifter to try for places which called themselves lesbian. It is a well known fact that like calls to like, when they advertise their calling. Theda would need dyke sustenance if she was to stay with her mother, and the episode with Ranier had left her needier than ever. She asked around, wrote to any addresses which seemed likely, bought a copy of *Lesbian Network* at the Feminist Bookshop and scanned every page. She learned an awful lot more about Sydney than her well-regulated life with its familiar corners had given her cause to discover: late night lesbian laundromats, hotels with 'homosexual doubles', but precious little for Perth. There was one café, which had recently closed down; one corner of a progressive bookshop; one pub which hosted a women's night once a month: it didn't mention which night although, fortunately, it did manage to let slip which pub.

Either everyone was in Sydney (at the late night laundromat?) or everyone in Perth had moved house, because none of the friends of friends, ex-lovers' ex-lovers, Perth dykes who'd come to Sydney to protest the bicentennial, replied to Theda's letters. Nor did they speak to her ansaphone. The only lesbian clues Theda was to carry with her on the three day bus trip across the Nullarbor Desert were the closed café, the once-a-month pub and the odd shadow in the straight bookshop. Luckily Theda was very determined, and a few days at her mother's, passionately though she loved her, was going to make her very desperate.

Only poor people and English tourists travel by bus. Theda would have driven, had not her license been suspended for a year, punishment for never, but never, paying parking fines. She would have flown, had her boss not refused to pay her in absentia. She settled in the long, slightly raised seat at the back and indulged in her favourite pursuit: dyke-spotting. It was a habit, it took Theda's mind off Ranier, and there was always the chance that someone on the bus could introduce her to the Perth lesbian community.

The only people she could cross off immediately were the men, but there were very few of them; all others were subjected to itemized examination at the first filling station. The Aboriginals sat apart, away from the roadhouse. The women pulled a picnic out of enormous baskets. Theda liked to imagine all five were dykes, so loud, so boisterous, so affectionate were they. She had to give it up when they launched into animated complaint about their respective men. There were schoolgirls bickering, which could as well mean sisters as lovers. There was another Greek woman, of whom Theda had had high hopes, ogling the back of her head on the bus. She had very short hair and no ring on her third finger, but she looked unswervingly straight, smiled so consistently, dressed so correctly, adjusted her make-up so carefully, would not drink tea with smudged lipstick. There were three elderly white women who asked politely why Theda was going to Perth and offered sympathy for her mother's accident. Theda felt the familiar *frisson* of culpable complicity in accepting the sympathy due the devoted daughter while concealing the broken heart of the spurned lesbian.

Where was the look, the open interest which comes from any age and any race, but always dyke to dyke? It was only when cut off from her lesbian homeland that Theda prized the thousand small signals of lesbian recognition. And soon a heterosexual drama was enacted before the whole coach, of such stirring pathos that it established this transit as a home-for-home for hets, pushing Theda even further into the never never.

A very small toddler trotted round the corner. She was dressed only in a man's shirt, the arms rolled up and the tail threatening to trip her at each step.

"Poor little mite," said one of the elderly women, "that fella oughta be horse-whipped."

"Calls himself a father," added another.

"Ronnie," called the toddler's mother. "Come here you. Come and look at the cockies."

But Ronnie was not interested in cockatoos. She ran toward the Aboriginal group where three children were tucking into ham roll and chips. She hovered on the outside, ogling the chips.

"Go on," said an old Aboriginal woman, "let the kid have one." Ronnie grabbed a handful and wolfed them down.

"Hungry aren't ya?" said one of the younger women, looking at Ronnie's flapping shirt and bare feet. Ronnie nodded. Soon both she and her mother were sitting in the middle of the Aboriginal group sharing the food from their picnic basket. The mother might have been as much as sixteen, though Theda doubted it. She wore the same kind of shirt as Ronnie, her feet were also bare. Her hair was long, and bleached out, falling straight from the crown of her head; her skinny brown arms and legs were all elbow and knee. She ate very little herself, making sure Ronnie said 'thank you' each time a new morsel was offered.

"You gotta eat too," said the old Aboriginal woman.

"Me?" grinned Ronnie's mother, "don't worry bout me but. I may look like a piece a straw but I've yet to meet the hurricane could blow me over."

"Do yous know her?" Theda asked one of the women at her table.

"She was talkin to us at the bus station."

104

"Baby's father left them by the side of the road north of Cairns."

"With only a coupla his old shirts to keep the sun off."

"No money, no food."

"Spect she was seein someone else and he didn't like it."

"Her own fault, really."

"Yeah, but he shouldn't take it out on the child. Not her fault her mum's runnin around."

Theda wondered how the kid's mother liked being talked about and still have to accept the food and kindness she was offered.

"What she do when he drove off?"

"Caught a lift into town and called her mum."

Theda looked again at the girl's bare, tanned feet, her straw thatch of hair and broken teeth. Just the sort of girl that sort of thing would happen to. A tragedy in waiting. If you were casting for the great Australian outback movie, you'd pick her to play the rags of the rags-to-riches heroine. After that you'd have to change actresses.

"Want some tea?" asked Theda. "I ordered a pot and I can't drink it all. I'll ask for an extra cup."

The girl smiled and sat down. Ronnie was asleep on the couch.

"What's your name? Everyone always talks about you as Ronnie's mum."

"I know. We're sorta celebrities aren't we. Ya always learn kids' names first cause their mums keep yellin at em."

"I'm Theda."

"I'm Billy."

"Billy and Ronnie," smiled Theda. "You make a good couple."

"Know why I called her Ronnie but?"

"Tell me."

"After the most powerful man in the world," laughed Billy. "Kid's got to have one thing goin for her."

Theda laughed. "Goin a Perth?"

"Yis. Mum's trine a get me a state housin flat. I'm goin ta ring her tomorrow. See how's it goin."

"Do you get on?"

"No," emphatic. "She's worried about Ronnie, her grandchild and all that."

"I guess so."

"But she sent me money for the bus," Billy added, trying to be fair.

Theda nodded.

"She's angry because Ronnie was born out of wedlock."

Such an extraordinary phrase. Theda'd never heard it said seriously. Straight out of Dolly Parton, like the rest of Billy and Ronnie. Theda shot a quick glance at Billy, but Billy was sipping tea. Maybe she was practising for the social workers.

"I'm crazy about my mum," Theda offered, then decided the best way of finding lesbians is to let them know you're there. "Except that stayin with her means goin into voluntary lesbian exile."

Billy looked up at that. Theda hooked glances with her.

"She live in Perth?" asked Billy.

"Yis."

"Big city. Lotta lesbians there. Ya just have ta look."

"I've been lookin," said Theda.

Billy only shrugged and nodded.

As the bus plunged across the desert, and the heat rose and the sweat dripped, Ronnie and her mother became a common cause for the women passengers. They seemed to identify with a mother's misfortune, even while blaming her for it. They fed Billy and the child, passed orange juice down the bus, offered advice, asked the roadhouse and garage owners along the way if there wasn't an old pair of thongs lying about for the child, a frock or something for the mother. Food, clothes, advice and homilies were all greeted with the same formal gratitude.

When Billy called her mum from Kalgoorlie, and heard she had a flat to move into, the rest of the bus cheered. There was talk of a collection for furniture. It was heart-warming, and after Ranier Theda's heart needed warming, but mopping up men's messes is a way of life for straight women. Theda would have liked it better if they'd done it for love of Billy.

The coach trip was a practice run for Theda's stay in Perth. Robust displays of female kindness: neighbours and relatives popping in to offer help, bringing cakes and jam and veggies, sending husbands to cut the lawn, sons to water the garden and clean the windows. But always that peculiar distance, of lives lived apart, a reticence, reserve. Theda was tempted to ring Ranier long distance just for the intensity of the connection. Why didn't straight women go mad with restraint? They must be the loneliest creatures on earth. At least men don't notice there's anyone else out there. It's amazing what you take for granted while you have your own community around you.

Theda's mother, Olga, was very frail, could not walk more than a few steps, so Theda spent most of her time in the house. Once, when an old friend of Olga's came to spend the day, Theda had gone into town to seek out the café, the pub and the bookshop. She had begun to wonder if straight women's atoms weren't more loosely connected, and lesbian valencies stronger, tighter. If so, her own molecular structure seemed to be slipping, hollow sockets producing a dry crack instead of the usual smooth spring. Perhaps this is what is meant by the phrase 'falling apart'. As she walked along the street in the brilliant sunshine she searched every female face for a sign, and in every one she saw Ranier. Her despised infatuation seemed now the most lesbian part of her; she had carried Ranier with her from Sydney and that face had not broken up into an assembly of dots but was as solid and resolved as before. As she walked, she felt Ranier beside her; Ranier shared the excitement of finding the location of the café, the disappointment that it had become a gleaming new car rental. Theda had hoped there might still be posters stuck up on the window advertising other events. The car rental was not a lot of use to one whose licence has been suspended. Then it struck her that Ranier did not want to be with her and Theda was left alone on the streets once more. At the bookshop she found lesbian novels to supplement the stock she had brought with her. All books she had read before, and no magic realism, but the sight of the word 'lesbian' was a boon, an escape from her mother's kindhearted friends who politely refrained from asking after Theda's husband, boyfriend, sons, knowing these positions to be vacant, not liking to sound the depths of Theda's emptiness. Back at her mother's she rang the pub and discovered there had been a women's night the evening after she arrived; she would have to wait another month.

As the weeks passed, the women's night grew in significance. Theda worried what to wear, how she would get there, whether she had the nerve to go on her own, and what if no one spoke to her when she did get there. She would just have to speak to them. Fill her loneliness with her own effort. She thought about Billy and Ronnie in their new State Housing flat. She wanted lesbians to tell the story to. Her mother had remarked how there were always reports in the papers about rapes by the U.S. Navy up at the flats. Well, she'd said, it's just a lot of women and children living alone so of course the sailors think they're all prostitutes. She said it was understandable. All of human life can be understood, why does comprehension eradicate blame? Why was Billy so certain Theda would find dykes in Perth? Maybe she thought lesbians were like mountain gorgonzola, a specialised taste but available in any large metropolis.

It took a three-hour bus ride with two changes to get to the pub. When Theda spotted the crowd of rowdy dykes queuing to get in, she beamed with the kind of joy she would have radiated if Ranier had said "Come right on over," in response to her epic phone call. After a month away from the smell of lesbians, Theda felt she could put up with almost anything. She was wrong.

"You can't go in there," said a voice.
Theda was about to unload a month's wrath on the owner of the voice when she turned and saw Billy and Ranier with a placard.
"No To Australian Apartheid."
"What's goin on?" demanded Theda, six questions at once.
"They're searchin Aboriginals for knives. If they refuse to be frisked, they can't go in. Whites just pay and enter," said a Black woman with another placard.
The promised land receded into a grey horizon.
"Why?" asked a white dyke.
"Manager's orders and the manager's a racist scumbag."
"I've waited a month to get here," said Theda, "only lesbian thing I could find in the whole of Western Australia." This was no longer the point, even for Theda, but events had so far overtaken her that she clung to the last clear thought she had had, until she could decide how to arrange her emotions.
"If ya wanna meet dykes," said Billy practically, "ya oughta join the picket."
If intensity had been lacking this last month in Perth, it was crackling here red hot.
"Why didn't you tell me you were a dyke?" Theda demanded,

finding Billy an easier target than Ranier. "Especially after I told you."

"I reckoned ya could see for yerself."

"Your smokescreen was pretty thick. Tellin the other women Ronnie's father'd caught you with another man."

"They took one look at me and made it up themselves. And so did you. 'Poor white trash,' as the Americans so sweetly put it."

"I never said that."

"Didn't have ta."

"Yous two know each other?" said Ranier.

"I wouldn't say that," said Billy. "Okay, I'm sorry to run you up the garden path, but I didn't reckon those women would look after Ronnie so nice if they knew her mother was a dyke. You'd made up ya mind what a lesbian looked like, and I wasn't it. Go on, admit it." Theda shrugged.

"Spose you'd like to know what I'm doin in Perth?" said Ranier.

"Oh no," said Theda, "I can make it up all by myself."

The Antidote

Janet Aalfs

I am the lesbian daughter of a lesbian mother. This has not always been true.

Jeanne once told me that if she and my father had been friends, instead of husband and wife, they might have gotten along. If he'd been somebody else. If he hadn't been a man.

My father, a stranger to me, sends my mother a cartoon. He posts it to my address where Jeanne receives her mail since, at the age of 57, she packed up her belongings in the middle of the night and drove away from the life they had shared. The cartoon shows a man holding a baby on his knees. The baby looks up at him and says, "I sure am glad you and Mom got together because I would hate not to be here." My father writes, "Show this to our daughter if you think it's appropriate," fearing that without us he will cease to exist.

Origins and separations. Interpretations of the stories I've been told, the memories I excavate. Not one escapes contradiction. Here, let me begin again:

I am the lesbian daughter of a lesbian mother. This has always been true. I fantasize roving bands of Amazon warriors on wild horses stopping only long enough to give birth to parthenogenic girl babies. Romantic visions no more colorful than my own derivations. We are all products of unusual circumstances creating mythologies of our own to explain the unexplainable. Here is what I know:

Carla, my grandmother, leaves her mother's large family to marry a wealthy businessman. She and my grandfather raise Jeanne, their only child, in a large house in the midwest and send her to private schools. Carla dresses Jeanne in fancily embroidered clothes imported from Switzerland, unsubtle and unacceptable in the established uppercrust. Carla sends boxes of clothes to her sisters' and brothers' families. She tells Jeanne never to make comments about how her younger cousin Julie looks in Jeanne's hand-me-downs. When Julie comes to visit, Jeanne cannot talk to her at all.

Photograph of Jeanne and Leslie, another cousin, on a wharf. Julie is there too. Jeanne wears a new dark tanksuit with white stripes around the edges and at the waist. Julie wears Jeanne's suit from two years before. They pose for the camera. In another shot, the camera catches them unaware. Jeanne poised at the end of a diving board, arms raised. Her two cousins watch. I imagine her a split second later, splashing through the water's surface, then reappearing, shaking beads of water from her face and hair. She begins to swim, arm over arm, towards the middle of the lake. Ease of her movement attests to the comfort she feels.

Carla takes Jeanne on a trip east in the car. Carla's sister Arlene and her daughter Leslie join them. Jeanne and Leslie amuse themselves by counting license plates, collecting matchbooks from roadside cafés, making up stories about the people they see. This is not the first trip they've taken together without the fathers nor will it be the last. Jeanne draws cartoons in her travel log and accompanies them with a short description of each noteworthy event along the way. Leslie and Jeanne in a rowboat fishing/ Jeanne at the post office sending a card to her grandmother/ Jeanne and Leslie slinging mud at each other by the ocean/ throwing water in a motel room/ Jeanne, Leslie, Carla, Arlene eating lobster.

Jeanne the record-keeper, archivist, historian, chronicler/ keeper of diaries, journals, letters, recorded conversations/ translator, transcriber, compiler/ curator of dreams.

Jeanne the painter, musician, scholar. Who rises before dawn in memory of all the years when this was her only time for solitary work. Who now paints for hours every day in her apartment alone without major interruptions. "It's taken me all these years to realize that when I

111

go back to a painting, I won't be stuck in the place I left off. I see progress daily. It's the keeping at it that makes the difference." She who perseveres in the face of annihilation.

Jeanne learned early how to paint. Fell in love with her high school art teacher. Learned how to make friends and keep them. Girls, then women. She gave me this.

At the New England college she attended, Jeanne would talk in the early morning hours with an artist friend. They were in love and it showed. Other students noticed. Someone informed the president of the college. He promptly sent letters to the two women's parents. Denial. A meeting with the dean, a woman, who could not look Jeanne in the face. Jeanne who escaped by saying, "Do you know what it's like to look someone right in the eye and know what that person is feeling?" Who turned the accusation back on her accusers.

Jeanne, who learned essential lessons in the arms of women, sided with her father and blamed her mother for complaining about the wind, rain, fog, isolation. She had no tears for the first woman she ever loved. For Carla, the mother, who locked herself in her room for days. No amount of coaxing would budge her. Carla's best friend Kay could only say, "She gets like that sometimes. No one really knows what to expect from her." Carla's tears for her own mother never ceased. The doctors said that Carla's grief was the result of an "unnatural attachment." In her unhappiness, she looked away from Jeanne toward the past. Long after Jeanne was already grown, living far away with a family of her own, Carla, age 70, packed her bags and moved to New York City to stay with an old college friend. Carla's husband coaxed her back, only for her to stop her heart the night before he was to fly her with an oxygen tank at her side to the west coast away from all she knew and loved.

From these women I learn to break patterns, destroy false allegiances. Dinnertime when my father wasn't there we talked about how it was better without him. Upon return, he sensed our betrayal. In retaliation, he brooded until the silence became unbearable, the way pressure builds before a storm until all it takes is one small spark for the lightning to strike, thunder to roll. No one could stop the deluge that followed. He slammed doors, broke glass, threatened to hit us, sometimes did, accused us of withholding information if we were silent and of being insolent if we spoke.

We are punished for our collusion. Made to drive splinters under the fingernails of the women we love. The pain a constant reminder of our defiance, our refusal to be torn apart.

Jeanne watched us at the water's edge, four children with sandy skin, making forts and sandcastles, screaming and laughing as the waves threatened to wash us away. Sometimes she played with us in the shallows. We climbed on her legs, shoulders, held onto her arms and begged for piggyback rides. As the years passed, she stopped wearing her powderblue bathing suit, the only one I remember her owning. She cut short her time spent sitting on the sand and walked long distances out of our sight. Then she stopped going to the beach much at all. My father liked to swim. He liked to tell us to be careful, don't run on the rocks, watch out for poison ivy, don't throw sand. But mostly he went off by himself, further and further as the years passed, and sometimes I wondered if he was ever coming back.

The girl in the boat who is me wears a smile, waves. She turns away into the wind, squints her eyes against salt spray, and tries to forget that she is not alone. The sleeves of her sweatshirt flap against her arms. She grips the top of the windshield and licks her wind-dried lips. What does she see in the glint of foam, streaked clouds, expansive water, gulls with bits of quahog in their beaks, geese flying south? Who does she become out in the open air?

The girl does not smile as she steers. She holds tight and maneuvers the boat carefully so as not to tip it over. Her father sits on one of the white plastic seats in the back of the boat. Her two brothers stand next to her leaning on the windshield. They lean especially far forward until the boat picks up speed and begins to plane. She is afraid and exhilarated, holds tighter and refrains from pulling the lever towards her to lower the speed. She knows they don't care how fast she goes, would go faster themselves if the motor had more power. They are not afraid or at least don't show it. She keeps her eyes straight ahead and her back stiff.

She follows iron buoys, remembering to pass them on the left, opposite of the way she would if this were a car and she were old enough to drive on city streets. She reduces speed to cross another boat's wake and is relieved to make it past the mouth of the river and around the sand bar. Her father calculates the tide and places the anchors accordingly, sometimes throwing them in and pulling them back several times before they are positioned to his satisfaction. She climbs over the side of the boat and wades to shore, glad that her mother and older sister aren't there. It was different when they were. Jeanne was nervous and clumsy getting in and out of the boat. Her sister didn't know how to tie the ropes, and when the fog rolled in, she didn't seem to care much that it was time to go home. The girl does not want to be like them. She lifts her sweatshirt over her head, exposing her scantily clad body, wishing she could become invisible, be rid of her round belly and thighs that rub together when she walks, her small breasts that do not fill the top of her two-piece. She drops her sweatshirt on the sand next to her towel and book and edges slowly away, hoping her father who is still anchoring the boat and her brothers who are skipping rocks won't notice and want to join her. As soon as she is around the corner where the beach opens out and stretches for miles along the coast, she begins to run.

I stoop to pick up shells. Some are half-hidden. I dig at them with my big toe. Others are filled with water left behind by the tide. I am selective, keeping only those that warm my palms, hum in my ears, invite my eyes to dance. I have held enough to know that even two halves of the same shell bear differences in formation. I train myself to notice a slight shift in curve here, faded tinge of color there, this one shaped like a bird's severed wing, that one glowing like the eye of a fish almost buried in the sand. Angels walk here and shed their toenails; mermaids roll in and back out with the tide, leaving behind their glistening scales. Every rock has a name, each piece of driftwood an origin. I gather these artifacts, evidence of all that has not yet been told.

We walk on a snow-covered road. Jeanne tells me about all the women she has loved and had to leave. Some by force and more recently by choice. Now that she has arrived here, she chooses to stay. To paint, laugh, make love with a woman for the first time, read topographical maps, explore back roads on foot, on bicycle, eat pizza, grow plants, feed her Venus flytrap chicken, write letters and papers.

I am the girl grown up and drawn to water in all its forms. I dream that Jeanne and I trudge through snow in a forest. We come to a frozen stream. I look at her face and wonder how much I would resemble her if I were wearing her white nylon parka with the hood. The ice cracks as we stand there. I wake myself up crying.

I am tired of answering my father's desperate phone calls, of covering for Jeanne, of being her escape route. My father tries to force me to tell him where she is. "Tomorrow is my birthday," he says, "I'm going to kill myself." Another threat, another slamming of doors only this time I do not shudder. Months later, a family reunion, orchestrated by one of my siblings who must imagine that the six of us have something to say to each other. A dark restaurant halfway between here and there, my father's quivering jaw, Jeanne's unwavering smile, my siblings' hope, my knotted guts. We fill our plates at the salad bar— spinach, black olives, steamed broccoli, bleu cheese—nothing wrong with the food, yet it is difficult to swallow. We finish dinner and do not linger, say our goodbyes. It is the first time I have ever seen tears in my father's eyes.

In the car on the way back to my town, our town now, Jeanne and I fight. I tear at her eyes, she at mine. We cut each other down with words. No more smoothing over, sweeping under, stuffing down. Bile bursts from my nose mouth eyes, shattering lies. Jeanne drives on into dark night route 202. A setup. Mother and daughter alone in the car after years of surviving abuse at the hands of the husband and father. Silence and speed on the highway. Eyes that don't blink, tight lips. Fluorescent dashes white on the pavement mark our distance. Monotony. Time stands still. I am awake asleep. My worst fear the frightening truth. Alone together we face our damaged selves, each other, choke on the poison we have swallowed for which the only antidote is love.

If I forget this history I will be forced to repeat myself.

Who ever thought we'd have this time?

I listen closely to what she tells me and remember:

Mother and daughter, both lesbians, make their homes in a small New England town in a river valley surrounded by hills. One paints the other writes. They spend time together talking. There are always more words than time. The daughter tells the mother that someday she will live by the ocean. "But you can always be there wherever you are," the mother replies. "Bring the waves to you. Hear them in your heart. This is magic. This is real." She who knows departure from both ends does not like to talk of separation.

The girl now woman hears wild geese calling up and down the coast just before winter falls. Inland I sit in my mother's apartment watching the tree framed by her back window sway and drop its leaves at the edge of the gravel parking lot. Something inside me dies leaving a new place for sound to grow. I am not sure of the words for this. We are girls again together. Each of us remembering herself for the first time.

Some Recognitions

Shelley Anderson

It's a typical summer day in north central Florida, twenty-five years ago. Ramona Cartwright and I climb the fence into her back yard. My little sister toddles behind. She bursts into tears seeing us disappear; reluctantly we go back and haul her into the yard.

It's a yard very different from our own; there's a garden, with the tomatoes neatly staked, green peppers and melons. There's also a red swing set in one corner and a tool shed in the other.

Today, just for Ramona and me and my kid sister, there's something new. Mrs. Cartwright and Randy built us a playhouse. The thin pine planks have been cut so the bark is still on the outside; inside it's light and sweet smelling, with a sturdy floor and one window. It's all ours. Only for us girls. Last week the neighbor boys wouldn't let us in the ramshackled shanty they'd thrown together from discarded tin and wood and cardboard.

Mrs. Cartwright has short wavy hair and wears men's trousers. Randy, who is younger, has short straight hair and wears khaki shorts and tennis sneakers. Neither one wears make-up. Ramona says Randy has always lived with her and her mother. The two women also work together at the hospital. Playing in their house one day, I look through the open bedroom door and see their double bed. I know this is significant but don't know why. I know I will not tell anyone else. I am pretty smart for eight years old; I know silence means survival.

I am silent when my father slaps me for not ending my sentences with "Sir" or "Ma'm." I crawl behind the couch and write in the air with my fingers. I write "damn," "damn," "damn" over and over again. Mrs. Cartwright says damn out loud. I heard her.

Mrs. Cartwright and Randy go fishing. Mrs. Cartwright spreads newspapers over the cement patio, puts the dented bucket full of fish on one corner, and shows me how to gut a fish. I enjoy handling the knife. I like the way she never asks me to smile. My mother says I am too serious, that I don't laugh like other little girls. Randy and Mrs. Cartwright seldom smile. They take their lives very seriously.

Ramona never called her mother "Ma'm."

So. Lesbians have double beds, don't teach their kids good manners, wear pants with zippers in the front, fish and are grim. I kept a sharp eye out for these women on the streets of Gainesville, Florida all through the late '60s and early '70s. I sent out signals, like carrying a knife and a wallet in my back pocket. I did not find any. I decided after high school to continue the search in the Army.

In the Army the signals got confused. Like with Ruth. Ruth wakes up an hour before formation to put on make-up and twist her hair into a regulation bun. Off duty she wears peasant blouses and red skirts that sweep the floor. Off duty, she drags me into dusty second-hand shops, looking for all the velvet, silks, lace to fulfill her fantasies. Off duty, in the narrow regulation cot with noisy springs, she teaches me lesbians are more than what they wear.

I had not recognized Ruth as a lesbian. Someone else told me someone very close to me was a lesbian. Then I opened my eyes and looked at Ruth and she looked back.

One fall night in North Carolina Ruth took me off base in search of a gay bar. We walked to the town's one hotel and I followed Ruth through the lobby and into the bar. The bartender frowned at us. We were the only women in the small crowd of old white men. We sat down, wondering what to do. Ruth asked the bartender to call a taxi for us. Outside, she leaned over the cab door, looked intently into the driver's eyes and said very seriously, "We are looking for a bar where women go." I made ready to run all the way back to the barracks. The driver laughed and said, "You want a lesbian bar? Why not just say so?" He told us to go to the dirty bookstore around the block and ask there. Ruth took my hand and we went into the store. I kept my eyes straight ahead. The guy behind the desk gave her the address of The Top Hat.

118

There were only two other people in The Top Hat that night. A pale guy with mascara drying glasses behind the bar, and a short black woman who immediately recognized us as Army. There was a poster of Tina Turner on the wall. Ruth and I had one beer and left.

At lunch the next day a woman I had never seen before sat down beside me. "Don't I recognize you from The Top Hat last night?" She smiled. I froze, visions of dishonorable discharges dancing in my head. I ran out of the mess hall, but not before another woman, in fatigues this time, winked at me and smiled.

Ten years ago, on a kibbutz in Israel. I am there to visit my lover and travel back with her to America. A ready-made community is waiting for me—six American dykes, all volunteering in the valley's three kibbutzim. Barbara has also come to be with her lover. She and I are the only non-Jews. We all share oranges, go to Jerusalem and get lost, exchange aura readings and climb the hills. Barbara wins the first annual Ms. Hairiest Legs contest.

Naomi and I leave, sad. We are very sick after crossing the sea. We visit Greece, where we know we are now the only two lesbians in the world. We take another boat, get sick again, and end up in Brindisi. Everyone tells us to get out immediately, unless we want to be robbed. In line waiting for tickets out of here, we spy two other women. Naomi and I look at each other. Instant recognition. Was it the short hair or the jeans? Or that intangible quality of intimacy between them, the sense of being exactly where they wanted to be, claiming their space and their bodies and each other?

Naomi walked up to them and asked, "Where are you going?"

"What do you want to know for?" snapped one.

Three days later Naomi and I wander through the Vatican museum, oh-ing and ah-ing at all the plunder these drag queens have made off with. We are in the Sistine Chapel, developing cricks in our necks, when we see them again. They are holding hands under Michelangelo's ceiling. It is my turn to approach them.

I think of passwords, of codes. Are you having a *gay* time? Or, my favorite color is purple—what's yours? In one corner of the room an Amazon is frozen in marble, one hand curled around her bow. Of course! I'll simply say the statues of Amazons are my favorite—wink, wink, nudge, nudge.

I walk up and say "Hi!" The shorter one looks at me and at Naomi a few feet away. She looks at her lover. Instant recognition. They smile grimly and we all go to look for some cheap pasta.

Three years ago. Naomi left me several years before. I walk into a non-violence workshop in a strange city. I am very lonely. I survive because of my friends, with the support of my community, lesbians all. A woman is laughing in the workshop.

She has a silver women's symbol in her ear. I smile and make a note to talk with her sometime during the workshop. Then I see the pink triangle dangling from a thong around her wrist. I make a beeline to her.

"I like your pink triangle," I say.

"And do you know what it means?" she says.

"Of course."

"And are you one, too?" she says.

"Of course," I say.

We like each other a lot. We become lovers. We are still becoming lovers.

Yesterday she reads this and says I find the more I recognize myself the more I recognize other lesbians. I think she is right. We have a double bed. We do not have children to teach bad manners to. We do not fish. But we do wear pants with zippers in the front. We do take our lives very, very seriously.

Soap

Jill Flye

I saw them pause for a moment as they came in. They squinted through the crashing lights, picking out the dark forms of dancers and drinkers, reeling slightly as they breathed in warm fumes of alcohol, sweat, and tobacco. I watched them cross the room, amusing myself by working out who they might be, in an effort to ward off desperate boredom.

Obviously students, being young, eccentrically dressed in jumble-sale remnants, yet still managing to look all clean-scrubbed and respectable despite their efforts not to. The shorter woman seemed to be the extrovert of the group. She marched into the room without even a look back to see if her friends were following her, which they were, three men and another woman. I don't take a lot of notice of men as a rule, but these were rather odd, not the usual sort in a place like this. There was a small one in faded dungarees and earrings. He had a healthy boyish face, short fair hair, and the innocent expression of a Walton. The other two were very tall and very thin, like they'd come out for the night after a week on the rack. One of them had long wavy hair, a beard, and a calm, rather holy air about him. In fact he looked remarkably like Jesus. And he carried a shoulder-bag, so he couldn't possibly be a local. Few Yorkshire men carry shoulder-bags. I decided he was a young socialist from Potter's Bar who wrote poetry to aid the revolution. The other skinny one was all jerky and nervous. He looked very out of place, in long baggy shorts and a crisp white shirt which was buttoned up wrongly. Something about his small, fine features and his awkwardness yelled out public schoolboy. The second woman hung back shyly by his elbow. She was tall and mousey and very beautiful. Her hair was cropped short and she wore no make-up. She had a long neck and long limbs and a long baggy dress which appeared to be made from an old pair of kitchen curtains. She and Baggy-Shorts were the most obvious couple of the group. The way she clung to his humorous bone told me this was new love. I didn't understand it. What could she see in him? Oh well, maybe she was into nervous men.

I looked back at the small woman who was at the bar, passing back the pints. I thought of a name for her, Josie. It suited the lively and vivacious woman, who was now talking to Jesus. She was up on her toes, yelling at him over the music, waving her arms about in wild gestures and pulling extraordinary faces to illustrate her story, which she at least found hilarious. It ended with her laughing uproariously, giving Jesus a playful shove, and spilling his beer all down him. He smiled calmly, pulled a hanky from his pocket and began to dab at his jeans with it, but Josie jumped back in horror, snatched it from him and held it at arm's length like it was something dead, pulling faces and making the others laugh until Jesus grabbed it back and stuffed it home in his pocket. He was smiling at her tolerantly. I decided Josie was a drama student.

By this time I was hooked. You see, it was a straight club. I had arrived with Sandy and Val. We had been out drinking together and didn't feel ready to go home at closing time. But here the music was so loud a three-way conversation was impossible, so I left them to it. I had been sitting there for some time with nothing to do except stare at boring couples and avoid the glances of single men, in case they assumed that a second of eye contact meant I wanted to spend the night with them. This crowd was more intriguing than the rest so I decided to make them my evening's entertainment. I was not to be disappointed.

Now the tall, shy woman needed a name. I found Ellen graceful and fitting. In contrast to Josie's stories and giggles, Ellen sat quiet and thoughtful. She smiled at Josie the way a fond adult might smile at an excited child. This made me smile, too. I like to see women who like each other, even if they are with their boyfriends. I named Baggy-Shorts Edward and the one in dungarees I called Max. Edward and Max were obviously old friends, with their heads together, deep in conversation. Max looked like a politics student from East Grinstead.

The record changed and Josie screamed and jumped up, tugging at Jesus' arm, but he shook his head so she flounced onto the dance floor by herself. Leo, I thought, or possibly Aries. Ellen, Edward and Max followed her and they danced together. They looked like two couples, Ellen and Edward shy and awkward, Josie and Max energetic, easy movers, clearly enjoying the music and themselves. I glanced over at Jesus. He was dreamily rolling a cigarette. I turned back to Josie and watched her with some interest. She was so self-possessed, with her black hair cut short and her long laughing eyes. She spun round to the music, quick-footed in tatty trainers, old jeans and a black silky top. As I watched her I had to remind myself that this was a straight club, and I was definitely not interested in straight women.

Then a strange thing happened. Josie looked across at me and there was a sure buzz of mutual interest as our eyes met. Startled, I looked away quickly and wondered, horrified, if in the dim light she had mistaken me for a young man. Only that morning a shopkeeper had called me 'sonny.' Soon I was watching her again, but she didn't return the look. Then I saw that Ellen was also watching Josie, or Max, maybe. Her head was turned towards them as she danced half-heartedly and she was smiling, but her eyes gave something away—anxiety, jealousy perhaps.

So, what's that look for? I wondered. I supposed she was sweet on Max. Edward followed her gaze, and he also looked lovingly over in the direction of Josie and Max. Now, I'm a glutton for soap, so I was glad to see there were sexual undercurrents amongst this group and I began to wonder who wanted who and how much. So I watched them as they strolled back to their seats. Ellen was talking with Max, their heads close. 'Aha,' I muttered, 'so that's it!' Then Max touched her arm in a very casual, familiar way, which led me to think they must have been lovers once. Right, I got it. Ellen and Max were ex-lovers, Ellen and Edward were lovers, Edward was Max's old friend and Ellen, Edward and Max were still good friends despite it all. I glanced over at Sandy and Val, my closest friend, with my ex-lover, totally absorbed in flirting with each other. And to think I'd imagined this sort of thing only happened amongst the dyke community. What was I doing here any-way?—Oh, yes, we were here for a late drink. I took another swig at my lager. Before long I found myself watching Josie and her friends again.

As Josie flopped, laughing, into her seat beside Jesus, he put his arm round her and gave her a squeeze. I was surprised to see her flinch and her face cloud over for a second, before she gave him a tight little smile in return. Well, well. So their relationship was in decline. Funny such a warm woman like her freezing at her boyfriend's touch. Didn't Jesus notice? He wore that same dreamy, contented expression as if he hadn't realised at all. Josie leaned away from him and touched Ellen's arm and I could have sworn I saw her jump and flush. Certainly she seemed keen to focus all her attention on Josie. Well, who wouldn't be? I decided I was getting a bit too involved in all this. Time to buy myself another pint.

As I came back from the bar, I noticed Sandy and Val getting very cosy. Not again, I sighed. Why was it my friends always got involved with my ex-lovers? It was time we had some new arrivals in our little community. After all, one in ten was the quoted statistic. So where were they all?

I looked around the room. Jesus was sitting there smoking, the other four were dancing, but this time the women danced together a little apart from the men. Edward and Max didn't seem to mind, they were dancing together with wild exuberance. Max had taken his shirt off, and was taking up more than his fair share of dance floor, but he danced so well no-one minded. Next to him everyone else seemed to be merely shuffling to the music. Except for Edward. He too was losing his inhibitions, along with his shirt. He danced in shorts and socks, drenched in sweat. He had no grace or fluidity whatsoever, but made up for that in energy, his long, thin limbs jerking about as if on the strings of some crazed puppeteer. Ellen and Josie seemed too absorbed in each other to notice them much.

Jesus fished a notebook out of his bag, then began scribbling. So I was right about the poet bit. Fancy doing it here though. It seemed a strange way to behave. Josie had noticed it, too. She rolled her eyes to the heavens and gritted her teeth. Ellen bent to say something in Josie's ear. Josie gave a shrug, followed by a dazzling smile and I'm sure Ellen flushed again. I chuckled; I was enjoying this.

The women moved off the dance floor, to lean against the stage and talk. Edward and Max were still flinging themselves about the room, and Jesus had gone back to smoking his roll-ups. I was getting bored again. I took a swig. Then I saw Josie staring right at me. Spilling lager down my chin and hastily wiping it off with the back of my hand, I looked up, embarrassed in case Josie had noticed. But she wasn't actually staring at me after all, but at my friends in the next seat who were now enjoying a slow, lingering kiss. Two women in one seat. Shit.

I looked round to see if anyone was watching. Luckily no-one else seemed to have noticed, yet. I breathed out. So, what was Josie thinking? She must have been shocked. However, I was surprised to see her close her eyes, smile and sigh. Then she opened her eyes and looked at Jesus and then her smile faded and she really looked miserable.

OK, I thought. So you're a lesbian. Why don't you do something about it? She turned back to stare intently at Val and Sandy. It made me a bit nervous. I looked over at Ellen. Now her face was a picture. Eyes like saucers staring straight ahead, mouth open. Following her gaze I saw the reason. The reason why no-one had noticed the women next to me. Edward and Max were slow dancing together.

Well, this was an interesting development. Perhaps I'd got the couples wrong and they were all gay. But the faces of the others denied this. Jesus looked worried for once, licking his cigarette paper over and over until his roll-up collapsed. Ellen just stared in amazement; she looked really shocked. She was, after all, watching her boyfriend getting it together with her ex-boyfriend. Josie, on the other hand, was clearly delighted. She was bouncing about, laughing and pointing, but even she looked surprised when the happy couple kissed, the kiss lasting well into the next record.

Josie grabbed Ellen's arm and pulled her onto the dance floor. Jesus got up and joined them. Josie snaked and curved and twirled across the floor until she was close to me and my friends. And she smiled at me. That dazzling, heart-stopping smile. Now this was more than I'd ever bargained for. It was all getting too close for comfort.

I scowled into my glass. Honestly, she couldn't keep going round with her boyfriend, eyeing up the dykes. Obviously she was a lesbian, so why didn't she do the decent thing and come out? What did she think I was going to do with Jesus there? Slip her my phone number as I walked past? Actually that was quite a nice fantasy, but really, she should sort herself out. I reflected self-righteously on this theme for a while, trying not to watch her dance. I was up to the 'after all, I had to do it, it isn't easy for any of us' stage when I remembered that it had taken me four years or more to come out myself. I knew, but I didn't know I wasn't the only one. What with her friends and my friends, Josie must be experiencing major explosions in the brain. I smiled back at her. Just for encouragement. Still looking my way, she reached up to say something in Ellen's ear. I knew she was talking about me even before the music suddenly stopped just as she yelled 'LESBIAN.' The word seemed to ring out across the room. I felt myself blush a little, but Josie had gone scarlet. Ellen stared intently at her like she couldn't quite take something in. Then she gave her a big, slow, wonderful smile. I felt myself melt into a puddle. I wished someone would smile at me like that. Then I realised what had happened. Ellen hadn't noticed me or my friends, so she'd misheard what Josie had said, and thought she was talking about herself. And that she was telling Ellen about it for a particular reason, and she looked extremely pleased about it. She took both of Josie's hands in hers, yelling back loud and clear, 'ME TOO.'

Now it was Josie's turn to look astonished. I saw it slowly dawn on her, the misunderstanding. She opened her mouth to explain, and I wanted to shout out 'NO! Don't do that, you'll ruin a beautiful moment.' But then she thought better of it herself. She looked down at Ellen's hands holding hers. She looked up into Ellen's beaming face, and she stared at her like she was seeing her properly for the first time. Then suddenly her own face broke out into a huge grin. They laughed, then they hugged, then laughed again and gazed into each other's eyes like they were the only people in the room. Neither of them noticed Jesus stagger, white-faced, to the gents. Another record had started up. Marvin Gaye. Josie gently slid her arms up Ellen's back, laid her cheek next to Ellen's, and they both smiled, closed their eyes, and danced, very slow and very close. I was enraptured. I could hardly take my eyes off them. Then I saw, among the other couples, Sandy and Val entwined together, and Edward and Max the same. I smiled and sang along a little, 'When I get that feeling, it's sexual healing.'

Josie and Ellen never looked up, just squeezed closer, caressing each other's backs, smiling. As the music stopped, they drew back a little, each gazing at the other like she couldn't believe her eyes. Then, slowly, hesitantly, they kissed. Oh, it was a lovely kiss. I felt quite churned up by it. They hugged some more, then suddenly, as one, they remembered and turned to look at Jesus. He was back in his seat, smoking a roll-up, with big fat tears running into his beard.

The last record was announced. Josie and Ellen stared at each other, stricken, not knowing what to do. They looked at Edward and Max, still wrapped round each other without a care. They looked at Jesus weeping. They conferred, then walked over to him, one sitting on either side of him. He pulled out his hanky and blew his nose. Ellen said something to him and he nodded. Josie said something to him and he stared at her, then nodded. He rolled another cigarette with shaking

126

hands. Edward and Max slunk to their seats like guilty puppies, the music having ended. Ellen leant over and said something to them. Eyes wide, they clapped their hands over their mouths and giggled. Then they saw Jesus and they sobered up suddenly, and stared at the floor. At last they left the room, Max with a hand on Jesus' shoulder, followed by Edward, Josie and Ellen arm in arm, a little way behind. As they left I realised I wasn't the only one who was watching them. Lots of people round here liked soap, it seemed.

So, I wondered, will Ellen and Josie become lovers? Or will Josie find she can't leave Jesus after all? Then will Ellen come to the lesbian group and fall in love with me?

Will Edward and Max become lovers? Or will Jesus and Max become lovers? Will Ellen then turn back to Edward, and Josie come to the lesbian group and fall in love with me?

If Ellen and Josie and Edward and Max become lovers, what will Jesus do? Will he become a best-selling poet through the experience?

Maybe I would never know. I decided it was time to go home, get a take-out on the way back, and take the Eastender's video to bed.

Rezubian In Tokyo

Linda M. Peterson

It isn't hard to find the foreign lesbians in Japan these days, because we are proud of our community and we are dying to be found. Our community consists of a small group of old-timers, women who have been here around ten years or longer, and larger numbers of women who stay for six months or a couple of years. We have a newsletter, commonly known as the *DD*,[1] dyke dinners and brunches monthly in Tokyo, monthly gatherings in Kyoto, lesbian weekends (informal conferences) three or four times a year.

Let me make it clear that what I am talking about here is primarily the English-speaking lesbian community. Of course, there is also a large and growing Japanese lesbian community, and there are many links between the two, but issues tend to be very different. I'll say more about that later.

The five main ways lesbians find us are listed roughly in order of frequency:

(1) Lesbian contact sources outside Japan. Specifically, lesbian contacts for Japan are found in *Lesbian Connection* (U.S.), *Lesbian Network* (Australia), *Gaia's Guide*, and other local information sources like lesbian resource centers. My lover Amanda and I are listed in *Lesbian Connection* and *Gaia's Guide* and we get around 50 calls and letters a year. We have put together an information packet which we send out with a copy of the most recent issue of the *DD*.

(2) Ads for lesbian events or IFJ (International Feminists of

Japan) meetings in *The Japan Times,* or other English language newspapers, in *Tokyo Journal* and/or *Kansai Time Out*, local what's-happening magazines. Any dyke brave enough and able to list her phone number in one of these publications can be assured of getting at least one and sometimes as many as twenty calls from lesbians not previously connected to the community. Sylph, a British separatist who has since left Japan, said she saw an ad for a Lesbian Weekend in *Tokyo Journal*. She was intrigued, but the date had already passed. However, in the same magazine an IFJ meeting was advertised, so she made a phone call and went to the meeting, where an announcement was written on the blackboard for a Dyke Dinner. At the dinner she gathered more specific information about when dinners and other events were held.

(3) Personal contact, usually by way of addresses and phone numbers passed on by friends of Japan residents, or by former Japan residents.

(4) Sometimes gay men or their publications lead dykes to find dykes. Pam Lane, who was in Japan with the U.S. military, found the general location of the gay men's bars in *Tokyo City Guide*, and after a couple of unsuccessful excursions to the area found Mars Bar for women. Some women have depended on gay brothers or friends for information. There is a Tokyo Gay Support Group, though sometimes the information they provide is unreliable. One woman said she went to one of their meetings and was told that there was nothing for lesbians. She tried again after a long time and met a couple of women who gave her a contact number for the Dyke Dinner.

(5) Perhaps the most unusual way lesbians come into contact with our community is by being found. More than one woman told me of coming to Japan with no intention of looking for lesbians, but then being befriended and brought to a lesbian event by a lesbian who had spotted her.

Those of us who have been here for a long time have seen the public lesbian community (as opposed to private circles of friends which have always existed) come into being. It started at a meeting called by a Japanese feminist group who wanted help in putting out an English edition of their magazine. Two American lesbians, Anne Blasing and Satrupa Kagel, who met at that gathering in 1978, were instrumental in creating the conditions which led us to where we are today. Anne was one of the main organizers and the first coordinator of the International Feminists of Japan. Satrupa, who stood up at the meeting and asked, "Where are all the lesbians in Tokyo?" later began having women's and lesbian parties at her house.

Until about 1984, IFJ was the main link for lesbians. A newsletter, also started by Anne Blasing, called *The Feminist Forum*, which later coexisted with *The IFJ Newsletter*, included information about the parties. Anne says, "From their involvement in IFJ, foreign lesbians in Japan, myself included, had their first real opportunity to meet each other and organize events specifically for lesbians. It remains a place to meet other lesbians, interesting feminists and to learn more about women's varied lives."

Satrupa remembers feeling terribly isolated as a public lesbian in the late 1970s. On a recent return visit to Japan, after an absence of several years, she was amazed at what she found by attending the fourteenth lesbian weekend held in October of 1988. As is typical of weekends, there were about 70 lesbians there, about half Japanese and half non-Japanese. Lesbians in Japan, both Japanese and foreign, are spread out all over the country. Even for those of us who live in Tokyo, it sometimes takes an hour and a half or more to get to each other's houses. Since the first lesbian weekend, held in November of 1985, lesbian weekends have become an important way to get together. Some events are in Japanese, some in English, some are bilingual. Weekends are a good way for foreign and Japanese dykes to get together, because there are opportunities for one-to-one conversations with women you don't know well. Between workshops and other "events," everyone sort of hangs out in the lounge area of the women's education center where many of the weekends are held. It's a relaxed atmosphere.

Of the 30 to 40 foreigners attending a given weekend, as many as ten will be there for the first time, as was Chris from Canada, who said, "This weekend—it's as if we walked into a different time zone, a different dimension. You can let your hair down, be exactly who you need to be. I don't know if it exists anywhere else in the world. It's damn nice that everyone's so friendly. I'm just floored. I don't know if my community back home in Vancouver is so friendly, even to me," she joked.

Often a woman goes from knowing no lesbians in Japan to knowing fifty or a hundred of them after spending two or three days at a weekend. The connections made at weekends can change women's lives: "I met my current lover at the 7th lesbian weekend. That has had an enormous, positive impact on me! It was her first lesbian event in Japan. She found out about it from two gay women who were introduced to her by her long-time gay male friend."

For women who live outside Tokyo or the Osaka-Kyoto-Kobe area, weekends may be the only opportunity to attend lesbian events. A recent decision by the Japanese Ministry of Education has brought literally hundreds of English-speakers to Japan, many of them posted to isolated areas where they are employed as Assistant English Teachers (AETs) to assist Japanese teachers of English in the local schools. Among the AETs was a woman who immediately recognized the potential for isolation, especially among the women. She started a *Women's Newsletter* for networking among the women AETs. This newsletter has enabled a number of lesbians to find dykes and to attend lesbian events.

As a result of finding the lesbian contact number in the *Women's Newsletter,* Karen Callahan from California came out in Japan: "I saw the number. I kept thinking I should call. I spoke to the woman who did the AET newsletter several times, about other things, but it was difficult to come out, having already talked to her without coming out. Then when the lesbian contact number was there, that was someone new. I wrote about my feelings about women in my diary when I was 12, but then I don't know what happened. My friends back home are very homophobic. Being here, being alone, thinking about myself, eventually I called and came out on the phone. After that I came out to another isolated AET lesbian, and then took a two-hour train trip to another city to meet her. That was a wonderful Saturday. We spent seven hours talking."

Karen is certainly not the first woman for whom the Japan community is her first lesbian community. Lots of women find being in Japan a release from the expectations and assumptions of their families and friends, which gives them the freedom to come out as dykes. Other lesbians, out only to lovers and a few friends back home, have their first experiences of community-type activities—dinners, weekends, working on the newsletter, workshops.

Lesbians who contact us here in Tokyo get a warm welcome. I think it's because we know we are a fluid community, and those of us who have been here for a long time are always delighted when new women come to town. In a sense we are a fragile community—the numbers stay about the same, but it takes work to keep track of everyone. We have a sense that someone might get lost—or not find us. We want to be found. One of our most exciting kinds of news is about who is new in town, or how many new lesbians will be at the next dinner or brunch or weekend. Knowing that women stay for short periods— sometimes only a few weeks or a month, commonly for a year or two— there is a sense of urgency about finding out who new lesbians are. What experiences and ideas are they bringing us? What impact will they have on our lives—on the next dinner or weekend? What issues will they raise? What new connections here or abroad will result?

We have evolved a sort of anarchic non-organization which allows new dykes, and even short-term visiting dykes, to facilitate a workshop, or even a weekend, or to do an issue of the newsletter. There are no permanent structures of any kind; everything is on an if-you-want-it, you-make-it-happen basis.

Our community is diverse and seems to thrive on diversity. One American lesbian who has lived in San Francisco, Ann Arbor and Northampton, all considered prime dyke locations, says that the thing about Tokyo is that it's a disparate community, but in a pinch we pull together. She thinks Tokyo is a coexistence of diversity: "There are strong opinions. There are circles but they don't feel like cliques. Exclusivity is so prominent in other communities. This community provides a place for *me* to explore all my facets. I get prickly because of all the strong opinions; I tend to get swayed, but at the same time the community allows me to be. I want to become me. I'm a crosser of boundaries. Diversity is one of the key enjoyments of my life."

We are diverse and we are not. The age range is usually from about 20 to 60, with the majority in their twenties or thirties. Many of us are middle-class. Usually there are a lot of English teachers, and a number of lesbians whose main purpose for being in Japan is to study something—Japanese language or art, karate, aikido, acupuncture, or shiatsu. There are women employed in fields other than teaching, such as business or publishing, and a sprinkling of U.S. military women. In terms of nationality, Americans always outnumber everyone else; Australia, Great Britain, New Zealand and Canada are nearly always represented, and at times there have been women from Thailand, Switzerland, France, Mexico, Ireland and the Philippines. The community I know is the English-language community, whether English is a first language or not.

English-language dominance has at times robbed us of connections with foreign lesbians from non-English-speaking countries. America-centrism is another issue, both because Japan is obsessed with the United States, and because Americans often seem to be more culture-bound than women from other English-speaking countries. Tracy, from Australia, commented, "Sometimes it's difficult for me to talk because women who are so blatantly a product of their culture react (not to what is being said, but to *how* it is being said), and then I react, thinking *I'm* strange. Women who are trying to be conscious will say, 'Oh, it's so terrible to be an American,' and that makes it difficult to say anything because it gets heavy." Karen commented, "I'm certainly meeting a much wider cross section of lesbians than I'd ever meet in California. I'm finding I had many preconceived notions of other areas, even other areas of the U.S. I'm glad to meet such a diverse group of women—both foreign and Japanese."

Pam, who was here with the U.S. Air Force, spent her first few months in Japan only with other military dykes. She commented, "Military women would enjoy and learn much more about Japan if they connected with non-military English-speaking foreigners. I wish that I had met dykes in the civilian community sooner."

Most of the close connections between the Japanese community and the English-speaking community are personal connections—lover relationships, friendships, language exchange arrangements, and information-sharing relationships. Foreign dykes often arrive in Japan wanting to meet Japanese lesbians, but not speaking much Japanese and having little idea of what life is like for women, let alone lesbians, in Japan. Sylph did some informal research using a questionnaire in English and Japanese about what she at first thought of as our bilingual community. She concluded that "bilingual we certainly are NOT," and went on to write, "Interaction between the two groups (though not necessarily between individuals within the two groups) is minimal." In her article, "Lesbian Weekends: Multicultural Gatherings," Sylph quoted a foreign dyke who said, "I wish there could be more interaction between the two communities, but they are different and have different needs. I would like more relaxed interaction, but that comes with time." Also in response to the questionnaire, a Japanese lesbian commented, "The interaction between the two communities is not especially good. The main problem is a difference of consciousness. For example, Japanese lesbians are more concerned with concrete things such as sexual relationships, jobs and day-to-day living. The foreigners are not so concerned with these things since they are traveling through. It seems to me that they are more concerned with ideology and abstract ideas about lesbianism." Another Japanese lesbian was even more forceful in her negative reaction to foreign dykes, writing, "I have a message for foreign lesbians. It is a complete waste of your time for you to live here if you persist in speaking only English and have no interest in Japanese culture and customs. You would be doing me a great favor if you returned home."[2]

In a way the existence of a foreign community has smoothed relations between Japanese and foreign dykes here; the Japanese no longer have to take care of or get rid of the sometimes persistent and insensitive tourist dykes, who think "finding out about Japanese lesbians" is their right, regardless of the trouble they may be to Japanese women who have enough difficulty finding time for their own projects. Also, I think that the tendency of foreign dykes to think they are bringing lesbian culture to "poor oppressed" Japanese lesbians is curbed by the existence of a foreign community. After a while it becomes clear that we have our community and they have theirs, we have our issues and they have theirs, but that links are possible between individual dykes who have sufficient language skills and the inclination.

From the point of view of a foreigner whose daily life may be fraught with language and/or cultural problems, the security of an English-speaking lesbian community is a welcome luxury. Chris commented, "I didn't seek any information before I came to Japan; I didn't know I'd need lesbians, but I did, just to maintain sanity." She got depressed one Sunday, called the IFJ number and asked if there was anything happening for dykes: "The answer was yes, and I soon found myself at a dyke dinner in Mitaka."

Anne Blasing, who describes herself as someone who has been around long enough to watch things develop and grow for the foreign dyke community in Japan, says, "I have found over the years much excitement and much anguish from this community, but I feel that it has grown to have a feeling of family. Many of us have known each other for years and we know each other's foibles and good points. We have laughed much, loved much, and survived much together. We have welcomed newcomers and said goodbye to many others who were dear to us. But I feel that we have come to a real acceptance of each other, a point where we know each other and where we have developd effective channels for communication. Whatever our differences and directions,

I feel that the dykes in Tokyo have created a real community—one that will survive and grow."

Notes

1. The newsletter changes her name whenever she likes, usually every issue. Most of the names contain two Ds, such as *The Discerning Dyke,* or *The Daisuki Dyke* (*daisuki* is Japanese for well-liked). For information write to Newsletter, CPO Box 1780, Tokyo, Japan 100-91.

2. *Disturbing Dykes*, No. 10, May 1988.

Desperate Dykes And Elevators

Julie Reidy

By the time C.Y. walked into the lift I had begun to expect the
unexpected. Chungking Mansion's over-exerted lifts transported a
global microcosm between their cramped, airless apartments and various vaguely illicit business activities. That was only one of the reasons
it was known as Junky Mansions.

Me, I had just returned from a smuggling trip to Nepal, bringing
out black market travel cheques into Hong Kong—the colony Britain
retained like a false passport to keep its own image clean. I had
smuggled a lot of the cheques out in a condom shoved up my vagina. It
had just entered my head to write a scathing article entitled "Yet another
way to make money out of your sex," when C.Y. walked into the lift.

As I said, I was used to turban, caftan and sari wearers, bearded
backpackers and ancient Chinese grandmothers, but she was none of
them. Even the mini-skirt didn't turn me off the way it normally does.
Her stride was confident and her cherry red lips ovaled into a cheery
hello. Surprised me somewhat. Normally it was the men who greeted
me—out of a sense of duty to their masculinity—as the lift descended
begrudgingly and we stood jammed together exchanging sweat.

C.Y.'s cat-green eyes met mine, innocent and bright. I spluttered
something audible in return for her greeting, mind busy searching to
remember which floor she'd stepped in at. Not being a practiced hand at
seduction techniques we arrived at ground before I could think of a
suitably impressive one-liner. A sea of bodies began edging selves and

136

suitcases into the undersized elevator almost before we shoved out and I lost her amongst the crowd.

Never did write the article on vaginas that day. No great loss to the annals of herstory anyway. Did a lot of thinking about C.Y. instead. It was most unusual to see an unaccompanied Korean woman inside the country, let alone outside of it. What was she doing here? How was I ever going to find out? Transience was the only permanent feature of the Junky Mansions. Upwards of ten thousand people shared the Mansion's decaying squalor with beady-eyed rats, spiders and other unnameable crawlies and scuttlers. Few people survived longer than a week; most moved on out while the money was hot. The scant faces that became familiar had a greying, unhealthy pallor under the only light that penetrated the concrete—fluorescent. Gazing through jagged edges of window I watched the concrete drip slime and ooze grime, wondering if the money was truly worth it. I will say, though, that several floors of the five-block, sixteen-floors-apiece buildings boasted the best Indian nosh houses this side of Singapore. Pungent aromas of curry and curd triumphed over the otherwise pervasive stench of pig fat oil and Chinese condiments. Regular shouting matches erupted over the discreetly placed mah-jong tables. Life was never dull.

Evening duly arrived, along with the usual load of crap on the TV. Judith, my roommate, was warbling on about her latest disastrous affair. At least with the TV soaps I could get up and switch them off, having the power of knowing only I could turn it back on again. Judith's love life was akin to watching repeat screenings of the same soap. She clung and they ditched her. I could have told her that men don't come to Hong Kong in search of commitment. But what credentials did I have? A celibate lesbian in a straight city. Ah, to hell with it. I thought I'd go out. Stalk the elevators for a while.

"Hello, again. You must be staying in this block too."

"Hi, actually my name's Nikki and I'm just collecting some stuff from the sixteenth floor. I stay over on A Block."

How's that for a cool opening line? I've been up to the sixteenth floor and back at least half a dozen times before she reappeared. I was beginning to look suspicious even to myself, let alone anyone else on that block, and had all but resigned myself to my rotten luck.

"Do you know where Rick's Café is?" she asked. "I am to meet a friend there."

"Sure," I replied. "Go out the back entrance, take the second left and then first right. You'll see the big neon sign."

"Thanks. Hey, why don't you come and join us? There is to be a band."

"That'd be great," I said, losing all cool and composure. "Let me just take these bags back to my room and I'll meet you there in about fifteen minutes."

"OK. I'll see you then."

That smile again and she walked off, still revealing the greater part of a pair of long legs. Should I quickly change? Maybe I looked too scruffy for her? I had on my black leggings, red basketball boots and a black waist jacket over purple T-shirt. My hungry ghost, a purple and red mask earring, hung cosily from my left earlobe. I wondered how Korean dykes dressed. I'd met one in a bath house in Seoul a few weeks previously, but she wasn't wearing anything at all at the time. Her only English was, "You want girlfriend?" Asian people often make mistakes in gender when speaking English, but there was no mistaking the intent that time. I'd felt too vulnerable, with my three words of Korean and my nakedness to pursue the matter at the time, but now ...

C.Y.'s English seemed excellent. I shoved my red carrybag into my room and slammed the door again. She would just have to take me as I was.

"Nikki, you are arrived." She shouted to me across the road from Rick's. "That's great."

I crossed over to join her.

"In here is too crowded and I can't find my friend anyway. Shall we go to another place?"

"Do you know any other good places?" I asked. "My knowledge of the social scene's a bit limited."

"Pardon?" she queried.

"Oh, sorry. I mean I don't go out very often. I don't know where to go."

"Follow me then."

I did. We walked into the Waltzing Mathilda. I felt male eyes turn to follow C.Y.'s stride, thighs rippling mini-skirt and heels a little askew. I felt like punching them. It was a long time since I had been with a woman who attracted that sort of devouring attention. It struck me that this same feeling caused blokes to get into barroom brawls over wimmin. Did I want to possess her? All I knew was that I didn't want to want to possess her and I certainly didn't want any man laying greedy

138

eyes on C.Y. either.

She seemed oblivious to it all. I bought us a beer each and we perched on stools in one of the corners.

"Do you like these earrings?" I asked, fishing several pairs out of my pocket and handing them over. "I sell them in the market."

"They're large, aren't they?" she said. "Do I look good this pair?"

"Absolutely. I like the way they curve around your cheeks and the colours match your skin. Have them."

"Oh, no. I will pay you for them."

"No, really, I want you to have them."

"Oh, no. I couldn't."

"Sure you can."

"But you are trying to make a living, no?" she asked.

"Well, yeah. But I do well enough."

This was not the time to talk about my real source of income. Some people can be funny about smuggling. I'd already lost two Chinese friends and a place to stay.

"They're a present."

"Thank you. I'll put them on."

"Hey, I don't even know your name," I said.

She clipped the second earring into place. "My western friends call me C.Y. My Korean name is too difficult to remember."

"C.Y.," I repeated. "That should be easy enough. What are you doing in Hong Kong?"

"I don't like to spend all my time at home. We are young and it is good to travel. I worked for a while helping my brother who is learning also the business. I can go back any time to that but I get trouble. My father wishes me to marry. He says thirty is too much old to be single."

"You're thirty! You seem more my age, twenty-five," I replied.

"We women in Korea lead sheltered lives, you see. I think women in the west mature more quick, see more of living."

"Maybe. I wouldn't have minded being a child a bit longer," I said, adding "I don't want to get married either."

"I have a boyfriend here in Hong Kong," C.Y. said. "He's German."

My hand tightened around the bottle and tilted it, draining the last of the beer into my mug.

"Oh, would you like another beer?" I squeaked.

"I will get it," she replied and slipped off the bar stool.

Come on, Nikki, I told myself as I emptied the mug. What did you expect? This is Hong Kong, you know. Straightsville, Arizona. What if I tell her I'm a lesbian?

"Please don't think I am doing this often, inviting strangers out," she said on returning. "But when I saw your face I could tell you are a warm, open person. It is so good to have women friends to talk with here."

"Amen, sister," I said fervently. "Er, I mean, I think so too. Were you supposed to meet your boyfriend tonight?"

"No, he has gone out to play music with some friends. He spends much time with them. When I am not in Hong Kong he sees also other women."

"How do you feel about that?" I asked.

"It is good to be a free spirit, free to travel and do what we need to do. But I don't see other men and I try not to think about those other women."

"Sounds like he makes the rules for the relationship," I said.

"Perhaps," she replied. "I feel that love is stronger between a man and a woman if they can just love each other, don't you think?" she asked.

"What do you think about love between wimmin and wimmin?" I asked, veering a little off the subject.

"That's a different kind of love, isn't it?" C.Y. replied.

"Not for me it isn't."

"How is that?"

"I sleep with wimmin. I'm a lesbian."

"Oh."

I rushed on. "Often when I say that to other wimmin here they don't want much to do with me afterwards—even though they say it's OK, they don't mind."

Blazing goddesses. I must have been getting drunk or have been desperate to talk to have said that out loud. I hardly knew the woman but she seemed to be drawing me out with her frankness.

C.Y.'s red nails tapped the side of her glass.

"I think," she said, "that it is a good thing to be open in love. But you are so beautiful, so warm. You shouldn't limit yourself. There are a few good men around. Why don't you try?"

"You make it seem as if I just need the right man to come along. It's not like that. Besides, why don't you open yourself to wimmin?"

140

"Ah, you have caught me there. I do not feel able for that. But you are beautiful, I like you." C.Y. put her arm around me. "Let's go and dancing."

Well, dancing had been my only avenue for releasing sexual energy since I'd arrived in Hong Kong. My lover and I, like so many others, had parted company less than amicably back down the backpack trail. I was subsequently a regular at the Cave Club now, appearing and disappearing to my own timetable. That had had its own freedoms but lately, on the crowded dance floor, I had felt myself a rocking liferaft, adrift on a vast ocean—thirsting; for while the water surrounded me none of it was of the right kind for drinking.

"Might as well," I said.

In the low-ceilinged smoky club, a funky African jive bounced off the walls and there was barely room to pogo on the dance floor. 'Chinese are nothing if not overstated,' I thought, watching mini-skirted and painted marionettes clinging to men who were only notice-able as such by the fact that they wore trousers. Everyone aspired openly in these clubs—would-be models, rock singers, and how many times had the local men introduced themselves to me as "business-men"—even if all they dealt in were copy watches in the local market. Big bucks—made during the day and spent flashily at night.

I felt cynical. C.Y. seemed distracted. Over the boom of the bassline I yelled, "Are you hungry?"—food being my habitual panacea for lust.

"Starving," she yelled back, hands cupped around lips pressed up to my ear.

Was I allowed to interpret that answer metaphorically? No time to ponder for, as we made to leave, a body came tumbling haphazardly down the stairs. It hit the foyer with a thud.

"I'm scared," C.Y. said, grabbing my arm. "What's happening?"

"Don't worry," I soothed. "Probably just Triad stuff again. They're the local bully boys, bit like the mafia you know, and they like to throw their weight around."

Her look told me that she didn't know at all what I was on about.

"Never mind," I said. "Let's go out the back way."

Tsim Sha Tsui, in all its plastic glamour, glittered blatantly as we emerged. Breasty cut-outs of white women on two metre hoardings dominated the now quiet Sony, JVC and Hitachi neons of earlier hours. Chinese morality ended with the daylight, took itself home to the respectable suburbs and left this area strictly to the thousands of transient sex seekers.

The noodle shop was still open, serving soup bowls of greasy water and noodles that, being vegetarian, came with just a few sad strips of spring onion. C.Y. used the phone to ring Mick.

"He's drunk," she reported on return. "I don't want to go back there just yet."

"You don't have to go back there at all if you don't want," I said. "Come home with me."

She didn't reply and the image of myself as a desperate ugly lesbian surged into my mind. How much more Amazonian to be the gallant Georgette, rescuer of wimmin from the dragon's fiery lair. But I'd sold my steed to finance these travels and all I had to offer in the way of a castle was a single bed in a poky little shared room. What if she said yes? How would I get rid of Judith for the night? She didn't even know I was a dyke. Oh, shit, maybe it was all too complicated. I began to hope she would say no.

"Do women ever hit each other?" she asked.

"Do you mean he beats you up when he is drunk?" I queried.

"One or two times it happens. Just a bit rough."

"The bastard. Well, wimmin are not peace-loving all the time but I think there's a difference. I mean, a man can really hurt a woman, kill her—and they do—but I've never seen a woman take on someone much weaker than herself. Wimmin are also taught to fight with words, not fists. I'm not saying that can't be just as painful."

"You say that wimmin fight but not harm each other?" she said.

"Well, yes, physically. I think wimmin have more reason to harm men than each other—not that we do often enough."

"At home," C.Y. said, "I watched my father go out drinking with his friends. You know it is custom in Korea? He would come home, talking loud, telling my mother to bring him this, bring him that, throw plates at her if she was too slow. I hated to watch. I thought perhaps western men were different."

"It's easier to think that western men are different when you meet them. They have all the right words and have learnt how to pretend," I replied. "But the more I travel, the more I begin to see that they are the same all over, just some are more honest about it."

"You say there are no men good to know?" C.Y. asked me.

"Well, maybe there are one or two somewhere but why waste

your time trying to find them when there are so many gorgeous wimmin around? Besides, wimmin's bodies are more attractive than men's anyway. Yours, for instance."

She blushed. "You say too nice thing to me."

"It's true," I protested. "I don't want to sleep with you because I can't find a man."

"Where is your room?" C.Y. asked.

"On A Block, remember? Does that mean yes?"

"Oh, Nikki, I like you. I don't know," C.Y. pulled at the straps of her bag nervously. If I had a bag I would have been doing the same thing. As it was, I slipped my hands under my thighs, arms hugging sides, preparing for possible rejection.

"I don't know what to do," she said, looking down.

"You're a woman. You already know," I countered, rocking slightly.

"What will I tell Mick?"

"Nothing," I said.

She looked up. I stopped rocking.

Had she seduced me or I her?

They Came In a White Convertible

Beth Karbe

It was 1961. It was a time when the adage that "children should be seen, not heard" was firmly embedded in my ten-year-old body. My sister and I had been well-trained—to whisper in restaurants, not to interrupt the conversation of adults, to speak primarily when spoken to. My world was a mixture of enough of the patriarchally old-fashioned mingled with what seemed so new in 1961—bouffant hairdos and black stockings under pointed, white sneakers. 1961 was a hair too early for the rise of the Beatles, too soon for much of the impassioned political activism of the latter part of that decade, and way before feminism had begun to ride its "second wave." And if children, back then, were to be seen and not heard, some measure of this applied to women in general—grown women, married women, women with children, with full-time jobs, with men, without. Women, *also*, were to be seen and not heard. But lesbians . . . Lesbians were *not* seen. Lesbians were not heard or heard *of* or even dreamed about. Lesbians were the Invisible, the profound and total denial of a culture I was growing up in. Yet if truth be known, and it surely wasn't back then, in 1961 I *was* a lesbian, and I was most definitely not seen, and not heard, and not heard of. But I dreamed.

There was a church in the Long Island town where we lived. There were actually many churches. But to my parents only one church, this particular church, was worth any mention—and it was here that we

144

would sometimes go to spend Sunday mornings. Most everything about this church was properly "acceptable." The vast majority of the people were white. They belonged to nuclear families, they were married, they worked "respectable" jobs. But to this rule there were exceptions, and the predictable sight of two extraordinary women who came together to church like clockwork every Sunday was surely one worth mentioning.

Joanne was a woman in her early 30s, attractive enough, but boldly different in her manner and appearance. So was her younger friend, Trudy. Long before I understood or had even heard the word "butch," Joanne and Trudy gave meaning to it.

The women wore d.a. haircuts, short and slicked back, tapering to a point at the nape of their necks. Neither of them wore any make-up. They dressed in slacks and tailored shirts and mannish shoes. They came on Sundays dressed this way and always together.

The presence of these two was a source of great fascination and unnameable comfort to me. Joanne, the older of them, was a gym teacher at the local high school. I knew that some day, when I was grown, I would be a student of hers. I dreamed of that day, of showing off my athletic abilities, of pleasing her with my enthusiasm and spirit. It all seemed so far off. But still I dreamed of it.

Her friend, Trudy, was obviously younger—maybe in her early 20s. She lived at home, with her parents. Joanne lived alone, in a house she inherited from her mother. But the two came to church on Sundays together. They came in a brand-new car that Joanne always drove. Somehow I knew it was *her* car—a 1961 convertible. It was a white Chevrolet, shiny and sleek with long, thick lines and big, round tail-lights that glowed a fiery red when she touched the brake. And a red interior to match. Joanne was very proud of that new car.

After church on Sunday mornings my mother and I would walk across the parking lot to the meeting hall for the usual, after-service coffee and sweet rolls. This was a grand treat for a child who had been seen and not heard long enough to deserve a sugary reward in the form of a bakery bun. How easy it was to be quiet with a roll of sweet, white dough covered with gooey icing, spiraling round and round and looking so huge. But on the walk across the parking lot I would always be alert for Joanne and Trudy and their fancy, new car . . . because one of the most startling scenes I'd ever witnessed, over and over again, was the way Joanne got *into* that shiny, white convertible. I would stare as she approached the driver's side of the car with an even, steady pace, walking confidently in flat shoes. Nothing unusual. Not *really*. Until she got a few feet away from the gleaming, topless vehicle. Then she quickened her pace just a bit, took the last few feet with short, even jump-steps, almost like skipping. When she reached the door she laid her left hand down on top of it and lifted her entire body up into the air, swinging like a pivot on her balanced, muscular arm. Moving through the air like this, she swung herself into the driver's seat without ever having to open the car door. At the age of ten, this was a graceful sight. And the movement itself became more and more perfected over time. With practice, Joanne was able to move her body over and into the car with increasing ease. It never ceased to fascinate me, though most of the grown churchgoers were, by this time, noticeably uncomfortable with her "mannishness," and both my parents were among the disquieted.

Trudy, too, soon learned to mount the passenger's seat in like fashion and with equal prowess and grace. There the two would move sometimes simultaneously through the air, landing in the lush, red leather seats, seeming happy with their game and with each other. But one Sunday it was only Joanne who came to church in her shiny, white convertible. Trudy wasn't with her. And the next Sunday she was alone again. And the next, and the next, until at some point, I was aware that something was terribly wrong. Weeks after Trudy's absence, I overheard a whispered conversation between my mother and father. I strained to hear exchanges such as this, knowing that muffled words were meant to keep secrets from my curious ears. My mother was telling my father what she had obviously heard from others that very morning. It was about Trudy. Her parents had known something was wrong with her. I remember my mother using the word "unnatural" to describe Trudy's condition. Her parents wanted her to be well, to be like everyone else. I heard my mother tell my father that Trudy's parents had taken her to a hospital, to doctors who knew how to cure "sicknesses" like hers. Mother's tone was very serious. I don't remember anything my father may have whispered back. But I knew that they shared a belief in Trudy's unnaturalness, that she suffered, surely, from an abnormality that needed curing.

Those few lines of whispered words sent me into a mild terror, and a silence I would not break for years and years. And in the weeks that followed, I watched and waited and quietly hoped Trudy would come back. I secretly dreamed that one Sunday she would simply reappear in the passenger's seat of Joanne's white convertible, just like always. I imagined her riding there, with her hair short slicked back, wearing her thick, silver i.d. bracelet and men's shirt and pants . . . riding there, next to Joanne . . . the two of them, I dreamed, like heroines in a storybook not yet written in 1961.

Many, many months went by and, like clockwork, Joanne continued to appear on Sundays. I watched her, alone now, without her friend. But it was as if only a *minor* change had occurred—that Trudy, always having been with Joanne, was simply gone. Nothing else had changed, nothing that I could notice—until the day Trudy *did* come back. But not in the passenger's seat of Joanne's white convertible. Not with a d.a. haircut and her silver i.d. bracelet. Not looking, as she had, in her slacks and tailored shirts. Instead she came with her hair bouffant and all made-up, wearing a dress and stockings and high-heeled shoes. She came back in a car driven by a man, and she carried an infant in her arms and wore a wedding ring on her left finger. And everyone, *everyone* acted as if nothing different was happening, as if nothing at all had changed.

For one horrible moment, I woke from my dreaming and knew that something terrible had happened, something too awful to ever talk about. I never understood what I saw, but I continued to watch, to wait, and keep very, very quiet. And I saw that Trudy never spoke to Joanne again, nor did she ever look in her direction, as if the two had never known of the other.

After this, I watched Joanne with a particular care, a particular seriousness, as though keeping guard that nothing else, no one else, would disappear again. She continued to come to church every Sunday and continued to come alone. She still wore her hair in a d.a. and dangled a thick, silver i.d. bracelet around her muscular wrist and wore men's slacks and tailored shirts. She even continued to drive up in that grand, white car with the fiery red interior. She kept it waxed and shining, too. Only one thing changed. She stopped moving her body through the air. She stopped jumping over the car door in a one-handed pivot in order to slide into the driver's seat. Instead, she deliberately opened the door . . . and stepped in.

Just like everyone else.

Last Night Of The Core

Adrienne Lauby

The Volcanic Core echoed with sound as people prepared the old warehouse for tonight's show but Teresa hardly noticed. She rocked back on her heels, tore a two-foot strip off a big roll of silver duct tape and contemplated her lover Shay, squatting a yard away among a tangle of thick electric cords. Balanced easily on her strong calves, spiked hair dyed raven black and rising six inches off her forehead, you couldn't miss Shay. A few other punks had expensive hairdos, but no one else's hair framed a pair of neon green eyes and Shay's luminous skin. Teresa laid her tape the length of an electric cord and flattened it firmly against the old carpet which covered most of the stage. She was taping the cords to keep someone from tripping over them, but safety wasn't exactly the main thing on Teresa's mind.

Now, Teresa didn't usually get all ga-ga to see Shay's even white teeth across a few feet of stage. Sure, Shay was the first serious lover she'd found in six action-packed years of looking, so settling in with Shay meant something special. She didn't deny it. But Teresa wasn't the type to get all excited by romance. Lots of punks thought Shay was hot. Lots of them would practically die to have a chance at what Teresa got. But she didn't get Shay in the first place by falling down in ecstasy every time Shay strutted around in front of the band. And lots of punks didn't have to put up with Shay's down side either. The fact was, unless she had a guitar strapped to her chest, Shay kept most of her inner fire securely damped down. Most punks didn't know that.

So why did Teresa's stomach clench as she tore the tape across her thumb? Why did she feel like someone had just run over her with a Porsche? How come she was tearing off tape and laying it down, same as she'd been for the past ten minutes except, now, feeling like time had stopped and a cool breeze had swept aside the sticky summer heat? Maybe her hands were still working—and they better, too, because she had a ton of shit to do in the next hour—but her mind was possessed. She might look like she was smoothing out wrinkles in plastic tape, but actually she was in a horror movie and an alien creature had slithered into her brain. She was going through the motions while inside, something entirely different was going down.

Inside, Teresa was praising every sweet departed saint of rock and roll because this woman, this gorgeous breathing bigger-than-life goddess of a woman, was working only three feet away from her in a common everyday kind of intimacy. Shay glanced in her direction and, for a second, Teresa wondered if she'd smudged her mascara or plastered dust across her black leotard top. But Shay only wanted to see how much work was left. She scanned the stage, then swiveled back to her cords as Teresa tore another length of silver tape.

Covertly, she watched Shay's blunt hands sort through the thick black strands, as though Shay remembered which electronic box each one powered by touch. Teresa added Shay's hands to her praise, these hands which could pluck a single string from the fret of a guitar, then one string after another, until the notes came fast and you could barely follow the fingers. Shay's hands could fill your head with the exact music she intended you to hear. Her hands made the guitar look like the Christmas toy she said she'd wanted when she was five. They were so large they inevitably captured your attention. Then, once she'd snagged your awareness, her entire body leapt forward. Teresa finished a stretch of cord and looked around for another.

A couple of guys from the music store called from the back door, announcing the rental amp they carried. Some of the tension left Shay's body and she hurried over, laughing, teasing them, "So, you finally found one that worked good enough to bring it out here."

She joked with them and they had no choice but to laugh back, but at the same time she directed them, clear as any boss, exactly where she wanted them to set the heavy amp down—not by the door where they planned, but clear inside, up five steps and to the right hand side of the stage. It was the kind of thing Shay could get away with.

The music store guys left happy, but Teresa wasn't. She wasn't thrilled when Shay kissed up to strangers, play-acting another loud-mouth, just one of the boys. Shay liked to joke, liked to laugh, but Teresa suspected she mostly liked to get her way. And what did that mean when a joker could turn so quickly into a sensitive set of fingers which sorted through Teresa's heart as smoothly as they counted electric cords? How much of their love was another instance of Shay getting what she wanted? Teresa quickly laid three more strips of tape, laying her doubts away. To Teresa at least, Shay was the right combination of tough and luscious; her big bones enveloped in plenty of soft flesh, her broad shoulders spread with a soft fan tail of hair . . . How else to explain? How else to accept that one casual glance from Shay could curdle Teresa's guts, and this, after they'd been going together almost a year? Praise Saint Janis. Praise Saint Jimi. Let it keep on being true!

While she worked, the warehouse had slowly filled with kids and Teresa looked out to see who else had come. Tonight was closing night and that meant a big crowd. No one wanted to miss their last chance.

The Dykes, with the help of Lava Rising, provided what kids wanted. Everyone knew it and mostly what they wanted was the music. When the Dykes sang, people shouted the lines of their songs back to them. Their music was hard, fast, and loud as they could make it, getting everyone thrashing and screaming in the pit in front of the stage. When the Dykes played, dancers climbed on stage all around them and, after a few songs, began diving off into the heaving body of the crowd. The Dykes were the best punk rock band in town, no questions asked. And when Lava Rising added back-ups and covered the band breaks, everyone went home with new blisters on their feet and blasting encouragement in their heads.

It wasn't easy to pull off weekend after weekend. The Volcanic Core was the only all-ages club in the city and Teresa's friends, Lava Rising, ran it themselves. They raised the money, leased the building and sent out the advertising. For three months they'd produced shows for the Dykes, other local bands and twenty-six bands that traveled through. On the day of a show, Teresa came to the warehouse by noon and worked her butt off for fourteen hours or so. And she wasn't the only one. They'd done it for each other, and all the kids in this nowhere city who cared about something different, wanted something real to happen for a change.

Half of Lava Rising were in Teresa's line of sight right now, ready at the door to collect money and stamp hands, putting the food counter together, doing a last minute sweep of the painted cement floor. A couple of others were on patrol outside. Although they expected a friendly night, they were ready just in case.

By the front door a girl yelled and ran toward a heavily made-up guy. He lifted her in the air as light bounced off the jewelry in her nose and ears. Fran stamped a row of purple volcanoes across the high cheekbone of a tall skinny girl and the bare shoulders of a guy with muscle arms. It was early yet. The kids who'd come to check out the scene before the show got together in small groups which eventually broke apart and reformed into different groups at another spot on the floor.

"Like minnows," Teresa thought. "Like minnows swimming together . . . a school of minnows giving each other some grades . . . like minnows . . . varsity swimmers . . . formations . . . not the army, like minnows . . . unformed armies . . . like fish, we swim . . . like fishy friends . . . "

Shay broke into her thoughts, scattering them like a . . . school of minnows.

"That's the last one, Tree. Thanks," Shay said. "Toss the tape over, and I'll get the small stuff from here."

Teresa stood up, stretched and, a minute later followed Shay's broad back to the dusty alcove where a bank of dials would manage tonight's sound. She stepped carefully around the equipment which littered the stage. Shay was protective of her expensive electronic equipment and Teresa was very protective of Shay.

"How're you doing, Honey?" she asked, sneezing as she reached for Shay's sticky coffee cup. They liked the same kind of coffee, liked a bit of sugar and lots of cream.

This cup was very cold.

"Are you set up now?"

"Almost," Shay said, turning her emerald eyes on Teresa though her body still faced the sound board. "I've got to clean up the mess and run another sound check is all. How about you? Don't you have six people waiting with stuff you're supposed to do?"

Teresa dug a tissue out of a tight pocket in her jeans and blew her nose. Her curls bobbed across her forehead and she was glad she'd put in bobby pins before she went to bed the night before. Her hair was shaved above her ears and on the bottom half of her skull. The style depended on a perm in the remaining hair to soften the lines around her face. Lately the curls had had a tendency to go flat.

"Don't forget you wanted to take a shower," she told Shay, reaching in another pocket for an old envelope, skimming the penciled list which covered most of it. "It's almost nine."

"I'll have to skip it."

"You want me to run out and get you a clean shirt?"

"Skip it!" Shay's sharpness surprised them both. "I only meant I was okay," she said defensively.

With one hand she slowly took the cup out of Teresa's resentful palm.

"You're sweet to try, but I'm too old for a mother." This time she managed a gentle tone.

She set the cup down and reached over to rub the skull under Teresa's curly thatch. "The amp blew. It's just one of those things. I guess the band is used to smelling my sweat by now."

'Mother,' was it? But, at Shay's familiar touch, the alien beast of love crowded past her irritation and took complete possession of Teresa. She tilted closer until she nested securely against Shay's chest, resting her eyes on Shay's scruffy black boots as fatigue raced across her shoulders and neck.

"How are *you*?" Shay asked. "Does it look like we'll get a crowd?"

Teresa flinched and the alien disappeared. No crowd would be big enough to keep them open. By tomorrow the Volcanic Core would be history. No wonder she was exhausted.

"It's okay," she whispered belligerently. "Whatever else, we've got tonight. One more night of music. Nothing can stop us from the party we're going to have here tonight." She tried to keep her voice from cracking as Shay awkwardly patted her back.

"That's the idea. Chin up and think positive and all that," Shay said, turning her thump into a rub. "Remember I love you and don't worry. You did your best, Tree. You gave your life to this place. If anyone could have made a go of this, it was you and Lava Rising. Don't you ever think different!"

Teresa straightened her back.

"Now who's Mama-ing who?" she said, mocking Shay's protective tone. "I'd better get out of here before this Mama stuff gets addictive."

But, she took a step backward and stood on her own feet again before she risked another look at Shay. Yep, still there. Straight-cut fingernails embedded in rosy pink skin, sweatshirt purposely torn open to expose a line of collarbone. Shay returned to her dials but not before Teresa had fixated on the tiny indented spot in front of Shay's ear. She couldn't help herself. She plunged forward and kissed it.

Back in the warehouse Teresa checked the time against her list and tried not to feel guilty. At first, she didn't notice when a small woman, wearing a leather jacket too heavy for the season, left a group by the back wall and strolled over.

"Hi, Tree," the woman said. "You dropping a few roots in this spot or are you off to something you have to do?"

"Hey, Pen." Teresa changed the weight on her feet and grinned. "There's not much hope now. But I've got this list." She wiggled the envelope covered with scratched out words and recent additions. "Have you noticed any new kids here?"

"Lots. Another weekend and you'd have every kid in town. Do you know the ones coming in now? At least one of them goes to Sojourner."

"See? What'd I say?" Teresa said triumphantly. "Finally we get popular enough to bring a crowd from the hoity toity magnet arts school and that's the night we close. Who knows? One of them might have a daddy on the Planning Commission. Well, too bad. It wouldn't make a bit of difference now." Her eyes roved around the room. "It sure took them long enough to notice our existence. I guess unity isn't a word those guys care much about."

Pen, short for Pender, alias Kathy Pender and nobody better call her Kathy, or hint by word or deed that such a name existed—hid a grin, resettled her jacket and let the silence lay.

Then she said, "You're bitter, Tree. But you won't hang on to it, no matter how you try. You don't have that much meanness in you." She looked down at her grease-stained sneakers and back at Teresa's face. "I have to say, it's not like we exactly trot across town to hit events at Sojourners. Not me anyway. But, never mind that. It's been hell for you, putting this place together and losing it. Who wouldn't be bitter?"

Teresa felt the pricks in her nose which meant any minute she'd be bawling. She talked as fast as she could to stop the rising tears.

"I understand about Mr. and Mrs. Simon. They had a baby and we were too big for them. After we found this place I was even glad we didn't rent out there. But nobody's trying to sleep in this neighborhood! Stupid zoning laws! What's the point? They just like to keep us in the streets where they can hassle anyone they catch walking around alone. Great! I love respectable decent people who pay cops to do their dirty work. And they have the nerve to say they're only following the law. As if laws come from heaven."

"We never thought it would be easy," Pen interrupted gently. "But this is the hardest. You'll see. Tomorrow we start over. All we need to take away from this building is what we've learned. And money, of course." She turned out a pocket to show its empty lining. "You guys got any money saved to start over?"

"You kidding?" Teresa said, genuinely amazed Pen could ask. "If there's no surprise bills on their way, we get to keep what comes in that door tonight. All we've really had time to get from this place is 'Thanks for the memories,' and 'Keep on trying.' "

She looked around, tears beaten back, and allowed a touch of nostalgia. Three months. They hadn't had time for much decorating but, filled with kids, the Core didn't look so bad. The first day she walked into this place, she'd imagined an apocalyptic anti-nuke mural large enough to cover the smoke damage on the south wall. And there was the same old smoke. Bold as ever. They should have made a better bargain, got free rent the first month in exchange for the three full weeks they'd spent hauling away crap from the auto shop that had the place before them. That month's rent would have bought paint for a couple of walls at least.

But, all things considered, they'd done okay: decor by Lava Rising! Lory had had the idea to tack posters behind the stage on big orange and green cloth rectangles she'd found in thrift stores, and Ray's artistic slogans classed up the graffiti the kids added to the walls each week. Yesterday he'd gone all out. His words ran the length of each wall in blazing red: "Music Cannot Be Planned!" and "DOWN Is Not OUT!"

Something was happening at the door. A few people stopped talking and ambled over for a closer look. Teresa craned her neck to catch a flash of long purple nails at the end of a short brown arm. Nah, no problem there. Just Iwilla clowning around as she took over for Fran. Anyway, time to work.

"Forget the sad stuff," she told Pen, absently scratching an itch in the shaved area above her right ear. "How's your rant? We only gave

154

you three minutes like you said. But there's still time to ask for more."

Pen grinned and set her brown suede butch cap more firmly on her head.

"The only change I could make now is to back out completely," she said firmly, "and Shay made a point of telling me she'd never speak to me again if I did. Did you find enough of us to heat up the crowd before you big girls come on to play?"

"Every basement band in town wanted to go public while they still had the chance," Teresa said. "We scheduled six spots and half of them I never heard of. And, you don't need to get all snotty, either. Lava Rising is gonna lead off with our chant and a new bit before you come on."

Relieved from the door, Fran made a beeline for Pen and Teresa, only stopping when Iwilla shouted at her to bring back the volcano stamp. Fran had dyed her hair fresh for tonight, a brighter orange than usual. With her worried round face and purple lipstick she looked like an out-of-season Halloween pumpkin.

"Lory's been trying to find the extra cups, Teresa," she said. "Do you have them? I saw them go into the station wagon but, as far as I know, they never came back out."

Teresa threw her shoulders back with an exaggerated deep breath.

"Excuse me, Pen. Discussion of deeper issues is hereby complete for the night." She turned to Fran. "I think they got put in a box with the stereo. Don't ask who or why." She stopped herself briefly before taking off after the bustling Fran. "See you under the lights in half an hour, Pen. And thanks for letting me blow off steam. You're a real pal."

Pen beamed.

It was more than an hour before Teresa finally stood on stage with Lava Rising, Iwilla pounding her congo drum as they chanted out their theme. Lava Rising had started as a gag, a way to get in on the fun, a doo wop line, Shay called it. Iwilla and Lory made up a few raps, including a chant about the Hawaii volcano eruption, and with a few friends, started traveling around with the Dykes. Teresa joined them about the time they got thrown out of a few places for being under twenty-one and decided to produce some all-ages shows on their own. Before long the scene had grown big enough for its own building, so they'd started saving money to open The Volcanic Core.

"You can't ignore volcanoes, when they rumble ocean bound. You can't control the lava, when it makes its bubbling sound. YOU

CAN'T HOLD DOWN A MOVEMENT, WHEN IT BURSTS FROM UNDERGROUND!"

Fran stepped forward, grabbed the microphone and pumped her other hand up and down to change the rhythm for the new part, something Teresa wrote especially for tonight.

> We came to your hearings
> fifty punks strong
> you called us all hoodlums
> said we did not belong
>
> We're simply your children.
> Why refuse us a place?
> You say we make trouble.
> Yeh, we
> Ignore your rat race.
>
> The nuclear family's
> collapsed into space
> In this shattered city
> Everyone's got their own mace.
>
> You mumble and grumble
> While we're making a change.
> We've got ideals and answers.
> Barbaric?
> We're out of your range.
>
> There's plenty to do.
> We tried and got a start
> Made music and dancin' while
> you built another K-mart.
>
> Now don't think it's over
> the day you close us down
> Like stirred up old hornets
> We're moving all over town.

After the applause, Pen replaced them on the stage for her ranting poem. They walked off stage, squeezing past the band waiting at the edge.

The Core was well past crowded. Kids who tried sitting on the floor practically got trampled by those standing on tiptoe to see. They clung to the center poles and each other. Everyone Teresa knew was there, Kali Das, Crystal, H.G., Todd . . . Most of them, people she'd met since they started the benefit gigs to get open; friends of friends who always showed up to help, musicians, Shay's old buddies from school, a few street people, the girl who only wanted to mix the sound . . . If the Core had stayed a fantasy—been nothing but a dream, the club every punk wished would open in their city—she'd never have known these people.

She might have hung out with some of them, gotten wild and drunk some night at some mall and taken one or another of them up on a sexual invitation; maybe stood in a corner and admired Shay's music or danced to it until she fell in a heap. But she would never have spent a certain afternoon with Shay driving all over hell picking up cookies for a damn bake sale in her Dad's old rusty Buick. Without the Core she'd be where she was a year ago, no reason for her life and no rhyme to make it move. She wouldn't have Shay and these friends, never in a million years be looking at a stage where she'd just been shouting and chanting out her opinions.

"To write something good, you gotta have a reason," Pen said, and "It helps to have people willing to listen." Teresa had a crate of diaries going back ten years under her bed to prove Pen's point. Only this year was different. This year, she couldn't find hours in the day for all she wanted to do. She didn't have to moon around her bedroom thinking up a fantasy to hide away in some secret book; she had to choose between ideas, and get one down in words before it got crowded out by something new.

The best part was how it didn't happen alone. It wasn't just having Shay, being in love and all that. It was something more than one or two. That's why the place was packed tonight. Everyone knew it was their last chance before they turned back into a bunch of isolated fools, dressed up like punk clowns and doing their act on the street: 'Hey, it's cool . . . I can take care of myself . . . I've got it all down . . . '

Pen finished her rant and Teresa realized she hadn't paid much attention. She shook her head. She'd heard Pen's poem before but the group tuning up was new. Most of the bands sang stuff about themselves, like opening a window shade and showing off a play about their lives. Tonight, even the old bands would probably play something new for their last night at the Core and Teresa didn't want to miss a bit of it.

These guys were shy. They had twelve people on stage but no one got close to the microphones. Everything they played came out blurry, mostly noise.

She counted the crowd, trying to guess the take from the door and Iwilla flashed by to say the cops had arrived. So she followed Iwilla outside where Fran said the guys drinking and hanging out had taken off. The cops left after a quick check around but Teresa still missed the frizzy-haired girl come on with her band. Despite her good intentions, she'd missed the beginning of their first song.

> I went down
> I went down
>   down down
> I went down to Rose's
>
> Where the rose
> grows and the rose knows
> what Rose knows
> Soft her thoughts
> Kind her heart
> I took myself down,
> my troubles outa town
> and went to Rose.

The girl stood on a chair at the tallest microphone. Nothing shy about her! The song didn't have much music, just bells and wooden clappers sounding off behind the singing like Chinese New Year. The noise pushed the girl to speed up but she kept the same steady pace, looking over the audience as she sang. One by one her dark eyes checked them out, like teachers when they watch for people cheating—almost before you knew she had you, her eyes moved on. And she had a smile, like she was personally inviting every punk in the room to a party.

Down, down, down
I went down to Rose's
    soft heart

With my hurt heart I said
Rose, who knows,
how down I've been
Rose knows
I've been down, down, down
Rose, who knows,
    knew how
and softly took me down.

down down down
    soft hearts
Softly down

down down in the down
    of Rose's
    soft bed.

    Just for a second, near the end of the poem, her eyes landed on Teresa. Then it was over. She stuck a marker in a small bound book and riffled the pages for the words to another song, apparently unaware of the applause and catcalls which joined the bells and clappers in one long din around her.

    Teresa stood with her mouth open. Down in the bed! Talk about nerve! This girl slipped sex into a sweet song about flowers and announced herself the first time she sang at the Core. She'd made sure everybody heard it too. No covering it over, no strutting around with a loud set of drums to drown out the words. The Dykes were blatant but when people yelled up to Shay to sing something about sex, she yelled back it was none of their business.

    The band was the Frizzy-Haired Girl and two others. One of them, a floppy guy wearing a T-shirt six sizes too big, hit a roll on the drums. Seemed like the next song was gonna have more music. When it began, somebody plugged Frizzy Hair into an electric socket. Her shoulders bounced, her hair wiggled and jiggled, she bent stiffly at the waist; the stage lights turned the tips of her hair transparent as her voice jumped from high to low, putting the words between drum beats and guitar chords where you could catch most of them.

It sounded like somebody this girl knew had been locked in a mental ward.

"They took you away screaming/ We'd been talking about life/ They took you away/ angels on the left of you/ angels on the right . . .

"You said it was places like this/ got you crazy/ in the first place . . .

"The shit/ the thorazine/ the lithium/ the shit/ the mellaril/ the shit . . ."

Teresa looked around, but Pen had disappeared. Pen had been locked up. When Pen was fourteen her girlfriend got caught with some letters and spilled everything to her Dad. Being a whole six months older, Pen got the "corrupting a minor" rap and her Mom bought the idea she needed psychiatric help. The upshot was four months in a state psychiatric prison playing humble until she got ground privileges, then three years on the street as a runaway. Pen said that was why she didn't have a girlfriend now, at her ripe old age of twenty-five. "Not about to mess with any minors," she said, "and nobody my age is worth the trouble." And what she had to say about that so-called hospital . . . This girl had it right, "Shit." Where was Pen anyway?

Teresa scanned the crowd, amazed at how people were paying attention. Usually, unless the Dykes were playing, or some great band on tour, half the kids were off in the corners, socializing. And, there were always ones standing around with frozen, embarrassed faces, pretending to be oh-so-in-love with what was going on, when you could tell they didn't have a clue. But, this girl, this girl only had to half turn to give a solo to her drummer, and twenty people rushed for the pit to dance. This girl had them in the palm of her hand. She raised her right fist in the air as she read the last verse and half the crowd put fists up too. Amazing!

"They came to take you away/ Screaming/ Seems there's no place/ screaming is allowed!/ No place/ no place/ no place . . . "

The guitar screamed and the crowd screamed. The girl smiled, starting in the corners of her mouth because it was a serious song but finally letting her pleasure stretch out across her face. She bowed in little dips, almost as if she wanted to hide, like she was surprised to make such an impression. But she knew what she'd done. She'd got them in her palm and bounced them all up and down a few times, hadn't she? She might be humble but she wasn't actually turning down any applause.

What was her name? Fran had scheduled the bands so Teresa hadn't seen it. The girl swung easily off her folding chair. Who was she?

Three other bands played ten-minute sets but Teresa mostly watched the crowd to see where the girl went, trying to find out who her friends were. Then Kali Das, even taller than usual in a pair of leather hip boots, announced the break with a speech about how great Lava Rising was and how much she and everyone hoped they'd get the Core back together in a new place soon. She coerced Lava Rising up on stage again and the tears Teresa'd been stuffing down streamed off her face.

When she climbed off, Pen was waiting.

"She was pretty hot, huh, Tree?"

And, Teresa didn't need to ask, "Who?"

"What's her name?"

"Don't know. I don't remember seeing her before. It doesn't look like she's hanging with any group in particular."

They both looked again, hoping to find out something. Shay was already onstage with the Dykes. The guitar player struck a few chords to get the crowd listening and Teresa jumped up and down, ready to begin. She landed easily on the balls of her feet, so happy she could have reached over to give Pen a big hug.

Not that she would, of course. As usual, Pen stood stiff as a two-by-four. Even with her police jacket slung casually over one shoulder and her sweet half-smile, anyone would know it was hands off. Pen was relaxed tonight, but you treated Pen with careful respect or you didn't treat with Pen at all.

"I guess I got to get cracking," Pen said. "You guys had your new piece all memorized, didn't you? I think I'm pretty hot with the words, but that new woman . . . "

That new woman . . .

Sequences

Terri de la Peña

May 2, 1983: Anticipation

Monica Tovar had eyed her mailbox daily, yearning for its cramped interior to reveal a bulky envelope postmarked Novato, California. Each time she returned home from the office, finding only department store bills and Publishers' Clearinghouse come-ons, she had slammed the unyielding mailbox and dejectedly climbed her apartment house stairs. Finally, after three frustrating weeks, she had been rewarded with the longed-for delivery. Snatching it from the mailbox, she had darted upstairs. Once inside, she rushed into her airy bedroom and ripped open the thick envelope.

Carefully she removed a bound booklet bearing *The Wishing Well* in elaborate calligraphy on its otherwise plain cover. For seconds, she stared at her treasure, before searching its finely printed pages. And then, with a gasp, Monica recognized her entry:

Pisces, 36 yrs.: I am a shy, sensitive but zestful, dark-haired, dark-eyed Chicana desiring deep friendship with other introspective feminist women. If you possess a sense of humor, enjoy books, films, theater, long walks, eclectic conversations, bike rides and chocolate, please write. I am allergic to cigarette smoke, so prefer non-smoking friends. No drugs, mind trips or role-playing, please.

She slumped on her narrow bed and critically reread her ad, doubting if anyone would reply. She chided herself for that negative thought, but it nagged her when she noticed that the few ads with photos showed smiling white women. Would any of them write to a Chicana? Monica tried not to think about that while she paged through the booklet. She had decided not to submit a photograph with her ad; self-confidence had never been one of her strong points.

In her twenties, she had been rejected by the only woman she had loved. Monica had remained celibate ever since, hiding her sexuality from anyone but herself. Although she was convinced of her lesbianism, she lacked the confidence to love again, afraid of additional rebuffs. For most of her adult life, she had been a lesbian in name only, "passing" as a shy Catholic spinster. Two years of feminist therapy finally had encouraged her to submit an ad to *The Wishing Well.*

Turning the pages, Monica grimaced when she realized that many ads were out-of-state entries. But, recalling her request for friendship, she grabbed a pen from the dresser top and scrawled check marks next to the selected ads' code numbers, regardless of geographic areas. For half an hour, she remained engrossed in her task until her back and shoulders began to ache.

Moving to a more practical position in her nearby desk chair, Monica flipped another page and abruptly paused, her gaze focused on a southern California submission:

Moon Child, 31 yrs.: I am interested in finding someone to go on a carpet ride to explore the faces of reality by going through the plane of illusion to find out what is. I am a sincere, college-educated individual who likes to be intense, playful, humorous and creative. I am interested in the political, economic and social consciousness of the Women's Movement. I am a vegetarian non-smoker who enjoys quiet evenings, theater, movies, sports, reading, traveling and other people.

Monica meticulously withdrew pale blue stationery and matching envelopes from her desk drawer. She noticed her brown hands shook slightly. With her favorite felt-tipped pen, she started composing her first introductory letter.

Friday, May 20, 1983: Meeting

Clutching two cellophane-wrapped peach-colored roses in her sweaty hands, Monica stood beneath the open casement windows of the Old World restaurant in Westwood, not far from her UCLA Medical Center office. Trim in coffee-colored pleated slacks, blue oxford shirt, and buff corduroy blazer, she wished she had had a haircut; her coarse black strands hung heavily against her button-down collar.

"I'm too early," she scolded herself, shivering despite the spring weather. She scanned the passing traffic, oblivious of the diners' leisurely chatter, and recalled the two letters she had received in short succession from Jozie Krozinski.

In the first one, Jozie had dubbed herself "a transplanted Easterner," living in a mountain community outside Los Angeles County. A later paragraph had offered a sketchy physical description: brown curly hair, blue eyes, fair complexion, average height, "a little on the chubby side."

Monica glanced at her own brown-skinned frame, her delicate-looking wrists and racehorse ankles. Would Jozie cruise by, see a skinny Chicana standing there, and keep going? Insecure and nervous, Monica realized she really knew nothing about Jozie, not even what type of car she drove.

Jozie's second letter had added a few more details. She counseled adolescents at a privately-owned school, and preferred to socialize "off the mountain." She had included her phone number in that letter.

On the telephone, Jozie's voice had sounded warm and friendly, flavored with a crisp New England accent. She had joked that she knew no Chicanas. Yet in the same breath, she revealed she had just finished reading *This Bridge Called My Back* and been moved by it. Hearing that, Monica had cast aside her doubts about their having nothing in common, and agreed to meet her for dinner. But now, leaning against the restaurant's stone wall, Monica mentally paraphrased a Streisand lyric: "Will she like me?"

Time crawled. Relentlessly, Monica stared ahead until the frequent passersby and constant cars became blurs. Close to 7:00 p.m., the stark outline of a brown minibus appeared from the midst of the steady Westwood traffic and halted before the restaurant. Monica stared, her heart palpitating. The side of the bus bore the legend "The Wildwood School for Girls." A curly-haired woman, ignoring angry drivers' blaring horns, leaned across the empty passenger seat and gazed at her.

"Are you Monica?"

She heard herself stutter. "Yes."

"I'm Jozie. Sorry I'm late. Took the wrong off-ramp."

Monica stepped to the edge of the curb. "Were my directions hard to follow?"

"No. I looked at them after I'd made the wrong turn. I thought you'd said 'Western,' not 'Westwood.' " With her wide blue eyes and rosy cheeks, she seemed frazzled, endearingly so.

Approaching the minibus, Monica smiled and offered to help find parking. Jozie looked relieved. Fumbling with the door handle, Monica managed to wrench the door open and settle into the bucket seat. With some awkwardness, she remembered her romantic gesture of buying flowers. The wrinkled cellophane clung to her wet hands and crackled as she handed the roses to Jozie. The other woman blushed and thanked her. And Monica liked her at once.

Over dinner at The Good Earth, they began to learn about each other, exploring and sharing. Listening to Jozie's witty account of her Polish-American Catholic childhood, Monica realized she felt at ease with her. Besides the common ground of religion, they both had emerged from ethnic, working-class families and had cherished close relationships with their now-deceased matriarchal grandmothers. Because of these similarities, Monica was drawn to the gently humorous Jozie, yet she sensed a secret sadness behind those easy smiles. From Jozie's first letter, she remembered a fleeting reference to "unsettling depressions that everyone has periodically." Perhaps homesickness for New England or job stress affected Jozie from time to time. Her unexpected question interrupted Monica's speculation.

"Why did you write to *The Wishing Well*? I can't imagine you'd have trouble making friends." Jozie toyed with an ear-length tendril of her curly hair.

Monica avoided her frank gaze and squeezed more lemon into her iced tea. "It seemed a safe way to meet women. Like I said in my letter, I've belonged to N.O.W. and other feminist organizations, but most of the women were either already involved or straight. Being the third party gets to be boring after a while—and lonely. And I'm not the bar type either." She shrugged, dumping the lemon slice into her tea.

"Does anyone in your office know you're— "

"They think I'm a nice old maid."

Laughing, Jozie took another sip of coffee. "That's basically what people think of me, too. Neither of us fit the stereotype, Monica, so we're considered asexual. It's pathetic how much people rely on stereotypes."

"Really." She wondered if Jozie considered her a non-stereotypical Chicana, too. Jozie probably had some preconceived notions about Chicanas; most Anglos did. Monica enjoyed surprising them, particularly male employers, by revealing the assertiveness lurking beneath her initial shyness.

She focused again on Jozie, admiring the changeable hues of her eyes; in the restaurant, they were greener than they had seemed outside. Anglos had such clear, vibrant eyes; her own black ones appeared impenetrable.

Scanning Jozie, Monica noticed the detailed embroidery of tiny multicolored birds on the other woman's muslin blouse. They fluttered capriciously across her lavish breasts. Jozie had told her about buying the blouse in Puerto Vallarta the previous summer. With amusement, she wondered if Jozie had worn it to their meeting in deference to Monica's ethnic origins. Oddly enough, Monica's own attire looked Ivy League in comparison.

"Jozie, is meeting women a problem for you, too?"

"Sure. And I have to be very discreet, since I actually live on school property. During the summer, most of the other faculty go off campus. In a couple of weeks, I'll be one of the few staying on. Anyway, it's been a long time since I've met anyone, Monica."

"Me, too." She looked away, studying the intricately designed macramé wall hanging adjacent to their booth. For a moment, she wavered, debating whether to mention exactly how long it had been. Maybe there would be time for that discussion later. She was uneasy about being candid right away.

While describing her sprawling rural campus, Jozie abruptly asked Monica for a weekend visit. Pleased by the invitation and with her own spontaneous reply, Monica smiled, liking herself for being impulsive, but knowing she would worry about her decision later.

For the rest of the evening, the two women wandered through Westwood, laughing at the raucous circus atmosphere characteristic of the neon-lit village neighboring the UCLA campus. Amidst the springtime crowds, they glimpsed brightly colored pedicabs and sleek convertibles, jam-packed with rowdy adolescents. On street corners, a variety of white-faced mimes and jugglers entertained unending lines of moviegoers. For once, Monica enjoyed playing tourist guide, showing Jozie this unique sampling of Southern California life. Ambling into "Aahs," a one-of-a-kind-store which displayed a bizarre blend of kitsch and film notalgia, they inspected outrageous greeting cards, amazed to find several lesbian-themed ones.

Later, lingering over cappuccino and chocolate mousse, they tried to postpone ending their evening. But they both knew Jozie had a long drive ahead and had to work the next day. Together they strolled to the university parking lot. In the moonlight, they faced each other, suddenly self-conscious after their previous camaraderie.

"Can I have a hug?" Jozie's voice was almost a whisper.

Although she nodded, Monica felt tense, encountering her long-held, unspoken fear. She tried to be calm, reminding herself that they had shared an enjoyable evening, but the current reality did nothing to quell her lack of self-confidence.

Viewing the anticipation in Jozie's clear eyes, Monica hesitated. Did Jozie honestly find her attractive, or was she simply being friendly? How could Monica be certain?

Yet, when Jozie offered her an encouraging grin, Monica stepped closer. Jozie's strong arms surrounded her at once, and Monica wanted to cry from the pure pleasure of that luxury. Clasping Jozie's soft, enticing body against her, she longed to relax her own rigid muscles; her neck and shoulders were coiled tight. Sighing to prevent a sob, she wanted to hold Jozie forever, their breasts pressed intimately together.

If Jozie had noticed Monica's earlier conflicting emotions, she said nothing. Her arms were wrapped securely around the Chicana's slight body.

"We'll talk during the week?"

"Yes." With reluctance, Monica slowly released her.

Through the evening mist, she watched Jozie depart. Her incipient happiness was accompanied by a sudden stab of loneliness. Would they be able to recapture the evening's rapport when they met again?

Subdued, though uncommonly excited, Monica drove home. Before sleep enfolded her, she made love to herself.

Weekend: Friday, June 3, 1983

Leaving her office, Monica hauled her hefty overnight bag to the medical center parking lot. Would Jozie be there? Or had she changed her mind? A couple of nights ago, they had discussed their weekend plans, but neither had mentioned anything about sleeping arrangements. Monica's therapist had been especially curious about that. Monica had preferred to change the subject.

When she glimpsed Jozie waiting by a blooming jacaranda tree, some of her apprehension faded. Approaching her, Monica searched for any tell-tale signs of nervousness: a tapping foot, a facial tic, but she could not perceive any. She hoped she could conceal her own. After a long day at her typewriter, her neck and shoulders ached from accumulated tension; but she realized today's strained muscles were caused by a combination of fear of the unknown and outright sexual anticipation.

Jozie greeted her with a smile, patting the lusterless hood of a much-traveled green Honda Civic. "I drove my own car down this time. It's easier to handle in traffic. Let me put your stuff in the back, Monica."

"Thanks, Jozie."

Once settled within, the women made small talk and decided to eat dinner later. Jozie seemed particularly eager to leave. Her pink fingers impatiently drummed the steering wheel at each traffic light, and on entering the freeway, she drove very fast.

"Am I being kidnapped?" Monica thought wildly.

On the road, they spoke about their separate weekday worlds, sharing anecdotes. Though she was comfortable with Jozie on a conversational level, Monica pondered her own churning nervousness.

While exchanging comments, she continued her own worrisome interior monologue. "It's been years since I've been with a woman sexually. I want to make love with Jozie because I like her, but I'm scared. Maybe I'm crazy to be even thinking about this. What if she just invited me to the mountains for companionship—to go hiking like she said? After all, we haven't even discussed making love in specific terms."

She glanced at Jozie, half-listening to her conversation. Monica liked the way she tilted her head while speaking, as if addressing an unseen audience. Monica imagined her lecturing in a classroom, reaching her students with warmth and witticisms. Jozie was probably a popular teacher. Monica smiled at that thought. Did the boarding school students develop crushes on Ms. Krozinski?

Monica was developing one herself. Laughing at Jozie's humorous remarks, she wondered what it would be like to hold that curly head against her breasts, to cuddle that ample body close. She wanted to touch her now, but did not dare. What would it be like to kiss Jozie, their tongues flirting? What would it be like to be with her in the same bed all night? Monica trembled. Would she even remember what to do? For years, she had been self-centered, only pleasing herself. Would she be able to arouse Jozie tonight? And what kind of lover would Jozie be?

Monica could not articulate this aloud, dreadful of seeming naïve and foolish. She was even unsure about discussing it later, if need be. Instead, she struggled to keep her mind blank, free of self-defeating thoughts. But despite her doubts, she did not regret accepting Jozie's invitation.

Halfway towards their destination, they dined in an ersatz Mexican restaurant, Jozie's favorite. Monica found the sampling of chile rellenos atrocious. To soothe her nerves and stomach, she ordered a Carta Blanca; Jozie had coffee.

With darkness enveloping them, they eventually left the freeway for a narrow two-lane road leading to the mountains, and at last began to speak candidly about their sexual pasts, their current celibacy. Listening to Jozie's revelations, Monica realized that she herself had been celibate much longer. At the same time, she recognized Jozie's awareness of her unspoken apprehensiveness, and she was grateful for it.

During their discussion, Monica diligently kept her eyes on the curving road, not on Jozie's gentle face. Silently, she wondered if the weekend would be disastrous; but she did not want to change her mind.

"Tonight," she promised herself, "I want to open the door, not hide behind it anymore. And she holds the key."

On entering her rustic apartment, Jozie flicked on the lights and paused in the tiny foyer. In her jeans and parka, with her curly hair framing her rosy-cheeked face, she presented an appealing outdoorsy portrait of a country dyke against the backdrop of the knotty-pine wall.

"Monica, I wouldn't be offended if you preferred to sleep on

169

the couch."

With more confidence than she felt, Monica turned to her, voice firm. "I'd rather sleep with you, Jozie."

And although she smiled in response, her Slavic facial contours seemed taut. Then Monica knew that Jozie was nervous, too.

"I'd really like to take a shower."

"The bathroom's to your left. I'll see you in a bit?"

Monica nodded, set her overnight bag on the living room carpet and removed toiletries and her nightgown. The brisk mountain air seeped through one of the louvred windows, and she shivered. She heard Jozie enter the adjacent bedroom and turn on the TV.

In the tiled bathroom, Monica relished her few moments of solitude, allowing the hot water to rain upon her tense body. She rotated her head from side to side, her rigid shoulders creaking in the process. Yet, once alone, her troubling doubts returned. "I don't want to go backwards," she insisted. Instead, she went to Jozie.

In bed, they sat stiffly viewing the 11:00 p.m. news, side by side in flannel nightgowns, two unlikely bookends. Monica's heart thudded within her thin chest, causing her entire body to tremble; she wondered if the double bed shook as a result. She wished she could joke about it, but she felt closer to crying than laughing.

During the weather segment, Jozie turned to gaze at her, those changeable eyes bluer in the subdued light. Her voice was quiet.

"Can I kiss you?"

Not trusting her own voice, Monica nodded, her eyes moving to Jozie's own. She recognized the gentleness there, sparked by an unfamiliar, but thoroughly arousing, fervor. Jozie's beckoning lips parted, and Monica found herself leaning closer, less than an inch away. Tentatively, their lips met, and Monica savored their fleeting touch. Both women smiled, eyeing each other conspiratorially.

"Again?" Monica murmured.

"Yes."

They edged nearer, sinking into an unavoidable embrace. That second kiss was suddenly surer. And Monica sensed that everything would be all right.

Agilely, Jozie outstretched a muscled leg and turned off the TV with her big toe, causing Monica to laugh outright. Their mutual amusement gave them another excuse to kiss, more than once, deeply and eagerly.

Minutes later, they undressed with some urgency, turning to each other rather cautiously. In the dimness, Monica was amazed at the fullness of Jozie's breasts; hers were miniscule in comparison. Lying there, she surveyed the sweet, smiling woman beside her and noted their contrasts: Jozie was pink, round and soft; she was brown, lean, and bony. But that didn't matter. They were women, and they had found each other.

My Private Search

Rosemary Reeves

Just weeks before my seventeenth birthday, my Scottish-born mother talked my father into moving us to England. It had taken all the money they had somehow managed to save over the years, money they had put away for their old age. They sold our row home in Philadelphia and left behind six of my adult brothers and sisters. In just two years my parents would be financially drained. Blurry photographs and a few treasured souvenirs were virtually all they had to show for it.

In England, my life was changed forever. Maybe it was turning seventeen that made me relax a little, stop hating myself for being gay. Maybe by that time I had so many years of emotional pain, thinking I was some kind of disgusting pervert (wasn't that what everybody said lesbians were?) that I was tired of it. Maybe denial had exhausted me. Maybe it was reading a book by Quentin Crisp called *The Naked Civil Servant.*

I saw it in a bookstore in the little English town where my parents chose to live at the time. My mother was with me. I picked it from the shelf because of its curious title. I couldn't believe it when I read the inside cover. A book about a homosexual! I was astonished. I didn't think such a thing existed in the world. I bought it, mentioning the subject matter oh so casually to my mother, like it didn't matter to me at all, though my heart was pounding so hard in my ears I could hear it.

I couldn't sleep until I read every page. Crisp wrote about his life as an effeminate gay man in London, some of it sad, and some of it quite fun and endearing. I didn't agree with a lot of his cynicism, but I understood how he had been hurt by prejudice and bigotry. After reading his book, I felt like I had permission to be myself. I decided then and there that when I was eighteen I was going off to London to find others like me.

I left my parents' house five days after my eighteenth birthday. I stayed at a bed and breakfast place in Earl's Court, a busy section of London with easy access to the center of things. I was awed immediately by the beauty, cleanliness, and diversity of such a massive city. Ruins of ancient buildings commonly stood in the middle of traffic-congested streets. Churches centuries old peeped out among modern office buildings. There was history, nightlife, rich and poor, all manner of culture. If there were people like me anywhere it had to be here. There was so much to see and do, but my goal, the reason I came, was to find them.

In *The Naked Civil Servant*, the author mentioned he met other gay men at Piccadilly Circus and Marble Arch in London. The first thing I did was to go to those places. I had nothing to guide me but that book, so I used it as an aid in my search. I remember sitting on the steps of Piccadilly Square under a statue of Eros for hours scanning the crowd for gay faces. What a lonely feeling it was not even knowing what to look for. Downhearted, I headed back to my bed and breakfast before nightfall.

It wasn't long before I found a magazine that covered the various activities going on in London, from art exhibits, to group meetings, to civil rights demonstrations. It was a popular magazine that had, to my amazement, a personal column that included a few ads from gays and bisexuals seeking romance. The particular issue I picked up had no personal ads from lesbians, however. Too impatient to wait for the next issue, I summoned up the courage to answer an ad from a bisexual woman seeking other women for romance.

We met at a pub in the evening. She was blond, feminine, pretty. For a while, I thought I was doing pretty well. I guess after sipping some wine, I confessed I was only eighteen, but tried to pretend I was experienced. She seemed quiet, nice, polite, and understanding. This and the wine gave me a false sense of security. I don't know who suggested it first, but we ended up at her flat, which was rather lovely. It had glass doors that opened out into the street.

There she offered me more wine. We talked a little bit about

173

ourselves and then she mentioned that her boyfriend was a photographer. I reminded her that I wasn't interested in men at all, particularly not her boyfriend, but she insisted on showing me some pictures. There were some weird ones of knotted ropes and one picture of a naked man, her boyfriend. I thought, what the hell is this? Right at that moment there was a knock on the door, and she got up to answer it. The man in the picture walked in, and I knew immediately that I had been set up. I was panicked, yet I knew I had to stay calm. They were talking to me, but I hardly heard anything they were saying. I kept thinking, those fuckers, what are they up to? I kept telling myself not to freak out.

Very calmly, I announced I was leaving. There had been a misunderstanding, I said. I inched my way over to the glass doors that opened out into the street. They tried to convince me to stay but didn't physically approach me. I guess a warning was written on my face. I escaped hastily into the night, duped and feeling like the world's biggest fool. I realized then how naïve I had been, how little I knew because so much was kept from me. I was not, however, about to give up.

I lived for that magazine, and sure enough, found information in it one day about a newly formed support group for women who recently discovered their lesbianism and wanted to come out.

When I attended their meeting I saw, for the very first time, other women like me. I felt relief, joy, wonder, curiosity and incredible anticipation at the same time. I looked around the room at the diversity of faces with their various expressions, from timid shyness to friendly smiles. None of them resembled the image that had been drilled into my head of the mean, ugly, perverted lesbian who preyed on other women. They looked like anyone else. They looked like me.

The group leaders said they didn't recommend the bars for meeting other lesbians but we all wanted to see a gay bar so they agreed to take us to one. I don't remember the name of the bar but there was an outside door, then a flight of steps, then another door that opened up to the dance floor. There were tables all around and women drinking at them, and my eye caught two women kissing, real deep like lovers. I stood and stared at this remarkable, natural sight, forgetting myself for a moment, until someone from the group called my name. I joined the others at a table and before we knew it, we were getting pretty casual with each other. No one was brave enough to ask anyone to dance, though. I was kind of disappointed because I wanted someone to ask me.

The next night I came to the bar by myself and that's when I met Sue. I had been sitting alone at a table, nursing a beer, and when I got up to get another one, she had taken my seat by mistake! Anyhow, we started talking, and then she said in the cutest cockney accent, "Are you a Yank?" She sounded like the actress in *My Fair Lady* in the beginning of the story. It was fun just to listen to her speak. Sue had brown hair that rested on her shoulders and she was almost too thin, but there was a fire in her that held me. Besides, the moment I had been dreaming of was becoming reality. I sat transfixed, following her lead, pretending I was not new at this. I took her home with me that night.

Making love with her felt so natural I knew what I wanted to do. Touching her body was like exploring a beautiful uncharted terrain. She guided me with many subtle movements. I surprised myself by feeling an unabashed rush of hunger. It felt so right for me, like everything was finally coming into place. I no longer felt like I was lost at sea, waiting, waiting.

I thought, was this the terrible thing I had heard about in whispered warnings? Was this something deserving of the word "perversion?" Were I and this tiny woman in the bed beside me a danger to society? It was so absurd I wanted to laugh out loud.

We met again the next night and before long I was falling in love. I moved from my B&B into a one-room windowless flat in the basement of an old boarding house and found work at a cafeteria down the street from Big Ben and the Houses of Parliament making salads. Every morning I heard Big Ben mark the hour, hopefully after I got to work and not before, since I was often late. It chimed every hour on the hour and I thought it was a lovely sound. One day, on a whim, I decided to find out where the author Quentin Crisp lived. I flipped through the pages of the London telephone directory. Sure enough, there was one listing, with an address, only half a mile or so from where I resided. There was a shadow of a doubt in my mind, but I thought it was worth a shot.

I walked the half mile or so into the Chelsea section. I didn't mind because the walk was so pleasant. I found the address. The name Crisp was on the door and beneath it a buzzer. I reached out a finger to touch it, but retreated. Questions started swimming in my head. What if it wasn't him? What if it was? If he came out to greet me, what in the world would I say? I knew I wanted to say thanks, but how? I tried to rehearse the scene in my mind but nothing sounded right. I turned and walked away. I don't suppose I'll ever find out if he really lived there but the possibility, to this day, makes me smile.

Over the months I visited other lesbian bars, some alone and some with Sue. I remember five in all. There was even one or two on the outskirts of the city that I didn't get to see. It was so exciting, this new life. I wanted to explore everything about it. Sue introduced me to a lesbian novel called *Patience and Sarah*. I was stunned when she told me there were other lesbian novels. (Blimey, luv, you didn't know that?) At about the same time came the emergence of a song called *Glad to be Gay*. The song was banned on English radio stations, but Sue had the record. Sometimes, when I visited her in her flat, we played it over and over. We'd sit on the floor, clapping our hands and singing along. It made us feel special, indeed, like we were different from everybody else but in a good way.

Our relationship was brief, however. We broke up because of Sue's alcoholism. I still loved her and it hurt. I continued to go to the bars and even slept with another woman, but there was an emptiness in me that only Sue had filled. I hadn't learned yet how to fill it myself.

My helpful magazine, though, had information about a civil rights march that was coming up. It was intended as a protest against an organization known as The National Front, a fascist, homophobic group of white supremacists similar to our American Ku Klux Klan. While English women and gays seemed to me to have about the same freedoms and amount of oppression against them as those in the United States, I was constantly surprised by the strikingly overt racism that seemed to be taken for granted over there. The march was to be at Trafalgar Square, and I had every intention of going.

On the day of the event, the subway train was packed with people. Large crowds waited at every stop. I thought, could all these people be going to the march? Those unable to squeeze inside had to wait for the next train. By the time we arrived at Trafalgar Square, it took me fifteen minutes just to exit the station. I had anticipated a few hundred marchers. There were tens of thousands. I marched with all sorts of contingents before finally finding the gay group. I met all kinds of people. I was glowing, beaming with pride just to be there. I knew then that things could change.

One day, my parents announced they were returning to the United States. Homesick myself, I decided to go with them. I left behind the memory of Sue, the beauty of the Thames River, the happy greetings from Big Ben, my agony at Piccadilly Square, my victory at Trafalgar Square, and the possibility of meeting Quentin Crisp, the man who unknowingly gave me permission to be myself. But, oh, what I took with me.

Birth Song[†]

J. L. Williams

Bobbie shifted cautiously, attempting to wriggle further beneath the sleeping bag that half covered her shoulder. She absolutely did not want to disturb the woman tucked against her; the one whose buttocks pressed into her abdomen, the one whose neck she had breathed against these last few hours they had both consented to sleep.

Currents of cool, damp air washed over them propelled by each wave that collapsed on the nearby shore. This little piece of the Baja became a churning, college sub-community during the annual spring break. But, they had been lucky; by arriving early they had found a camping spot right on the beach. Bobbie propped her head upon her doubled-back arm and surveyed the miles of empty desert that stretched beyond the beach dunes.

The pearly-grey light of early morning softened the features of the woman who lay sleeping beside her. Bobbie's eyes caressed her face, tracing with loving familiarity the curve of her eyebrows, the high, round cheeks that, like small firm apples, were wonderful to bite. Her lips were full, inviting even as she slept, with an endearing sampling of freckles scattered above her upper lip. And when she smiled, well it was like neon. If she kissed you, the smile softened the almond of her eyes,

---

[†]"Birth Song" was first published in *Common Lives/Lesbian Lives* 28 (Fall 1988), 48-56, and is reprinted here with permission from the journal and the author.

while her tongue took whatever it was it wanted from you. Bobbie ran her hand gently along the woman's cheek and jaw line in a kind of dazed amazement. Was the first time for everyone anything like this? she wondered. She lifted her head and kissed the sleeping woman's bare shoulder.

STOP, she ordered herself. You have to let Cynthia get some sleep. Bobbie's hand paid her thoughts no mind, it continued to stroke the hip, the thigh of her companion. You're turning into a sex maniac. God, no wonder Mom spent all those years warning you to never DO it. She must have known you would be the type who would never get enough. As her inner voice continued to rage, her hand continued, undaunted, to wander the length of Cynthia's bare torso. The pathway from her breasts to the beginning of that soft, black mass of pubic hair was traveled over and over again. Bobbie slid her hand gently between Cynthia's thighs, marveling at the softness of her skin. Of their own volition Bobbie's hips began to move rhythmically against Cynthia's bum.

Oh shit, you are a nympho, she shrieked at herself. Stop, stop; you'll wake her up and then she'll know. She'll know you're selfish and disgusting. She'll say she was just incredibly drunk last night, and that she doesn't remember a thing. Or worse, she remembers everything and never wants to talk to you again for making her do such awful, awful things. Bobbie watched Cynthia's eyelashes flutter as she struggled awake. She rolled slowly over and her eyes smiled at Bobbie in recognition. Very thoughtfully Cynthia stretched out her hand and began to stroke the fine hairs along the back of Bobbie's neck. It was as if Bobbie had never before in her life been touched. Every fiber of her being was focused on the random play of those fingertips.

It was as if they had just met, had never touched. For three years they had been the starting guards on their high school basketball team. Initially, there had been an intense rivalry between them, as each vied for a starting position. One night, the usual starter was injured half-way through a game and Bobbie was subbed. From the moment she and Cynthia hit the boards together, something clicked. Their individual intensity that had seemed to repel them off the court was suddenly transformed into a sort of psychic ESP. They telegraphed whole game plans with one cross-court glance. No matter how embroiled they became beneath the basket, each seemed to know intuitively where the other would be positioned when it came time to pass the ball.

Until that game, they had warily respected each other from a distance, continuing in each practice to take the measure of the other. But, as the final buzzer had sounded and the gym resonated with victory, their friendship was born. Later, when she and Cynthia had left the school and begun the walk home, they replayed the game over and over again. Bobbie revealed to a skeptical Cynthia that she sensed she led a charmed life. "Luck constantly hovers around me," she crowed, "waiting to be plucked, like ripe grapes, from each moment." Bobbie pantomimed sinking another basket.

Cynthia had shaken her head in disbelief and said, "Look, don't get your hopes up, Bobbie. Next game one of us will be warming the bench again, for sure." But their freshman coach had noticed the on-court transformation and they had started together ever since.

The remainder of high school had brought them the sweetest kind of notoriety, as they fueled victory after victory. The school newspaper never failed to print their pictures and interviews after each game. Together they accumulated honors and trophies that never quite embodied what they shared; but then, they weren't sure what to call it either. Bobbie just called it magic.

Cynthia had run for student council, and in her senior year had been elected president. She had initiated committees that had protested the government involvement in Cambodia, and the low state welfare rates. Cynthia had channeled vast amounts of energy into school functions, and in return had gained the highest endorsement from her peers. Cynthia was, everyone conceded, popular; her smile alone could melt an army tank.

Other than sports, Bobbie had been content to remain on the periphery of the school hierarchy. As an athlete and Cynthia's best friend, she was routinely invited to important school social functions. Whenever a particularly critical dance or party loomed on the horizon she and Cynthia would spend hours on the phone beforehand. Bobbie would insist that this time she would not go, and Cynthia would attempt to dissuade her. This was not mere posturing on Bobbie's part; she was incapable of subterfuge. Her argument was that the evenings of parties and dances progressed with numbing predictability. But Cynthia would badger and plead and beg until Bobbie relented.

Once Bobbie had arrived, she would pour herself a token drink for the evening and then settle in to talk to friends. She sometimes danced with a particularly persistent boy; but mostly she talked and watched.

180

Cynthia always appeared later with a casual date in tow. She would hover near him initially while he found them both a drink, and then subtly desert him. The evenings invariably ended with Cynthia approaching Bobbie with an equal mixture of apology and irritation. "Danny's drunk," "Dave's drunk," or "Mike's drunk." The names changed but the scenario remained the same. When circumstances dictated it, they had bundled the hapless date into Cynthia's car and dropped him at home. Or, if that hadn't been necessary, Bobbie and Cynthia had simply left the party together. Everyone always knew that Danny or Johnny or Dave was too drunk to drive, and that Bobbie was always sober.

Last night, as they had finished dinner at their campsite, a couple had approached from down the beach. They were not friends, but she and Cynthia recognized their faces from campus rallies, football games and high school. It was obvious they had just arrived and were looking for a good campsite. They offered to share their jug of wine and had settled in around the campfire before Bobbie could think of any plausible reason to object. She was surprised at how fiercely she resented their presence. The four of them drank and talked and watched the sun set. As the chill desert night enveloped them, Tom rose and disappeared into the dark. He returned moments later with two sleeping bags and the briefest of apologies for expropriating half of their campsite. "Wouldn't want you two girls out here without a chaperone, would we Ruthie?" He chuckled drunkenly at his own joke as he draped the opened bag over his companion. Bobbie had poured herself another tumbler of wine.

Now her eyes flitted across the campfire to the other sleeping couple. After last night, it had become a moot point as to who were the chaperones. Bobbie gingerly draped her arm around Cynthia's waist. She sighed deeply and wondered just how attentive Ruthie and Tom had been regarding anything outside their own passion. Something inside her made her quickly squelch the thought.

As if hearing Bobbie's thoughts, Cynthia whispered in Bobbie's ear. "You probably should put some clothes on and zip up your sleeping bag. It's very nearly daylight." To underscore her words Cynthia retrieved the light cotton shirt that lay in an untidy heap at the opening of her bag. Bobbie listened to the sound of Cynthia's bag closing with a strange sense of foreboding. It was as if all that had happened between them last night was now sealed beyond her reach. Reluctantly, she pulled her T-shirt from the edge of Cynthia's bag and put it on. The rrrip of her own bag closing echoed deep into her sleep.

As the sun rose higher in the sky, Bobbie's sleeping bag became moist and tacky. She pushed herself awake and floundered from the bag. It desperately needed airing. Draped over a nearby mesquite bush it provided ample camouflage for her morning pee. After adjusting her cut-off sweatpants she ambled towards the abandoned Volkswagen that sat axle-deep in Baja sand. In the gaping trunk of the bug was a cardboard box of foodstuffs. She pilfered a jar of instant coffee and a bag of cinnamon buns. Um, scrambled eggs would be nice, too, she thought; but anything at all perishable had been left at home. That was the profound joy of camping, she mused, you always wanted what you couldn't bring.

On the ashes of last night's fire Bobbie bunched old papers into loosely formed balls. Over these she liberally scattered twigs and brambles gathered from the desert. A match snapped to life and the fire was soon consuming the small stuff as fast as she could add it to the pile. She carefully added larger and larger pieces. Once she was certain the fire was stable she placed the coffee pot on two flat rocks near the center of the fire pit. She flopped onto the sand to wait for the water to boil.

Directly across from Bobbie was a large, lumpy mound of sleeping bag that concealed Ruthie and Tom. It began to writhe and undulate and slowly Ruthie's tousled head appeared. Bobbie self-consciously ran her fingers through her own short hair. Ruthie sat up and stretched, her arms reaching for the sky, palms flat against the heavens. She yawned grotesquely, and then her face settled into a silly grin. Bobbie quickly made her own face impassive as she poked the fire nonchalantly. Ruthie crawled from her bag and nodded silently to Bobbie as she mouthed the words, "Good morning." She nodded a second time towards the lump of sleeping bag remaining on the sand and held her index finger over her lips. Flashing a wide smile at Bobbie as she passed her, Ruthie trotted out of the campsite in search of a clump of mesquite. Bobbie grimaced at Ruthie's retreating back. There was a certain briskness to her whole being this morning that Bobbie found mildly irritating.

As she poured boiling water from the coffee pot into a mug, Bobbie probed her annoyance with Ruthie. She stirred in a huge spoonful of coffee granules and listened to the clink of spoon against ceramic. It rang in the morning air like a meditation chime. Clink. So Tom and Ruthie had done it last night. She suspected that it was their "first time" as well. So, why didn't she feel a certain kinship with Ruthie this morning; a kind of extended generosity, instead of annoyance? Clink. Um, maybe because the thing between Ruthie and Tom felt so orchestrated. Why, last night Tom had even admitted that most of the guys on campus organized these camp-outs during spring break so they could get laid. Then he had winked at Bobbie and uttered his remark about chaperones. What had he meant by that? Clink. Oh, and what was he going to be like now; the great morning after? Bobbie anticipated rank smugness. She had overheard boys at school talking around the gym and she knew what it would be like, especially once his campus cronies began to arrive. Clink. Worse yet, what would Cynthia be like once friends and acquaintances began to filter down to the beach? What had it been like for her last night? What if the experience for Cynthia was as unrelated to Bobbie's as Ruthie's had been? Clink. Bobbie stirred her coffee.

Eventually, the rapidly escalating temperatures on the beach forced both Tom and Cynthia from their bags. Tom rose dimpled, rumpled and beaming; tousled hair framed his boyish face. Ruthie became outrageously affectionate with them all. Perhaps in silent atonement for last night's trespass, she busied herself with the debris from the evening meal. She hummed to herself all the while. Tom succumbed to her good humor and offered to help. She took great delight in loading him down with pans and plates and soap powder and then directing him towards the water's edge.

Cynthia, from the moment she had sloughed off her bag, had treated them all with a determined detachment. She sat across the fire from Bobbie staring into the cup of coffee she had been given. Try as she might, Bobbie could not engage Cynthia in conversation or eye contact. Bobbie felt a sense of panic fluttering in her chest. Always, always she had held a direct line to everything Cynthia thought through undenied access to her eyes. Bobbie sat staring at her friend, willing her to look up.

What are you thinking? Bobbie's mind raced. "Those two are too much," she offered. They could hear Ruthie's laughter carry from the tide line.

Cynthia sighed deeply as she set aside her coffee mug. She bestowed on Bobbie one long undecipherable look. "Too much for me to take today." She rose abruptly and mumbled apologetically as she brushed past Bobbie, "I had almost forgotten they were here, that's all."

She strode purposefully down the beach away from their campsite. Bobbie mutely watched as her figure blended slowly with the Mexican village in the distance. She felt more and more abandoned with every step that Cynthia took.

It was clear that Cynthia would not be returning soon. Bobbie pushed herself to her feet and circled the campsite aimlessly. She fussed with the fire and then the water jug, trying to give her actions some semblance of direction. Tom and Ruthie returned, giggling quietly between themselves. Their arrival propelled Bobbie from the campsite. She trudged to the Volkswagen and pulled her swimsuit from a duffle bag wedged in the back seat. She changed quickly and then dragged an old air raft from beneath the car and marched with it to the beach. She mounted it as soon as it touched the water.

With a flurry of strong, rapid strokes she guided her craft towards the open sea. Once Bobbie was safely past the crumbling wall of breakers she let herself collapse against the cool, damp canvas. She was acutely aware of the pressure of the raft where it touched her breasts and pubis. Acutely aware that it was all that lay between herself and complete, everlasting immersion in the undulating body beneath her. Aware as she had been the night before when she had hallucinated while in the midst of loving Cynthia. She had felt herself falling, melting, dissolving into the very marrow of her lover until her free-fall abruptly ended. Seven oceans span the world, both joining the continents together and keeping them apart. Seven layers of skin had been bond and impenetrable barrier and become the raft on which Bobbie had ridden out the night. She pushed her face into the cool canvas and cried until she slept.

When Bobbie awoke, some time later, the sun was high and searing her back and shoulders. Her stomach rumbled, demanding her attention. She reached over the side of the raft and scooped cold salt water onto her face, and then the back of her neck. It sizzled and crackled down the center of her back and ran off the sides of her waist. "Shit, only my second day out and I'm sunburned," she swore aloud. She deliberately flipped the raft over and stifled a gasp as the icy water covered her completely.

With one hand she firmly gripped the raft's edge while treading water until she was sure she was fully awake. Once she had gotten her bearings on the shoreline she tied the raft rope to her ankle and started to swim. As she closed on the line where the waves begin to crumble and heave themselves upon the beach she stopped swimming long enough to climb aboard the raft. She could feel the waves gather, collecting themselves beneath her like a horse responding to pressure from the bit.

Once ashore, she dragged her raft far enough past the tide's edge to ensure that it was beyond the reach of the silent, filmy fingers of the constantly thieving waves. Bobbie wandered towards the Volkswagen and the box of edibles in the trunk. Tom and Ruthie were tanning nearby and she realized that it was going to prove impossible to obtain lunch without having to interact with them. She pasted a flaccid smile on her face and waved weakly as she passed them. Tom was preoccupied in meticulously covering every visible inch of Ruthie's exposed skin with suntan lotion. He tickled and teased her at every opportunity and she giggled appreciatively at his ministrations. Bobbie winced in immediate irritation and turned her attention to the sand at her feet.

"Hi Bobbie, how was the swim?" Tom's beaming face was the antithesis of Bobbie's sour expression.

Bobbie shrugged in reply, then added hastily, "Fine, great. But I fell asleep and got burned."

Tom merely nodded in reply. The mention of sunburn seemed to spur more fevered attention to Ruthie's fair torso. He began a minute inspection of her dappled shoulders as if he were personally responsible for each additional freckle the sun awarded her.

Bobbie watched them a moment longer and then resumed her march towards the Volkswagen and lunch. The sand burned the bottoms of her feet, especially the tender skin between her toes and the arch of her foot. What was it about Ruthie and Tom that bugged her so much? she asked herself as she trudged towards the car. The feeling seemed to border on jealousy. But why? If nothing else, last night with Cynthia had given her the complete and absolute answer to why she had never been interested in boys. It was as if some part of her had known for years how she felt but had been afraid to tell her until now.

She had been loathe to ask either of them about Cynthia. Instead, when she reached the car she did a quick survey of its contents. Cynthia's towel and swim suit remained stuffed in a corner on the ledge along the rear window. Evidence seemed to indicate that she had not yet returned from the village. Bobbie pulled a large shirt from her duffle bag and tugged it on. She jammed a tennis hat on her head. She rummaged through the carton of foodstuffs without enthusiasm.

What about Cynthia? Bobbie's mind churned. She hastily shoved a huge section of cracker into her mouth. It was awful to know her friend, her lover, wrestled with thoughts, worries, arguments she might never speak of to Bobbie. Worse yet, Bobbie might never get an opportunity to answer. She pulled two tins of pudding from the box and balanced a load of crackers atop the tins. She shoved a couple of tins of juice under one arm and retrieved a paperback from the dashboard. She plodded to the far side of the Volkswagen, that provided a bit of shade, and deposited her goodies on its running board.

Bobbie sighed deeply and knelt down in the shade of the car, eyeing the sand judiciously. At the point where her bum would want to be to use the side of the car as a backrest, she scooped a hollow in the sand. "Presto, lazy-boy goes to the beach," she laughed to herself as she plopped into the trough she had created. It was not that she didn't like Ruthie and Tom. It was just that they had it so damned easy. The morning after the big night, their honeymoon continues. They're allowed to be as kissy-face and cuddly with each other as they want. Bobbie could feel anger churning inside her. That is what Cynthia had meant when she had said she had forgotten they were at the campsite. Bobbie's anger turned to remorse, a deep sense of foreboding that seeped throughout her limbs and settled in the pit of her stomach. She couldn't remember when she had felt so exhausted.

She finished the first tin of juice in four huge gulps, then started on the second. Perhaps Tom was right, she told herself. She was no better than the guys from college who brought their girls down to the Baja so that they could get laid. Bobbie set the tin of juice on her thigh and closed her eyes. For years she had thought of herself as a freak, a misfit. While everyone else around her had been discovering the thrill of sexual yearnings, the mixed blessings of being in love, she had remained immune. Not through any intent or purpose of her own designing; but she would not lie to herself. She had simply never met a boy that she even wanted to kiss, let alone do anything else. Last night the obvious truth had hit her like the proverbial thunder bolt; she had loved Cynthia for years.

What they had done last night had seemed natural and right. Everything they had discovered together as lovers had underscored that fact. But now, Bobbie's certainty was beginning to erode. Was it possible that she had been too pushy; that Cynthia had really had no choice?

Bobbie pulled the tennis hat lower over her eyes and conjured up the vision of the beach the night before. She remembered leaning over Cynthia, after they had gone to bed, and laughing because her eyelids were so white in the moonlight. They had spent the afternoon lying in the sun and Cynthia had used cottonballs on her eyelids to protect her eyes from the sun. They were both incredibly drunk from Tom's cheap wine. And Bobbie had thought Cynthia looked outrageous lying in her sleeping bag, arms solemnly folded across her chest, eyelids ghostly-white against her tanned face. Bobbie smiled underneath her tennis hat at the memory.

She had laughed and laughed until Cynthia had opened her eyes and asked with a sleepy smile on her face, "Are you going to tell me what's so damn funny?" Something had seemed to click deep inside of Bobbie, and instead of explaining she had answered, "Shit Cynthia, you are so beautiful." It was as if shutters that had kept her from seeing how much she loved her just fell away. Bobbie had looked into her eyes for the longest time, feeling the thud of waves hitting the shore, but no longer hearing them. It seemed as if she had seen what she felt mirrored in Cynthia's eyes; and she had kissed her.

Bobbie wriggled her hips deeper into the sand and wrapped her arms around herself. Something incredible had happened when she had kissed Cynthia. It started out that she had been moved to kiss her because she was simply overwhelmed at how long, how much she loved her. But in the middle of that first kiss Bobbie had been born; she had entered it as one person and emerged as someone entirely different. Years of questions became answered.

With the second kiss she had moved over to lie on top of Cynthia. Her mouth and hands had seemed to know exactly what to do, and so she had let them. From deep within her had surfaced the primal urge to touch, to be touched in a way long desired, but denied. It was as if they both had been thrown into deep water and discovered that they had always known how to swim.

Bobbie closed her eyes against the sense of powerlessness that swept through her. Part of her wanted to leap up and run and find Cynthia; say whatever it would take to make their loving alright. The other part of her, the part that kept her seated on the beach, knew that Cynthia would have to do all that herself. It was this part of Bobbie that crooned, that soothed her till she slept; saying over and over again, you are just beginning, just beginning.

dykeling merril meets dykeling penny

merril mushroom

the prologue:

the year is 1958. the place is dade county, florida. merril and penny are both teenagers. they have not yet met. penny is a notorious lesbian. merril hangs out with lesbians but calls herself straight most of the time. for many many months, merril has been hearing stories about penny from her friends. penny is so brilliant, they say. penny is so sensitive. penny's mother *Knows*, and penny has all-girl parties at her house where they play spin the bottle. penny is wild and penny is wonderful, and, most of all, penny brings everyone out. merril has to meet her says everyone. oh, yes, penny is definitely someone merril must meet, even though it is scandalous how she brings out straight girls left and right.

merril thinks about penny, even though no one has said anything about what penny looks like. the tone of voice they all use when they talk about her intrigues merril. with their admiring and critical comments, they make penny sound extremely attractive.

merril and her friends are coming out. they are in high school and college and are bringing each other out or coming out with some of the more experienced girls—like penny. merril messed around in bed with her friend dorothy when they were 13, but she has not been with a REAL lesbian, so she calls herself straight. she spends a lot of time with the gay kids in school and on the beach, and she thinks a lot about the gay girls she has seen around. she also has a lot of big time crushes on

188

her girlfriends.

the story:
one mild miami night in december, dykeling merril went out cruising with some of her wild gay girl friends. merril knew them from high school when they were all wild straight girls. merril and her friends drove around town for a while in the white convertible with the top down and their hair blowing in the wind, and then someone said, "let's go to The Manor."

"okay," said everyone else.

merril was delighted. she had always wanted to go to The Manor, which was also known as Sex Manor. it was a small apartment complex where a lot of the older gays lived. some of the gay high school kids hung out there, too, because there was no place for a gay kid to go where they could be themselves. it was especially difficult to find a place to make love when you both are in high school and living with your parents who would never understand; and some of the people who lived at The Manor would even give a couple the use of their bed for a few hours. this was very brave of them, because when kids were underage, adults involved in any way with them could get busted, especially if the kid was an undercover cop who was LOOKING to bust a place for homosexuality and "contributing to the delinquency of a minor."

merril's friends parked the car and they all got out, walked down the sidewalk and turned beneath an archway, then went through a patio and up a flight of outside steps. merril's friends knocked on the door at the top of the steps, and a thin man with pale skin and dark hair opened the door. he smiled. "come on in," he said.

merril followed her friends into the apartment. they all sat around and chatted for a few minutes, and then merril's friends went off to make love.

soon the gay guy went into the kitchen, and merril remained in the living room waiting for her friends and wondering if the celebrated penny might show up. the other girls had told merril that penny often visited The Manor, and merril was hoping that maybe tonight would be one of those nights. sure enough, in a few minutes, there was a knock at the door. then it opened, and this cute little butch number strode in. merril perked up, interested. the girl was short, chunky, and had straight blond hair combed into the traditional duck's ass. her eyes twinkled, her mouth grinned, and her cheeks were pudgy. she was alert, lively, and bubbling over with good energy. she looked directly at merril, smiled, and said in this sweet, high-pitched voice: "hi. i'm penny," and merril thought that she was simply adorable, and that all the wonderful tales about her were obviously true.

penny and merril talked for a little while, and then merril's friends came back and invited penny to come for a ride; which is how penny came to be sitting in the back seat of the convertible next to merril. their friend the driver, who always carried phony proof-of-age, stopped at a package store where everyone chipped in to buy a fifth of Southern Comfort which was passed around, especially around the back seat.

somehow, during the course of the evening, penny and merril sat closer and closer to each other in the back seat of the white convertible. they talked and talked, and they started to really like each other a lot. they drank and they drank from the bottle of Southern Comfort, and their hair blew in the warm night wind.

then came the moment when young-dyke merril, who lived with her mother who held her to a strict curfew, realized that she could stay with this wonderful girl no longer; that she would have to go home or risk the wrath of her mother. she wondered if she would ever see penny again. soon they would return to school—to different universities. they gave each other deep and longing soulful looks, exchanged addresses and promised one another that they would write.

and they did write. the first of their letters crossed in the mails, they were each that eager. the letters grew longer and longer. they poured out their hearts, souls, feelings each to the other. they shared dreams and disappointments. they were enthralled by their communications, their verbal explorations of their thoughts and feelings, their trust and sharing with one another.

then, penny called merril on the telephone, and merril invited penny to come visit her at the university she went to. penny accepted. she arrived. merril suddenly realized that this would never do—there was no way that she and penny could stay in her dormitory room with her straight roommate who was an old friend from high school. so she hustled penny into a taxicab which brought them to a motel where they took a room. then they went out to dinner. then they came back to the motel; and they got into the bed, and, after merril made her protestations of straightness and penny listened to them all, they kissed.

and that's the story of how these two lesbians found each other.

Opening the Door

Sheila Anne

The idea of being a Dyke or that there were women who were living as Dykes was not a tangible part of my reality when I was growing up. Looking back, I find that there were subtle but powerful messages being put across to me by the community in which I lived that certain ideas and people would not be tolerated. I knew this most clearly by who and what was not mentioned.

My concept of Lesbian—although I didn't really know the word until late adolescence—was formed by my unconsciously responding to the gaps, the silences and hesitations I was experiencing both in language and in "human" relations. As naming something brings a concept into existence, not naming something renders "it" invisible and nonexistent. Women related to men or ???—BLANK—there was nothingness. Nothingness was loaded with dread, the fear of the unknown.

These blank spaces, these pockets of nameless fear, had a lot to do with my learning process as I grew up irish-catholic in a working-class italian and jewish neighborhood in brooklyn, new york. My family was respectful friends with our jewish neighbors, but was adopted by the italian-catholics on the basis of our shared religious heritage. There was a bottomline sense of neighbor—meaning those who you knew and understood enough to live next to vs. "stranger"—someone who was unpredictable and nameless. Nameless strangers were always the perpetrators of evil. Persons known and named were alleged to be "good."

Not naming something gave the person, idea or activity a nonspecific, irrational, ghostly power and presence to be guarded against, protecting the agreed-upon and named values and individuals of the community from outside influence. If by some slip or misadventure you allowed yourself to fall victim to such "outside influence," the door would be open between you and that "other" world, allowing you to be haunted and pursued and possibly won over by the unknown forces of evil.

Once my mother whispered to me that my father was tired one morning because he had been tormented the night before by dreams of "demons." She couldn't explain to me what these demons were or why they'd be after my father but she implied that there was a connection between demons and guilty consciences and *she* proudly had neither. Beyond that, there were demons and if you weren't careful, they'd "get" you—just *how* was another terror. Enough said. "Best to be good, think good thoughts, and you won't have to worry about anything else."

There were many fears of danger in my neighborhood, both real and sensible to survival in the city, and then unreal and irrational ones that bolstered the cohesion of little ethnic, father-controlled nations called "families."

I was taught, through unspoken fears of difference, not to notice or appreciate the diversity in the many cultures that lived side by side, separated only by plaster walls, but to look for and relate to the commonalities that left my parents' beliefs unchallenged. Facts of life, contradictions and differences were perhaps stumbled upon, but were not for examination in my house. No one discussed why the doors were made of metal with tiny peepholes, or why the door had three locks that always and nearly automatically had to be relocked behind once inside the apartment—click, click and click.

Without much discussion or attention to a named or specific danger, we learned not to walk too close to the edges of sidewalks, near parked cars because "they," (the strangers, the outsiders), would grab us and do unthinkable things. Somewhere in-between those parked cars, but just beyond conscious knowledge, lurked the women who "liked" women; but I didn't know them yet.

Intuitively, we knew that, in addition to the human outsiders, there were also those ideas, contrary to neighborhood or family values; these were detours from the "right path" down the middle of the street. Even "thoughts" (a lesser transgression of the various sins mentioned in catholicism) could reach out and grab us and make us stray from safety and goodness—which were rumored to be one and the same. I learned survival tactics against dangerous people and ideas. To be unsure about anything was to present oneself as open and vulnerable to attack or worse—vulnerable to the swaying of morals and beliefs.

Street smarts: Never appear lost or unsure about your direction, never look scared or show any hesitation about what you think is right or wrong, about who your friends are and who are not. Don't smile, don't look like you need assistance, don't even look at strangers. Meeting their eyes is as good as accepting an invitation to unknown depravity. I learned to live unthinkingly and consciously unconcerned, behind heavy locked doors—shut against dangerous people and ideas. When I was out in the world beyond the heavy, metal door, I learned that, if a bottle crashed and splattered at my feet, I shouldn't look in the direction it came from unless I was prepared for violent confrontation. If I heard a whistle or sexual comment, I kept my vision straight ahead and unaltered.

I mostly did not register what was in my peripheral vision and often found it most functional to pretend that anything in my peripheral vision did not exist at all. Because Lesbians are on the periphery of what women are willing or encouraged to see, I can't conceive of how Lesbians found each other without first stumbling upon a known Lesbian community of some sort. I imagine that, for the most part, Lesbians found each other by trial and error. For me, it was mostly error until I came out as a bar-Dyke around 1979.

As I've said, before I came out, I didn't have an image of a real Dyke. Mostly, I had hellish flashes (those demons) that popped out with sudden stubbornness from behind tightly shut doors in hazy rooms of my imagination. I'd see an image and before it became clear or nameable, I'd shove it back hard and shut the door with a familiar click—a slam would draw too much attention to it. A sneering smile—click. Suggestive, enticing eyes, wanting too much—better not look back—click. Fingers that burn and entangle, vampires (my mother tried to warn me) that suck you in and turn you into one of them—click . . . click . . . and click. I wasn't conscious of how I was responding to these unclear images drawn *from* reservoirs of fears and defenses; but I did respond *swiftly* to push the images away—and it was easy, perhaps imperative at the time, to shout back (not too loud)—"that's not me, NOT ME and not ANYONE I could love!"

I could love all right. I fell in love with girl and women friends. I

loved them "totally" and "purely." My skin would shiver with electricity whenever one of my friends (accidentally?) brushed by me. I
explained this reaction to myself as happening because I just loved *them*
in particular *so* much, that it was a "natural" extension of our intensity.
Although I didn't allow my feelings to form more clearly, I had enough
of a nagging doubt concerning my enjoyment of physical proximity
with other girls to know that I should keep my mouth shut about it all.
The closest I came to expressing the waves of physical intensity I felt
was in a cowardly metaphor I wrote to the girl I loved when I was 17:
"The luminous sun touches the calm ocean gently, and in return, the
ocean shimmers and glistens in delight, . . . " She thought this was a
"*nice*" poem. (No Lesbian flushed out here!)

Another time, that friend absentmindedly commented to me,
"Too bad you're not a guy." I had no idea what was coming here and my
throat dried and tightened as she continued: "There's just so far you can
go—being friends with another girl. Too bad I can't find a guy that
would be like you . . . that I could talk to . . . " Her voice trailed off and
I was no longer hearing because I was paralyzed. The feelings I had
were conflicting and powerful. I was crushed by the understanding of
what I could not be for her. I was thrilled that I had come as close as any
girl *could* be to her. I could be her life partner and soulmate if it wasn't
for the fact that I was female. There was nothing about me that
otherwise obstructed our relationship, or the possibility of her love for
me. In fact, it sounded like she loved me as much as she could imagine
loving anyone—except some yet-to-be-known guy. In that wild, terri-
fying, paralyzing moment, I knew, but was not about to admit, that I
wanted her to love me as much, the same and *more* than she would any
"guy." I knew she saw a limit, a barrier to our love that I had already
slipped over. She had merely put my feelings into the question I had
been afraid to ask: What would be *wrong* if two girls loved each other
completely and expressed this physically, as committedly as they might
with some (yet-to-be-found) guy?

Sirens roared in my head, making it hard to think, screaming at me
to stop my questioning, that I had crossed some prohibited line by even
asking it. I was straying to the shadowy doorways; beckoning hands
were ready to pull me in, into the abyss beyond the world of rightness
and safety. But wait a minute. I caught a breath. These were irrational
fears. I wasn't afraid of my friend. Neither she nor I were going to hurt
each other or anyone else for that matter.

The pull and twist of emotions was so confusing I looked only at my most practical considerations—to survive that moment, to retain my secrets and composure despite the coldsweat terror. Struggling for control, I separated reason from feeling. Catholic upbringing and all, I couldn't find any *reasonable* answer that would make the wonderful and special feelings I had for and about my friend not be right.

This was more of a realization (albeit shock-induced) than I could really handle in those few seconds, but before I came back to the realities of time and place, I decided that if I ever met and loved another woman, who also didn't think that *any* kind of love was wrong, I'd do my "best" to be open to "it" (on principle, of course!). Then, tossing this idea to the furthest corner of my mind, I exhaled long and deeply as if to let everything out of me except that now-secured and hidden thought about loving women.

And so I caught myself teetering on the line that separates ideas from acting in reality. I could now have intellectual considerations about loving women . . . but I was far from taking any action about my fondness for females and making choices about how to live my life. I could *maybe* deal with a physical relationship if it "came up," but I could figure out that opportunities to challenge myself to physically love a woman (from this place of non-action) would be rare—if ever.

So I teetered, and then, with relief, planted my feet firmly but still on the edge of the imagined abyss of Lesbianism. If someone reached out and pulled me in, then I would go; otherwise, I wouldn't have to think about making choices that I'd have to stand behind. I continued to pursue special and meaningful relationships with "best friends." These friendships, with, of course, no direction on my part (!), were always on the edge of physicality, pulsing with the tensions of repressed desire.

I would not have dulled the edge on these relationships no matter how hurtfully unfulfilled because even if there wasn't release of our sexual energies, at least there was energy, feeling—a sense of being alive to each other. The burning of sexuality was fired in each casual or affectionate touch. My female loves and I "made love" for hours at a sitting—being close to each other with the electricity that is generated by near and tentative touching. There was not the touching of "bases" or the mappings of heterosexually-defined sex. Since this was a sexuality that wasn't defined by heterosex, the physicality could be dismissed as something entirely different and not "sex" at all. Even though we sat hip to hip and thigh to thigh with our arms about each other, sharing whispers and touches that caused my levis to steam, within a heterosexist context I wasn't being sexual with a woman. My wanting was not an act I could be held responsible for. I did not want any "accountable" or undeniable action to upset the fragility of these intimate sessions of barely touching. I would not risk these friendships by shoving them to a point where I or my beloved would have to acknowledge a sexual identity or have *my* love rejected with ingrained repulsion. The women I was loving would have to take the risk first and I was not enough beyond my own ingrained lesbophobia to know whether or not *I* would be repulsed by another woman's more "serious" physical explorations. Now I know that wanting, and that desire was very sensual and sexual in itself.

I don't know if these relationships dissolved because my "friends" gave up waiting for me to make the move I was unwilling to risk or because they were terrified by their own feelings about our closeness. I had a couple of these very painful and "unexplained" departures from my life in rapid succession. In each case my friend would hint that we should sleep together (whatever that meant) and then suddenly retreat, refusing to discuss what had happened—after all, "nothing" had happened. Beth entered the convent associated with the school we both attended. Pat solidified her relationship with her husband and bore him a son. They were both "safe."

The endings of these relationships hurt as deeply as the endings of any consciously-defined Lesbian relationship except we didn't name what had transpired between us and had no place to talk about it. I was staggered when Pat suggested that maybe we could spend our time together window-gaping at Shopper's World and have fewer "deep and philosophical" conversations (sitting on her couch entwined, listening to Karen Carpenter, in the semi-darkness while her husband was out bowling). I could only manage, "I don't think I could go shopping with you," before I hung up the phone. Then I hit the floor wailing and keening, wanting to push out this terrible pain, this terrible loss that I couldn't even speak of. I wanted it all out of me and done with so I would never have to explain myself and my grief to anyone.

By the time I pushed myself up from the floor of my apartment and so much as said, I'm done with feeling, it had grown dark. "Nothing" had happened and now there was nothing to feel. I became the steel door of my childhood home with only a peephole to get a blurry glimpse of the rest of the world. I clowned and laughed and partied raucously with my very casual, very heterosexual friends. No one was going to get to me any more. I was not going to make myself vulnerable to this incredible hurt again.

I was able to keep myself feeling numb for quite a while. In fact, I was so good at it two years of my life are a fog of memory made coherent by a profound sense of hollowness and boredom. Life was one big party with people I didn't know, who didn't know me. I wouldn't let myself give a shit about anyone and this attitude developed into a whole new angle of my personality. I was flip and easy-going and showered folks with automatic irish hospitality and politeness. For the first time in my life I was extremely popular. Many women (and even men) considered me to be their good or best friend; but whatever their level of caring was, I let it bounce off me—bored. Bored to death.

Slowly, the boredom and the hollowness, the absence of self, started getting to me and wore more heavily than the prospects of new love and loss. Within my lifeless void of inner self, a strength began to grow with the clarity of the realization—I had nothing, absolutely nothing, to lose and with whatever risks I took, I would only add to my life. I began to look around me. It was clear to me (although I hadn't up to this point ruled out the possibility of being intimate with men) that my intimacies and affection had always been directed toward women; but all the women around me were living the same boring and tedious male-directed lives. I wanted to find women. But not just "women." I wanted to find women who actually had the guts to *love women*!

Where was I to find them?

I had already spent a lot of time by myself at this point, trying to cut myself loose from the curiosity of my het acquaintances. I was my own company—exploring various neighborhoods of boston, the city I was now getting to know—walking absorbed in my own thoughts and explorations, very much as I passed the time as a teenager in brooklyn. Now, though, when I walked, I was looking for something—for signs of life on the periphery that I hadn't previously allowed myself to see. I had managed to see enough to know that there was something to look for. I became awake to all differences, to all and anything outside of the societal, the heterosexual mainstream of information, to what existed beyond the corner market, the *TV Guide* and *Boston Globe*. I began to notice women walking around cambridge holding hands. I recalled half-forgotten glimpses of books and periodicals that had once seemed weird or too far out to be noteworthy. I re-evaluated the existence of different types of people who stepped over the edges of society's welcome: artists, musicians, writers, political activists.

The periphery of society's welcome became my new world. I was digging and searching for new possibilities. I closely examined bookstores and cafes, devoured flyers hung in windows and doorways, watched people—especially women—for some sign of difference and defiance that I could engage. I found some local "alternative" papers that seemed to have interesting and broad-minded viewpoints. I hadn't guessed that there might be anything specifically or generically Lesbian or gay. I hadn't noticed the feminist movement while I was immersed in my personal loves, losses and subsequent numbness, and I was totally uninformed about Lesbian or gay liberation.

Yet, I knew there had to be a place—some place to meet, or just get to see women who chose to love other women.

I remembered years back, driving back streets and the combat zone of the city for thrills and dares with a college friend who thought she knew where the "lezzies" hung out. I was relieved that we hadn't found "them" that night, but now I was ready to find that place wherever it might be, where I might chance a look at my own reflection.

With persistence, I began to turn up clues. My first was finding a journal of poetry written by Lesbians; so Lesbians wrote poetry—a fairly tame and intelligible enterprise. It felt so daring to touch that book—even though it said nothing Lesbian on the cover—just *Conditions*. Perhaps other browsers had opened the cover and dropped the book quickly back into place when they had discovered what was inside. I was so unsure of myself and what actual Lesbians were and did, I didn't want anyone to catch me in this vulnerable uncertainty of being neither straight nor Lesbian—but "just looking"! Burning curiosity won out; retelling myself I had nothing to lose, I bought the journal and hurried home with my first concrete evidence of Lesbians, my first acquisition with the word *Lesbian* in print.

I was feeling more ready to find something that I could act upon. On my next expedition seeking signs of Lesbian life, I hung about in harvard square looking for more evidence and ended up buying bunches of post-hippie, leftie-type, progressive newspapers. I pored over the papers trying to decipher various calendar sections and personal ads: "lf," "gf," and "bi f" and "women's" this and "womyn's" that. Then I came to a short listing under "night life" and then to the bold-face letters, WOMEN'S BARS. I had to think about that one: women's bars? Bars for women? Why would women go to bars for women? To meet other women? Was this something different from "gay bars"? Were these... like ... feminist women? Women's this or that seemed to imply feminist women in a lot of the material I was searching. Perhaps these were feminists, having political gatherings of sorts or an independent night out without men. Or was this the place of my seedy lesbophobic imaginings where depraved females hit upon other depraved females and where outsiders and intruders would be suspect—unwanted, possibly met with hostility or maybe . . . Even in my ignorance I detected something important going on here—no men, no boyfriends or husbands to play second fiddle to. I told myself that a "women's bar" had to be a place where women went to enjoy the company of other women and that possibly *some* of these women would even have the guts to love other women—in some pure and refined way, of course.

I told myself about this welcoming place on one hand while on the other I was scared that in it would be the dreadful outsiders I was taught to guard against. The images became clearer to me as I examined them. The demons lurking on the edges of the sidewalks of my childhood took shape and form as women in leather jackets with greased hair, their sleeves rolled up around cigarette packs. I had just seen enough of what I wasn't supposed to to vaguely record these images and bury them amongst other terrors. I had refused to interpret these images as females and potential models of Dyke existence; but now perhaps there was a new context, a new understanding, a new explanation about why I wet my hair down and combed it back, pretending to be steve reeves/ superman. Perhaps, secretly, I was trying to be like these strong women but playing at being a man was far from reality. It felt like a safer game. I swallowed hard, bought a street map, and decided to find THE SAINTS[1] bar, to find these "saintly" women.

I drove around and found the address, the sign outside a nondescript building that told me nothing more than I already knew. I didn't dare linger in the daytime—peopled streets, fearing transparency, that everyone would know that I was trying to figure out if I was queer. I left, but I set a date with myself. I would come back and go into that bar on Saturday night.

So, now I knew that I was going and might find what I was looking for, but the whole time fighting the idea that these women were going to kill me! (They would know that I wasn't one of them and that

I had no business there.) I had always dressed kind of tough—jeans, flannel shirts, overalls and sneakers. I was strong and I had defended myself physically and fiercely when I needed to. I could definitely be "cool"; but this situation, facing unknowns and ingrained fears, was wilting and melting me. I couldn't figure out how to dress when Saturday night rolled around. I did not want to stand out in the crowd. Too tough? Too straight? I decided against the shiny disco shirt and chose the less flashy cotton, striped button-down, went for the neutrally casual look, and hoped it would work. I gave myself one final going-over in the mirror and slipped my long-handled comb into its usual place in the back pocket of my jeans.

I parked my japanese subcompact in a multi-level parking garage a good, long, nerve-building walk from the bar. There was now no fail-safe device to deter me from my destination. I was going.

I cut through the quincy marketplace, weaving my way through the heterosexual couples out on date night. I felt different, but invisible in the crowd. I felt myself leaving behind any pretense of likeness to these people as I entered the suddenly narrow, poorly lit and deserted streets behind the market area. It was hard to believe that any other women had come this way or that these streets would lead me anywhere I wanted to go.

My fists were clenched in my pockets and I thought about how high and how hard I could kick. Moving to the middle of the sidewalk now, old brooklyn street senses came back to me and told me it was very important to be cool *now*. Cool felt like cold sweat, but I was bobbing and swaggering at a good but steady clip. I had one more street to cross and once I turned the corner of broad street, I knew that no matter how I felt inside, I would walk directly and purposefully. No one would see me hesitate on this street.

Now I felt like I was working under cover, posing as a Lesbian, as someone familiar with this territory. I couldn't afford to be found out as a tourist or a browser. I wanted to do more than survive this experience; I wanted to be OK, I wanted to fit in—and I wanted to be able to become instantly invisible and disappear if anyone picked up that I was an imposter.

My footsteps echoed in my head—why had I worn oxfords instead of sneakers? I never stopped or planted my feet. I headed smoothly for the door handle barely illuminated by the light of the bar's sign. I reached for and pulled the handle toward me in one step, swung my body through the doorway in the next step and then released the handle behind me.

I was standing face-to-face with a serious-looking woman whose steady eyes scanned my face. She spoke only three words: "A dollar cover." A paper bill made it from my hand to hers and somehow my eyes left hers. In a blur of dim, yellow light I came to focus on the bar against the right wall and then the nearest bar stool. Seated, I could order a drink. Dewars and water sounded right. I spoke and managed the transaction, though I never tasted the liquor. I was aware of fairly regular (like me) looking women all around me, but I didn't look at anyone directly. When I realized that no hand was grabbing my shoulder to pull me off that stool, my muscles began to loosen ever so slightly. I finished a second drink and left with a sense of relief but also pride about having faced and survived the most fearsome half-hour of my life. It felt like a first attempt at sky-diving: finally getting through the door of the plane, finding that one could jump and fall and, in the end, experience the exhilaration of being alive.

I made a couple of more trips to The Saints before I got off the stool, kind of insulted at this point that no one was bothering me, instead minding their own business. How different from a straight bar! I began to feel safe walking around and exploring this new world. I learned a lot by watching. I learned that there were indeed all types of Lesbians— really hard-ass types with tattoos, totally into their pool game; het-looking women standing near the bar; older Dykes; preppy-looking Dykes with polo shirts and turned-up collars—quite an array. I found that I "blended in" easily. Soon, I was reading *The Gay Community News* each week at the bar as I sipped my Dewars and I found out about a Lesbian group at the Women's Center and heard about some Dyke basketball that was happening. This was getting more and more encouraging.

I still hadn't "met" any Lesbians. In fact weeks had passed and I hadn't spoken to anyone but the Dykes who tended bar—and all I said to them was "Dewars and water—please." I hadn't come all this way to be a wallflower, so I began to study the dance floor. With time I began to figure out how to ask a woman to dance and who was most likely to say yes. Figuring out who was with who and *not* in a couple was a challenge of my finer perceptive skills.

The first woman I asked to dance was someone I had been

201

studying for a while: definitely by herself, casually leaning against a pole near the dance floor, head swaying, keeping time to the music. "Would you like to dance?" She smiled broadly and collapsed into my arms as if to slow dance. She was too drunk to stand up! But I was "sort of" dancing with what looked to be a bona fide Lesbian. When the song was over, I placed her in a booth and figured that if I could survive that dance, I could survive anything that came my way here. So I asked women to dance, hours at a time, many nights a week. I was having the time of my life.

One of my first *conversations* was to come sometime later. Now I only sat at the bar to warm up *for* or cool off *from* the dance floor. Nancy and I had danced quite a bit and then she wanted to get a drink so we sat at the bar for a while making whatever conversation one can have in a crowded bar with a Lesbian when one really knows diddly-shit about Lesbians.

When the bar was closing, Nancy offered to give me a ride to my car and, as I drove off with this stranger, I was again wondering what to expect. Would she try to kiss me? Ask to make a date? Was I supposed to do something? As we came to a stop in front of the parking garage, it was clear to me that Nancy had only intended to give me a lift to my car—but here I was in a car, late at night, with a Lesbian. I was feeling curious and light-headed and I desperately wanted to know what it would be like to kiss her, to see if I would like it, to see if I was really going to be a Lesbian. And lest another opportunity to test this out would not occur, feeling slightly silly, I asked her, "Would it be OK if I kissed you goodnight?" She smiled and leaned toward me; I kissed her briefly and thought I felt her lips begin to part as I sat back in the bucket seat. Warmth and electricity filled my body like never before. YES! I COULD DO THIS! I didn't care how silly I was now. "C-could I do that again?" (I had to be absolutely sure and it did feel like we hadn't finished the first one.) Nancy was smiling good-naturedly and said, "Yes, but it has to be longer this time."

We kissed again. I fell back in my seat, and unbashedly proclaimed, "That was great!" I was very, very sure as I opened the door and got out of that car that I was going to be one hell of a Lesbian.

Doors were no longer barriers to hide behind or obstacles to keep me out, but gateways to find myself and my own kind. I've found more and more courage in myself to take risks—for something more than I've got, for something better than I'm supposedly allowed to have.

Notes

1. The Saints bar was heartbreakingly closed in late 1981 by its male owner. The Dykes who managed the bar and who are "The Saints" continue, in the wake of the closing of many women's bars, to struggle to open their own bar where they can operate as The Saints. In the meantime, women's bars all over are disappearing and I mourn the loss.

Pearly Bucket Moon

Eleni Prineas

Speeding on together
through wind, over water, under moonlight
the gentleness with which she places
her gloved hand over your cold, bare one
coming to a stop sign
And it's your first time
and she is so close
and you are so far away,
the moon thundering by
and she can't see you smile—
Don't know where I'm going but
I've been there a long, long time.

For instance, I sat very close to one for six months, in a history class, in
high school. She asked my brown uniform and plaits home to tea but
they said no because they were too shy to visit, had to stay home and
look after Mum and the kids. I dragged my feet home after them.

But it's moonlight night
and you with your camomile tea
now warming your hands
sit long in the lounge-room waiting,
watching

for her upstairs by the window watching,
waiting
for you.
You've only just met, after all.

My cousin was one all along. I knew it for sure at the last family
gathering. She brought a friend, as usual. "Poor Katina—an only child,
you know. We always encourage her to bring along one of her little
friends." Same one, from the age of 16.

Trail of rice on the lawn, another family wedding shaken from our
pockets. Catching the smile between Kate and friend in the flash of
cameras adoring the bridal party. "They make such a lovely couple,
don't they?" They sure do, Aunty.

But it's the first time,
so you're perching
uncomfortably on the lounge-room chair, gazing
distractedly at the lounge-room carpet, watching
the lounge-room door
opening
"What are you doing here, alone, in the dark?"
she says
So you go upstairs   to get closer   to the moon.

In 1986 Grandma was worried I wasn't settling down. So I told her I
was having a relationship—with a woman. "I am settling down, in my
own way." And the sunlight settled on the dust on the mantlepiece and
the cat settled in Grandma's lap and Grandma said there were two
nurses boarding in her mother's house in Yorkshire in 1916. And
Grandma said she was in love with one of them.

70 years later, she still remembered waiting at the bottom of the
boarding-house stairs to blush and smile hello at the funny, dark-eyed
nurse she loved.

Love between women? Unforgettable.

But it's your first time
so it takes a long time to
finish your camomile tea
as you stand by the window
watching the moon grow wide.
Then she says
and you say
Well, it's late, so you stay
catching sweet moondrops
under the pearly bucket moon.
Late, coming home.

Patti's Day Out

Berta R. Freistadt

On the tube the girls scarcely spoke. There was no need. Friends of
many years, they communicated more often than not by nudges, the
movement of an eyebrow, the twitch of a mouth. Words were too
precise, needed too much explanation, too much clarification. Good
friends who knew each other through and through could read each
other's thoughts; and today especially there was much to think of and
little to say. A nudge and a nod of the head at Baker Street meant,
'Come on, we change trains here, don't we?' And the answering eyebrows as they leapt through the closing train doors said, 'Bloody hell, I
was miles away, thank goodness you noticed.'
It was a warm June, it was going to be a lovely day. In the tube train
though it was close. Lesbians were a heavy subject and they were both
sweating a little. It had been Sandy's idea originally. She'd seen some
leaflet or other. It would be, she'd said, a golden opportunity to broaden
their education. Maths and English and Physics were OK in their way,
but you never learnt about real life at school, did you? Who else at
school would ever have seen a bunch of real live lesbians together?
They ought to go, to see what they looked like, so they could be
prepared later on in life if ever one tried to jump them.

They were both dressed in trousers and T-shirts, flat shoes and no
jewelry. Sandy, who knew about such things, knew that on marches you
needed to be able to run in case of trouble. Patti always relied on the

judgement of her sophisticated friend, but knew what she knew. That if the chips were going to be down it would be her aunty who'd just happen to be passing and who would see them. In the silence and the noise of the journey she went over the story she'd prepared just in case. She'd just been to John Lewis's to get some special silks for her home economics project when this crowd of women passed by and she'd just stopped to watch them. She knew it sounded phony and if she got asked for the silks she was sunk. She didn't say anything to Sandy, but at High Street Kensington in the crush of the Saturday shoppers Sandy squeezed Patti's hand and winked at her and Patti felt better after that.

Sandy had reckoned about seventy. At ten to eleven there were four lesbians. At five past, twenty-four. At eleven fifteen there were a hundred and twenty-nine and by eleven thirty two hundred and eighty-three lesbians so outstripped Sandy's estimate that the two girls sat on a wall not knowing whether to laugh or cry. Patti and Sandy didn't look at each other, but sat very close. That seemed alright, quite normal in the circumstances. Women were meeting and greeting each other with cries of joy and squeals of delight. With hugging and kissing. Patti wondered to herself if this counted as being jumped. But in the end she thought, no, not if you knew the person who was kissing you and you liked it. The kissing seemed a way of saying hallo, like shaking hands. It wasn't like the stuff they did on telly.

There were so many kinds of women here, and none of them looked how they were supposed to look. Where were the tweed skirts and the women who looked like men? Where were the dirty ones, the ugly ones too ugly to get a man? And what were all those children doing here? How could there be children if you were a lezzy? Some of them were very old, though no-one seemed to mind. One old woman was wearing apricot velvet harem trousers and every time she moved her henna'd ringlets quivered like springs. She was tanned and when she laughed a gold tooth caught the sunlight. Another with white hair cut very short also wore velvet trousers, black and cut tight to her body. Her waistcoat and white shirt with flowing sleeves turned her into a fairy-tale prince. Or was it princess? And velvet in the middle of the day! Patti thought of her granma with her thick brown nylons, her tight blue perm and the feel of her corseted waist.
There were lots of women in their middle years, too. Sort of teachers'

age. Patti wondered if any of them were teachers. She tried to imagine it, her at her desk and one of those women giving out books and writing on the board. She couldn't do it. It seemed too unlikely, none of her teachers could possibly be a dirty lezzy. Her thoughts were interrupted by the sensation of being looked at and she saw that both she and Sandy were being scrutinised by a group of young women who were gathered near one of the biggest banners. While she and Sandy seemed to be the youngest here, the group who were staring at them were much younger than most of the other women. They were seventeen, eighteen, one maybe twenty. There were about nine or ten of them all dressed very casually. Patti couldn't help but compare their easy style with the very precise and immaculate way most girls at school dressed. She was just beginning to think about turning out her wardrobe when she felt a nudge from Sandy. Turning her head she saw Sandy acknowledge the stares from this group with a big grin. At that moment one of them smiled and waved. She was small, black and wore a bright yellow T-shirt. She also sported a bright yellow mohican, but before she could follow up the wave with an introduction the march began to happen and she disappeared. Patti grabbed Sandy's hand, 'D'you know her?' 'No, of course I don't.' It was as if a spell had been broken. Up to the moment of the wave they had both been mesmerised by what they'd seen; as though they'd been watching a movie or a play they were too polite to interrupt. The wave was a sign, a welcome. It said, come down off the wall, join us. Sandy was the first to make a move. 'I'm stiff,' she said and jumped down. The next moment she darted away and Patti's heart climbed into her mouth. This was the worst nightmare, being left by your best mate in a crowd of funny ladies. But no sooner gone than she was back again, laughing at Patti's face and giving her a badge to wear. 'I thought you'd gone.' 'Don't be daft, put the badge on.' It was green with purple writing. The green was dayglow and the purple against it looked black. 'Lesbians Are Everywhere', it said. What an idea! Patti thought and put it in her pocket.

High Street Ken, Green Park, Piccadilly, the march meandered like a fantastic caterpillar. Women laughed, joked, sang. They hugged each other, quarreled, kissed, pushed children in wheelers and let off balloons. Along the way people stared. Sometimes they smiled and cheered, sometimes they cursed and shouted insults. But mostly they stood and stared, unable as Patti had been at first to put together myth with reality.

Patti could see them thinking with screwed up brows, 'Where are the dirty lezzies?' Patti felt quite pleased to be walking along in such company. She hadn't meant to walk with them, she'd only gone to look. But when they'd got off the wall she and Sandy sort of drifted along with the rest. They didn't discuss it but it felt as if Sandy had meant to walk with them all the time and just hadn't got 'round to mentioning it. Anyway, it was warm and sunny and she felt nice, suddenly it didn't feel like a big deal anymore. She even stopped looking for fate in the shape of her aunty. It wasn't until they were nearly at Trafalgar Square that it happened. The trouble that Sandy had expected. There was the tall column, there were the pigeons and the seagulls, and there suddenly were more police than seemed necessary. All along they'd been there to help with the traffic, at least that's what Patti had thought. Until a dark green van opened its doors and they'd spilled out like ants do out of a nest when you stir it with a stick. Still in their heavy uniform they flowed, a well rehearsed dance troup to surround the squabbling crowd on the pavement. Why don't they leave us alone? Patti thought, we can sort it out, it's only a quarrel. She hadn't seen exactly what had happened, only heard a man's voice shout from a car. Then a crowd had gathered around it and there'd been an exchange of insults. He started it Patti thought as the smooth flowing march disintegrated and there was a kind of jerk, a jolt, a lump felt and not seen. It was like when you iron one side of your trousers smooth only to find you've ironed a crease into the other. As the marchers arrived at the point of conflict some of them carried on, but many didn't. Worried organisers flew up and down attempting to spur the march on, trying to smooth over the quarrel that was sparking and barking at the pavement's edge like water thrown in hot oil. At first there was only one friendly London bobby trying to get things moving. Then there were three, and then the van doors opened.

Patti could see that Sandy would never get away. She could see as an exquisite detail, like a drop of dew on a rose, how tiny Sandy's wrist looked, held as it was by the large red hand of the copper. She'd never noticed before how slight and bony Sandy was. She was remembering stories of Jack and the Beanstalk, tiny Jack against the huge giant and how he chopped down the beanstalk, when her dream was fractured by Sandy's scream. 'Run, Patti, run,' and as though another fairytale was about to erupt into reality she saw moving into her line of vision another copper, intent this time on her. His eyes held hers and he was moving with slow deliberation towards her. For a moment it felt as if the world had stopped except for that man. Her teeth were knives in her head and her eyes felt full of sand. What would her Mum say if she got arrested? Police, lesbians, trouble, fines. These words banged inside her head like an alarm, over and over. He was already near, lifting his hand to her when something deflected him. Something hit his leg and he cursed and looked down. It was only a second's inattention but he dropped his eyes and he lost her. In that second the spell was broken and Patti was gone. Away she flew, running as if the devil was after her. The street was crowded but she ran, seeing no-one and people stood aside as if the sight of a fugitive was the most ordinary thing in the world here. The force that she put into her escape was so vigorous that she scarcely knew what was happening until her shoe caught an uneven paving stone and she stumbled. It was the sort of stumble that is nearly a fall and she paused for a second to catch her breath and composure. A short slope put her above the marchers and, looking back she saw Sandy still waving her away. Nearby she saw the policeman who had nearly caught her. He had both hands full now; one clutched his shin while the other held the arm of someone who seemed part fallen, part protesting on the ground. It was a small black woman in yellow, whose hair was done in a matching mohican. As if sensing her presence the policeman suddenly turned his head towards Patti and she knew that standing still was dangerous. And she was off again. She ran up Whitcomb Street, along Wardour Street, darted down Rupert and came to a breathless halt in Green's Court. There, after gasping for a few moments she saw a tell-tale helmet that told her she couldn't stop. Turning immediately she bumped into someone, said 'Sorry' and burst into tears. Once started, the tears wouldn't stop as the full realisation of her position hit her. She was guilty of so many crimes towards so many people. She'd lied to her mother about where she was going, and what was worse it rather looked as if she'd soon be found out. She'd mixed with lezzies and had a good time and she deserted her best mate when she should have stuck by her. She wondered if Sandy would ever forgive her. And now here she was lost in Soho. She knew it must be Soho by the shops, the strange mixture of cosy Italian food shops, tacky punk stores that sold new clothes with rips in them and the other places with dirty photos outside. Soho was famous and she was lost. The tears continued as she thought of the police looking for her, and knowing she was really too old to cry made it even worse. Feeling a comforting arm around her she peered up through the wetness to see a woman's face gently smiling down at her. The smile was full of sympathy as if such tears of guilt and loneliness were only too familiar. 'You'll stain my blouse if you're not careful,' the woman said, and 'What you need's a cup of tea.' As she said that Patti realised that she was famished and wondered if the cup of tea might include a biscuit as well.

The woman took Patti's arm and led her from the main street to a side road that was even more lined with the doorways that displayed photos. Choosing one, she ushered Patti past a yawning man in a brown suit into a small foyer where there was a ticket booth. Here, there were two more doorways. One straight ahead had a string of small, white fairy lights around it and in place of an actual door hung strips of red and yellow plastic. The second door was in the side wall and was just a door, and taking a key from her bag, the woman opened it and motioned Patti inside. It was quite dark until switching on a light revealed to Patti quite the shabbiest and most rickety staircase she'd ever seen. 'Mind how you go' was all the woman said as they picked their way up over the threadbare carpet and past broken banisters. The staircase was still dark even with the light on and so Patti's eyes were quite dazzled by the lit room at the top of the stairs. There, it was like a festival of lights. Around three sides of the room they'd stepped into was a wide ledge, and along the three walls were three large mirrors in wooden frames. Around these frames were fixed light bulbs, most of which were on. On the ledge in front of the centre mirror was the most glorious mess of personal and intimate things that Patti had ever seen. Before the mirrors were spread a selection of towels and on one was a profusion of make-up, bottles, lipstick, letters, vases of flowers and what looked to Patti like the Crown Jewels. The woman told Patti to sit down and took a kettle and filled it from a sink behind the door. Patti chose a chair that had a little space on it and hoped she wasn't creasing someone's clothes.

The woman gave Patti a large mug of tea and from somewhere she also produced an equally large sandwich. 'Never seen a dressing room before, have you?' Patti shook her head, her eyes and mouth too full to answer. 'Are you a dancer?' she managed eventually. The woman laughed, 'Sort of, dear. But what about you, what have you been up to?' So Patti told her. Everything. About Sandy and the march, and the balloons and the dirty lezzies. At this point the woman laughed again, but this time sounding as if she wasn't really amused. 'Yes,' she said, 'people don't mind who they hurt as long as they feel superior.' Patti thought that was one of the wisest things she'd ever heard. She wanted to ask the woman if she'd ever been a teacher but just looking at her earrings told her it would be a silly question. When Patti got to the bit about the police the woman looked quite worried and she sighed and nodded as if she understood. Then she got up and said 'You wait here a mo', I won't be long,' and she left the room.

The woman was gone ages. Patti finished the tea and the sandwich and read a bit of a paper that was sticking out of a waste bin. She felt sure that hours were going by and she wanted to go home. Sandy might ring, or the police, and she couldn't help anyone, let alone herself, by hiding in a dancer's dressing room. So, carefully maneuvering the stairs, she opened the door and found herself back in the little lobby where, in contrast to the dressing room, the light was almost dim. The man in brown was gone and her friend was nowhere to be seen. The lights above the other door twinkled innocently and the coloured plastic strips lifted and fell slightly in an invisible current of air like waving fingers. Patti stuck her head through the plastic curtain. Disappointingly, there was nothing more than another short corridor and two more doors. Going to one she turned the handle and slowly opened it. Rows of seats faced a small stage. There was a wooden chair on the stage on its side and one of the dusty curtains that hung either side of it had a long threaded tear in it. 'That needs a darn' she thought. It was only a small theatre, and she wondered what sort of plays they put on there, not connecting that bare space with the bright lights and the lovely jumble of the upstairs room. On the side of the room was a bar, unlit and uncleaned. She smelt the stale air, saw the abandoned glasses with their melancholy dregs and, wiping her fingers on her trousers, she backed out and shut the door.
Thinking that her new friend might be looking for her she turned, ready to make her way back. But at that moment the other door caught her eye. She knew she ought not to be peeking and prying and at any moment someone might appear and ask her what the fuck she was doing here. But the very sight of the door so firmly closed, so shut against her, aroused her curiosity. So she opened the door just as she had done the other one and looked. It was crowded and unlit and there was a smell that she didn't recognise. At the end of the room away from the door was a large screen and on it was a man and a woman. Patti knew what

they were doing. But seeing it so plainly and so clearly somehow numbed her. She could only think 'How strange.' But that was not all. As her eyes grew used to the gloom she began to see the rest of the room and realised that all the other figures in it were men. They were seated on benches in rows, their faces strained up towards the flickering screen. She stood there for only a few seconds unseen in the shelter of the doorway and for the second time that day felt terror and was unable to move. In that awful room there was no sound but that of the screen performers, and yet there was. Patti seemed to hear subdued rustlings of cloth and flesh which steadily became more sinister as she realised what they were. She knew what it was, remembered school jokes, but had never before known it could be like this. What frightened her was the men's silence and their intensity; they seemed isolated, each from the next, yet they were a crowd with a secret and common purpose. Then she remembered that no-one knew where she was and even with their backs to her she felt in danger. In a moment she had closed the door as silently as she had opened it, had gone out through the plastic and up the stairs. Looking at the clock on the wall she saw to her amazement that only fifteen minutes had passed since she'd gone downstairs. She sat down and looked at her face in the mirror: it betrayed nothing and she thought of the women she had walked in the sun with earlier. Then suddenly there were footsteps on the stairs and there was the smiling face of her friend.

'Been alright, love, have you? Sorry I was so long, I just got some bad news. Come on, I've got a taxi, I've got to go somewhere and he'll take you home after.' And with a smile and a squeeze of her shoulder the woman shooed her downstairs and into a waiting black cab. She sat on the smooth padded leather and wondered what the bad news was. But it seemed rude to pry. To be in a taxi was a treat; so shiny and black on the outside and so sleek and dark within. Though just now her mind was so mixed up that she couldn't concentrate on the pleasure of the journey. Feeling stifled by her thoughts and the smallness of the cab she leaned forward and pushed down the window in the door letting the rushing air cool her face. The thought of the small room with its flickering screen kept coming back and she wished she could phone her mother and ask her to run a bath in readiness for when she got home. But she knew that when she did get home it would be talking to's first and bath, if at all, second. Anyway, the first thing she had to do when she got home was

214

somehow to see if Sandy was safe. How small she'd looked next to that policeman. She'd always thought of Sandy as big, taller than her, even though she knew they were the same height. If only she knew what had happened. The image of Sandy alone in a prison cell leapt into her mind and her heart began to thump painfully. If only they were together wherever it was, Patti thought she could bear it better. I'll never leave her behind again, she thought. Never. And immediately in her mind's eye she too was in prison, sitting next to Sandy on the narrow bunk with her arm around Sandy's shoulder. The taxi bumped over a pothole and Patti pushed the picture aside in case she started to cry again. She didn't want to appear ungrateful after all the woman had done for her and the woman might ask her what she was crying about. She might think it a bit funny if she told her. Then springing up like a collection of bright birds she saw again the women in the park; their laughter, their affection for each other seemed like a consolation for all her sufferings. They weren't ashamed of putting arms round each other, Patti thought, so why should we? 'Here we are, dear.' The woman's voice broke into her thoughts and Patti looked out of the window to see where 'here' was. Amazingly, 'here' seemed to be back among the crowd of lesbians. She wondered if she ought to tell the woman. The taxi came to a stop at the edge of a great crowd. Patti looked at them eagerly, but they were no longer bright and carefree. Although their clothes and hair and badges were the same, their gaiety had gone and in its place was a very different mood. They were standing in groups, some sitting on the pavement in huddles, hands in pockets against the cooling air. She could see their faces, now serious and stern, and where before they'd seemed to bounce with happiness as they moved, here in their stillness they seemed poised to spring. 'Where are we?' asked Patti. 'Vine Street, dear,' and Patti looked out at the building beyond the gathered women. A blue lantern hung in the stone doorway. 'That's a police station, isn't it?' she said. 'That's right, I've come to fetch my friend. I tried to warn her, but she would go.' Patti looked at all the lesbians that she'd thought so often about all day. They almost felt like friends. She wondered if it was very clever of them to hang about outside a police station considering what had happened earlier. She wanted to rush out and tell them to be careful, or at least to say something like goodbye or thank you. But they'd think she was crazy if she did that. I wonder, she thought, if any of them know where Sandy is. She smiled to herself; we've certainly broadened our education today.

Just then coming down the steps of the police station, Patti saw the small black woman in yellow. Quick as a flash she was out of the taxi and dodging through the crowd. At the bottom of the steps she stopped abruptly, not knowing what to say. The woman in yellow was talking vigorously to some others, Patti caught phrases: '. . . the pigs,' '. . . bail,' ' . . . kicking against the pricks.' Great gusts of laughter turned heads but seemed to drown Patti's 'Excuse me . . . ' But still the woman in yellow looked down at Patti and, seeing her smiled and raised her eyebrows. 'Ah,' she said, 'it's the sprint queen.' Then before Patti could reply a hand landed on her shoulder making her jump. It was only the woman. 'Don't run off like that, we've got to get you home.' With that she began to pull Patti back to the taxi. 'But . . . ' Patti began, her head twisting and turning back and forth between looking where she was going, stepping over legs and back to the woman in yellow. She still stood there on the bottom step looking after Patti. 'Sandy?' yelled Patti. 'Your friend? She's OK. Her parents came.' And with a final wave the woman in yellow stepped down and vanished into the crowd.

Back at the taxi the woman opened the door and gave Patti a gentle push inside. 'Now you give Tom your address and he'll see you home. You're safe with him, he's a mate of mine. And don't worry about the fare, I've seen to it.' She closed the taxi door and turned away, her shining earrings glittering in the last rays of the sun. 'Thank you, thank you,' Patti said through the open window, almost too late as the driver started up. 'But wait, I don't know your name.' The woman turned again and smiled a smile that reminded Patti of someone, though for the moment she couldn't think who. 'It's Glenys, dear. Now you keep out of trouble and watch out for those . . . ' But what or who she was to watch out for she never heard as the taxi rounded the corner and slipped into the early evening traffic.

One Mirror, Three Reflections: A Movement in Dance

Donna Allegra

People just looked better in mirrors than they did dead-on in the flesh, Rafiki mused, her eyes returning from the vision of Laura on whom she discreetly gazed. Once she was in class, a major pleasure was the sight of herself and others learning their steps from Grace's image, checking her own movements against the other students'. She had been away from class for almost a month and it felt right to be back in her spot by the barre, in front of Paula's drums. She felt so good that she wondered why she'd stayed away for so long. She belonged here in this class, with these people. After all: she was one of "Grace's girls," as she'd once heard a ballet student refer to another dancer with some admiration.

Rafiki wasn't all that crazy about modern dance, but she loved Grace and what this woman was teaching her about movement. She also liked the sense of having additional technique to take to the Brazilian, Haitian and West African dance classes she went to as regularly as she lived and breathed.

Grace's warm-up was a set ritual and it had become a meditation for Rafiki to repeat the pattern of movements over and again each time she came to class. Paula's drum accompaniment was usually alive with Africa simmering through a New York City stew of Puerto Rico, Haiti, and Brazil. Rafiki believed she was probably the only one in class appreciating the subtleties in Paula's samba. She could recognize the Congo, Nago, and Ibo Haitian rhythms that Paula often served to an audience consisting mainly of white women doing Grace's brand of modern dance movements.

Rafiki warmed happily to the stretch in the back of her thighs as she held the rolled-down position with her legs first in turn-out, then in parallel, and finally ending in a wide second position. The pliés between positions enabled her to pull her upper body erect. By the time she got through the brushes, relevées and isolations to the grand pliés, she felt nicely attuned with all her parts in place. She was ready to move. At this point she would have liked to leave modern and dance Haitian or Brazilian. She didn't feel she got a good and thorough enough warm-up in her traditional folkloric dance classes, but she didn't want to just leave Grace's class midstream. Besides, she liked it when Grace would come over and give her corrections. That was another pleasure of class: to be touched by that handsome spirit whose dazzling grey eyes held such friendly black irises. Rafiki wondered if she didn't fuck-up a movement just to get Grace's attention shifted to her.

Is she gay? Rafiki wondered, as she often did. It was so rare that straight women were comfortably touchy with each other that Rafiki felt surely Grace had to be lesbian. Still, Grace, with her articulate and alert body, clearly loved to teach. She would bend down in front of a male student to correct his pelvis alignment as unselfconsciously as in front of a woman. And each time Grace went down on one knee to adjust a pair of hips, Rafiki would shake her head at the sexual connotation she imagined.

Her lesbianism was such an important aspect of her being and one that had no visible reflections as she was growing up. Perhaps that's why it felt more urgent to nurture than being Black, which was plain and visible to anyone and never carried the necessity to hide, though it did call for courage, many a time, just to claim her place in the world.

Even though she taught the class, Grace had to exercise discipline to remain centered; especially today. She was so joyous over the turn-out for Friday night Modern I that she could barely contain herself with any professional calm.

Almost all her girls—not that anyone was that much younger than herself—had come to class. It was like a reunion of the old students and the new. Everyone from Gale, Brigitte and Danielle to Laura to the new Black woman with the Rastafarian hairstyle and stunning colors was stretching on the studio floor and inhabiting the moves she'd patiently repeated and drilled into their bodies. She loved teaching as a way to interact with the many sorts of people who were attracted to her style of modern dance.

Rafiki, the Black woman, paid serious heed to her instruction and was considerate of the other students in class. She's an angel, Grace thought, just like Laura had been in their early days. Rafiki was like an awkward adolescent in modern phrasings, but she tried hard and made progress. As was so often true, this dancer was good in her own discipline—African ethnic—but a gawky beginner as she tried her hand in another mode.

Grace had seen her dance like a raging goddess set free at the end of Marta's Afro-Brazilian class, which ended just before her 7:30 class. Marta put her students in a circle around the drummers at the end of her classes. Each student then did a solo to the drums and for the surrounding dancers. It was always thrilling to witness and to behold the vibrant energy infusing the room. Grace got to the studio early as much to watch them as to set up for her own class.

It had surprised Grace when Rafiki showed up one day for her modern basics class, when afterwards the nimble dancer she had regarded in Marta's class had thanked her so nicely in the shower for the attention Grace had given during class, and then returned to her class again and again to become a regular amongst her students.

Grace didn't dare be sure that Rafiki was gay, despite certain signs: Rafiki wore a labrys and didn't give any notice to the men in class when they made their loud noises and took up more space than necessary. The risk was real that this woman was actually very heterosexual. After all, she had the Rastafarian hairstyle and Grace had the impression that dred lock women held themselves aloof from feminism, poohpoohing women's liberation as white women's frivolity. Also, Paula had once pointed out to her that the labrys, the Amazon's double-headed axe, was also the sign of Shango, an African deity. Yet, Grace knew, some women took the dred lock hairstyle as a Black Amazon's badge of courage and of African identity.

Paula had conceded, "It's possible," with a questioning smile that Grace declined to answer. Grace had her suspicions about Rafiki, but still told herself to be cautious in her speculations. She kept her own love for women under close wraps because she could lose her livelihood all too easily if word got out. Her experience had been that there weren't very many gay women in dance class, but she'd also discovered some lesbians whom she wouldn't have guessed were so. Not a lot of dykes came out for dance classes, which seemed a sad irony to Grace. Dance was a realm where women could be strong in the connection to their bodies and take pride in competent physicality.

Rafiki took in Grace's corrections with the center floor work of class in her movement across the floor with obvious relish. For that alone Grace adored her. She seemed to welcome and expand to Grace's guiding touches. To top it off, she was gorgeous—strong, ripely brown, and quiet. She had good floor manners, a friendly energy, but remained contained within herself.

Laura had been like that too. And like Laura, Rafiki looked Grace in the eyes, woman to woman, as a peer, not taking the role of an insecure child, nor treating Grace as a servant, as so many students did.

Something in the mirror caught Grace's practiced eye. Laura was losing her alignment on the leg lifts. Grace went over to stand before her and guide the dancer back to center.

Laura, one of Grace's advanced students, performed with Grace's company and felt she had to set a good example for the others in class. This inevitably got in the way of her own body's work, so she was making the effort to release herself from this trap of her own devising.

"It's okay, baby; you're here to learn," Laura told herself as Grace showed her where her rib cage needed to pull back for proper alignment. Her neck and chest flushed warm streams of pink shame at needing this basic correction, but she strove to take it in.

"Why do I come to class when I'm this tired?" Laura asked herself, time and time again. She knew the litany of her answers: Fear. Fear of missing class, fear of losing Paula's favor and Grace's eye; fear of not exercising and of losing momentum and willingness to work; fear that others will progress ahead of me and I'll be left behind looking stupid; fear of the tiredness—that it is just laziness on my part; fear that if I don't push myself I won't go to class and improve; fear that I won't make it in the dance world, won't get recognition and a place to perform; fear that I'll be left out, won't be a part of the crowd; fear that just me is not enough.

And why this anxiety to be such an accomplished expert? Because, she continued the catechism to herself, I want to look good; because I believe that if I'm one of the best, people will like me. There's some truth behind my fears, but that's not the whole story or even the better part. I've never liked the snooty dancers. I might have admired their technique, but I felt put off by that style. I don't want to give off the smug attitude of the have-it-all-together. There's more to dance for me than looking good. It's also about the feel of learning and satisfaction of taking risks on how far I can go.

She watched Rafiki struggle to hold the adagio in the mirror. Laura enjoyed looking at her, this woman who'd been so strongly appealing to her during the past few months and thought, "She's got to be gay. What a waste for her to be straight with those muscles. And dyke or not, she sets my heart to dreaming."

Laura noted that she no longer held herself in check, trying to be the perfect, flawless dancer she believed it was her duty to portray. She sighed, "I just wanna look at Grace and some of the others in their paces. I love to watch dance. It's that simple."

"With Rafiki, I've got these warm and loving feelings and no name for them. I don't feel actually sexual, just drawn . . . It's an odd space, this not knowing. Sometimes that's the only answer. Ahh. Almost time to go across the floor with Grace's killer combination."

Rafiki finished the turn she'd wanted to try again and looked to examine her posture in the mirror before moving lightly across the room to join one of the groups of three preparing to do Grace's combination of movements across the floor. She saw a curly blonde head reflected. Laura was standing in front of her, so instead of scrutinizing her alignment, Rafiki retied her head wrap, the orange and black bird print fabric from Senegal, by memory. She struck a pose that she hoped wasn't too far from keeping with Grace's principles of alignment, but which was more intended to impress Laura.

"Okay, enough of that, girlfriend, let's bring the camera back front and center." She tried to chastise herself that she'd do better to pay attention to her own body in order to learn, but Laura was a sweet distraction humming on the other side of her mind. She directed herself to the task of repeating a movement from the center floor work they'd just done, which under Grace's guidance she'd gotten pretty good at. It was during the center floor part of class when everyone faced the mirror that Rafiki learned the lessons about movement that had become so valuable to her. She always had to concentrate to maintain her technique while executing the movements and this took real effort. It was painful too. She couldn't follow and duplicate the modern dance movements all that well. She wished the women in class could see her do the samba or a yan valou or mandgiani. Then they'd see how she could dance. Her reflections came back from the mirror looking so awkward sometimes, but it was going across the floor in modern that really put her to shame. Sometimes she could smile about her lack of finesse. To think she'd once thought there was nothing much to that modern dance bullshit when Marta had first suggested she look in on one of Grace's classes.

Still, she had to give herself credit: she tried and sometimes saw small improvements. She would often hearten herself by saying, don't come to any conclusions now. Keep going to class and working for three more months and then we'll talk about how you're doing. And with that, she'd hang in for the combination of Grace's movements across the floor, the finale of every class.

Laura watched Rafiki and thought, "I'll either get better as a dancer, or I won't, and through it all, I can at least enjoy myself in class. It doesn't make sense to be impatient at the rate I progress. There can be such beauty in the effort to grow or keep pace. I do this for fun, as a healing, as physical release and for emotional connection. Remember?

"Yes. It's like what I saw in those young boys in the park on my way over here. One was on a skateboard and he had to put out a lot more effort to stay with his pals who were walking and horsing around, having fun. He had to slow down in order not to get ahead of them or run into them. He was considerably more alluring, efficient on his machine, and yet having to do more work to match the slower pace of his walking buddies. There was paradox in that, life-poetry.

"That's how it is for me in this class. I'm a more experienced student having to come up with extra power to harmonize my pace with the level of this class and still stretch for my true reach. I know the basics and still have to take risks. I see something that corresponds to me in Rafiki. Her example reassures me that it's fine to be struggling and to not have it all together, to be awkward in the process of finding your balance. We're each in our own ways beings of beauty. I sure hope to high heaven and back again that she's gay."

Grace was annoyed that she had to go over the head count for class. She was eager to present the combination and teach about movement, but the cashier from the front desk interrupted her class to say someone had not signed in. Grace told everyone to take five. She was glad he came over before she'd gotten into the across-the-floor work, but what a pain.

While the class waited for Grace to go over the attendance sheet, Rafiki again tried out the adagio. She thought: "I'm even kinda good today. The turns were awful, but I'm finding my way around inside them. I worked really well throughout the warm-up and I actually had all the center floor work. I was following fairly well, but lost it at the end, and even that's okay. My brain is tired and tuckering out on me.

"It's good to be here. I feel welcome and at home in Grace's class. It's a safe place to be simple, appreciative and nice. I can dress up and enjoy myself in the mirror. And then there are the lovelies who come here: Brigitte is her absolutely beautiful self, unaware of anyone else; Gale seems even taller with her noble profile. And Grace. I love Grace. Is-she-gay-is-she-gay-I-wonder-if-she's-gay? Do other people love their dance teachers so? I think Danielle likes me, as a straight girl likes a straight girl. She's so good in modern; so light and confident in the way she moves that full, rich body of hers.

"And of course there's Laura. Such a beauty. And blonded or not, she looks like me. She waits and pays attention quietly. Something about her feels like home.

"I like it when class is crowded like this. The room is warm and alive, and I'm loosened up from that Brazilian class this afternoon. I love it when Marta pushes us to give her more. Let me try this adagio once more while I still have the heart."

Rafiki struggled with the extension and just as she was about to lose her balance, Laura put two hands on her shoulders and steadied her.

"That's it. Try it again. Plié, then lift. Keep in a small fourth. Use the turn-out from your inner thighs. That's where your strength is. Now, move your ribs back, here. Yes." Rafiki couldn't hold it and grabbed Laura's shoulders. "Just the right size," she thought and smiled to herself, reining in the impulse to flirt.

"That's okay. You're getting there. You need to gain strength but you're coming along just fine."

"Thanks. This is kinda hard for me."

"Yeah, but you're doing really well. Here's where you can pull up more. Yes. There." Laura searched Rafiki's face for signs as she spoke. Rafiki seemed to glow radiant with her red burnished chocolate coloring.

"Thanks. You're a really good dancer, really."

"Yeah, well, I've been at it for awhile."

"I mostly do African dance. I come here mainly for technique. And, Grace."

"That's like how I go to ballet classes, for technique. And—Grace."

"And ballet dancers go to ethnic classes to try to loosen up on the technique and have some fun—but no grace."

They both laughed.

"You doing anything after class? Wanna have coffee?"

"Yeah! Let's try this again."

As she came back, rounding up her students, Grace noted Laura helping Rafiki with the adagio movement from the center floor work they'd done earlier in class. Rafiki lost her balance as she attempted to hold the passé before the extension from the tilt. She reached companionably for Laura's shoulder to support herself. Grace heard them laugh and Laura say, "That's okay, hold onto me, but don't let go of your alignment. Yes. There. Remember to focus on your center."

"Well," Grace thought, "this makes a lovely pas de deux." She was ready to move the class across the floor with her combination. She observed the two in the mirror, Laura adjusting Rafiki's alignment, Rafiki holding to Laura to steady herself. Watching with both interest and longing Grace thought, with some satisfaction and no small irony, "It seems I have taught my girls a thing or two about alignment, centering, and making the necessary connections for dance."

Beginnings

Jay Reed

She liked to think of herself as a gambler, but Dani always hedged her bets. Like naming her children after archangels: was that arrogance or merely celestial insurance? Before and following those two christenings, her adult life was a model of predictable progress toward security via the dictates of propriety, aimed at the not-unreasonable expectation of measurable contentment. She could view her approaching maturity with a satisfying prognosis of success as she plowed a straight, steady course through the well-mown meadows of mediocrity, avoiding the lures of extravagance and the annoyance of excess criticism. Well, almost.

There was a veer in this terrestrial treadmill—one brief period of brilliance, a dazzling burst of excess, flaring and exploding beyond the usual confines of her everyday world, like a supernova leaving a bright splash seared against the darkness. I live in its wake; I can testify.

That summer morning, as she was shampooing in the shower, I'm sure Dani could not have imagined that a simple encounter would mark, even alter her future direction. The pelting water revealed a wide, exposed brow never seen in public under the long, straight curtain of blonde bangs, bleached to a lighter gold with a comb-in chemical to "cheer me up," as she later put it—the wet hair now seal-dark, sculpting a head appearing small above broad, pale shoulders, beneath the massage of her large, freckled hands—hands that could be tender but seldom gentle. There was a gaucheness, a clumsiness about her that came across as a kind of awkward charm.

Mind you, I'm trying to tell this with objectivity, to see her as someone else might have seen her that July day in the kids' swim-lessons sign-up line with all the other mothers, as I saw her for the first time. Not knowing one another, a cluster of us made small talk about our children, about summer activities. Dani began to project a sense of her insecurities into the conversation with questions about safety and sanitation.

She had a nordic look, not tall but with an angularity overlaid with the barest lazy layer of excess softness at biceps and hip, like an athlete taking a season off. The deep-set, green eyes filled with concern under the frown brackets impressed just above a straight nose set prominently between the planes raised by high cheekbones. An outdoor type, obviously, but not tan, it was as if the generous sprinkling of freckles had fused in patches to acknowledge her time in the sun, giving her an uneven brownness to burnish the year-round buttermilk complexion.

Her concern was for her daughter, soon to enter kindergarten for the first time: how clean were the toilet seats? How could one be sure a child would not pick up a disease in the school bathrooms? I watched the thin, sunburned lips framing clean, somewhat irregular teeth, her scattered, aimless hand gestures, the frequent laughter of unease or embarrassment at her own anxieties voiced to strangers. I made a mental note: this appealing young woman will not age well; she worries too much. Later, to my surprise, I learned she was already seven years older than I had surmised, a few weeks away from her thirty-second birthday. Time had brushed her with its lightest touch.

Because of our children, we kept running into each other all that summer, at swimming and ballet and trampoline—like people who take their dogs out for predetermined walks from opposite directions and converge, their leashes tangling inevitably. By fall, despite her frustra-tion at not getting the highly-touted teacher she'd wanted for her daughter, she found the child enrolled in the same class as mine and began to relax a bit over her disappointment; we discovered we were around-the-corner neighbors. Since I was older, with other older chil-dren, Dani invested me with an assumed wisdom from greater experi-ence, for which she accorded me a measure of unwarranted awe.

So began a year of tangential acquaintance, circumstances throw-ing us together in peripheral ways until we started consciously making our contacts intentional. Still, there was a randomness to our meetings, as though we needed some external excuse to initiate an occasion. Parent-teacher conferences, bake-sale and school carnival committee car-pooling extended into an excuse for a drink and conversation to delay the evenings' end. We exchanged the customary anecdotes, baited and set our hooks to secure mutual attention and compassion. The conditions were favorable. We were each caught up in the urgency of our internal timing; we coincided.

As I try to tell this, standing back further and further to sharpen the perspective, I realize I have gone too far; the figures fade; their edges blur. I'm not trying to revise history. I feel a need to preserve it, to place the events within their moment and attempt to leave them there. This is the thing I have to do: tell my version as well as I'm able, being fair to Dani's own, as clearly as I know it, resisting the dulled lessons of what later ensued or my sharp longings of the present. All that happened then has bled into my subsequent experiences, coloring and staining my perceptions. Did I say Dani was marked by what followed from our initial encounter? I can speak only for myself.

Goethe said, "Beginnings are always delightful; the threshold is the place to pause." If I could pause there, rewind, retain only selective memories! All those afternoons of sunlight streaming in through her west windows, the redwood deck and sliding glass doors opening off the blue-and-white kitchen bathed in golden rectangles, the children playing and chattering in one room or another, and Dani moving in the way that always made something catch in my throat, gave a twist to my gut: Dani sauntering ahead of me up the stairs, ambling down a hallway, barefoot across an expanse of carpet—"something in the way she moves . . . " The Beatles sang of it, knew all about it, but I never figured out just what it was that assured a visceral response I could not own or identify. She said she'd had trouble all her life on account of that walk; it wasn't my imagination.

So now I try again to reconstruct it, the way the two of us became more than the sum of individuals. It's difficult to say exactly how or when it started, the spiraling intensity, as it changed from the casual connection, the off-handed but convenient combining of daily efforts to run our households, tend our families, to the intimate consolidation of our equally-pressing needs for change.

Those long evening drives had ceased to begin with legitimate motives of altruism or self-improvement. We ran out of PTA meetings, of yoga classes; we ducked out of volunteer forums and planning sessions. Riding along the back country roads wherever we could wind within a few hours and still return at a reasonable hour, we talked in breathless spurts, our stored-up hopes and hurts and history tumbling out in reciprocal release. But what was growing between us and not being said extended the gaps, crowded into the pauses, heavier than the sweet, fragrant spring air. Finally, the car trips were freighted with the imminence of parting; my new companion and her family were going to the east coast for two months to vacation with relatives.

The night before they left, Dani, her husband and I sat around their living room smoking pot—something she seldom did and only at Nick's coercion for her company. He thought it would be fun to get me high, since it was my first time, but his enthusiasm was more genuine than mine. For me it was an excuse to be with Dani a little longer. Relaxed and sleepy and extremely cozy, I hung within the arc of the hour, not wanting to think about the next day and their departure.

As it grew cooler in the spacious, candle-lit living room, Dani threw an old quilt over us where she and I lolled on the carpet, as Nick fussed with the pipe or relit a joint, between trips to the kitchen for snacks. Suddenly I realized Dani's toes were touching mine, and soon thereafter our ankles linked and locked in covert communion. Nick became bored waiting for my reaction to the adventure of Acapulco Gold and finally wandered off to bed, excusing himself with the prospect of a long day's drive ahead. Dani and I lay sprawled in the shy semblance of innocence, sheltered by our persistent ignorance as to what was happening to us—close, in a spacey limbo of comfort without the fore-knowledge of consequence, not wanting to move.

Presently, Nick came back out to the living room, roughly pulling the pillow—apparently his own bed pillow—out from under my head, a not-too-subtle hint indicating the lateness of the hour. As if in instant reflex, in an almost instinctive gesture of protection, Dani threw her arm across me as Nick retrieved his possession. I didn't see what glances were exchanged between the two of them. Touched, but too groggy to analyze this sequence of actions, and noting Nick's grumpy return to the bedroom, I yawned, gave an appreciative hug to my unexpected defender, and commented to her that it was time for me to leave. Dani exacted a promise that I would return in the morning to say goodbye before they left.

The next day I retraced my steps reluctantly, weighed down with my own uncomfortable interior baggage of stifled sadness, of impending loss. I am no good at farewells; as a rule I avoid them, aware of my ungraciousness in tendering something I'm unwilling to give: aid in my own deprivation, colluding in the facilitation of a loved one's exit. I remarked on their preparations as they loaded the van and silently observed with some mysterious satisfaction that Dani was still wearing the daffodil-yellow shirt of the previous night, had probably slept in it. Seized by a rush of anguish at the thought of not hearing her sweet, cheery voice on the phone to start my mornings, of not seeing that beaming face every day, I rushed to leave, stricken.

This next part sticks in my brain like a needle in a defective groove, replays repeatedly the same passage:

. . . I rush to leave, stricken. And then she runs after me forever in slow motion a möbius strip of seamless recall down the driveway down the dip of pavement in front of their house and garden past the long bank of ivy past the azaleas and oaks from the van to where I am moving to go back home running running after me insisting on a goodbye unwilling to have me slip away so easily and somehow in my arms and running into my arms over and over—and that part I, the stuck needle, have to be lifted beyond—for she is running running in her daffodil shirt a bright yellow flash of color streaming toward me and I always see it in my mind's eye from above as though I'm watching two people one moving away so as to be the leaver and not the left and the gold hair flying back from a furrowed forehead above the daffodil arms waving and reaching above the running and the other one caught and someone always running and someone always leaving . . .

That summer the letters flew back and forth across the continent and everything was between the lines. When August arrived, returning Dani and her family, there were two people running toward each other this time, and all the ambivalence, the doubt, the ambiguous circumlocutions and hesitancy were at an end. We didn't know what we were doing or where we were going, but there was no uncertainty as to the mutuality of feeling, the rightness of its concurrence.

One September weekend, Nick left for ski-patrol training in the Sierras, and Dani invited me over to keep her company. This was after many more long country drives during which we kept the wheels spinning under us for miles, baffled as to what to do if we stopped. One night we did stop, and so did the words. The first tentative touch of her hand on mine was received with such a flood of joy and excitement that I was stunned and could only drink in the pressure of those strong, firm fingers, as frightened as my own, in a mute osmosis of love, like a thirsty desert traveler who discovers the oasis was not a mirage created by lifelong drought and immediate want.

That night at her house we felt deliciously close, the children asleep and the two of us, awkward in our sudden freedom, finished with dinner, not interested in TV, with the opportunity of having the place all to ourselves almost too much to take in.

Then Dani said, "Let's go in the other room and be more comfortable." I followed, unquestioning. At the end of a long hall, the master bedroom was dominated by a large waterbed under the blue-glass panes of a hanging Tiffany-style lamp. Without knowing the script, and too embarrassed to look at her as she began undressing, I quickly removed my own clothes and slid under the covers, then noticed Dani was still in T-shirt and panties. She made a point of indicating which was 'her' side of the bed and where I belonged; I found my head once again on Nick's pillow.

In no time, Dani's legs were entwined with mine. It felt as if they had always known where to go, as though we were resuming a familiar position which would anchor us in this unpredictable sea where we twisted and tossed. Soon there was no fabric, no false modesty between us. And then our arms knew where to go, and our mouths. Oh, those mouths—*all* of them: rosy entrances to a fateful labyrinth, intricate and unforeseen!

Like a patient, perceptive prospector stumbling upon a buried mine shaft, Dani discovered in me a vein of previously undetected passion so rich, so limitless its ready treasure seemed inexhaustible. My hands and lips began to learn the contours of a face I had looked at for a year and never really seen, became acquainted with a body infused with a compelling eagerness of sensuality I had never dreamed existed under the concealing, yet tantalizing clothes she always wore. As I traced the surprising roundness of Dani's shoulder with my tremulous fingertips, I asked, "What would happen if I touched your breast?"

She whispered, "I'd scream." Chastened, but with caution and curiosity, I explored other areas of her creamy, delicate flesh, increasingly aroused and surprised at my own actions, seeming so natural and happening of their own volition. It was like a coming home, a sudden mirroring in her of my own deepest self. As I lay with my head on her concave belly, overcome with rare emotion and the wonder of what was unfolding, she lifted my face and said softly but distinctly, "I want you to touch me everywhere." And eventually, I did.

That's the essence of it: a pure gift of grace before dreams and plans had surfaced and crystallized, where, hovering on the brink of the unknown, all doubt, all thought was suspended in the absolute fullness of the moment. In an awakening of amazed delight, we opened to each other with the acceleration of a flower in time-lapse photography, revealing the innermost petals. In a crescendo of intuitive creativeness, each movement had its counterpart; every daring advance by one of us met its corresponding and equal extension ventured rashly by the other. Dani called it "the ratchet effect," for despite our equal shyness, our tactile attempts proceeded in a brave, forward ascent. We never looked back.

Whatever intrinsic or educated capacities and appetites we each brought from previous initiations became whetted and incited, heightened by our increasing physical harmony and enriched by the growing depth of our caring. We spent hours unhinged from the awareness and demands of time, journeying to dimensions of discovery and fantasy beyond any prior experience or imagination. Spirit had found its vehicle. It was all I wanted; she wanted us anchored on earth.

We brought forth untapped resources in one another in other ways, as well, unlocking, provoking, encouraging our complementary facilities for playfulness in words and work, always lightened by laughter. Dani developd a faith in outrageous possibility which was contagious. Her belief in us convinced me to believe; it was so strong, so capable of surmounting the improbable, that it became a part of me, lasting longer than it did in her. Therein lies the beauty and the irony of such conviction.

The profound feelings evoked in those early days remain intact, as though what Dani and I distilled were a heart-and-mind-altering ambience surrounding me, seeming to be always out there, part of the air I breathe, when actually it's only the rarified atmosphere of my inner landscape, unavoidable. All I may do now is honor it keenly and fairly, giving it its due. As Milan Kundera wrote, "What exists is what we allow ourselves to remember."

Thus, I fight against admitting, for it does not ring true for me, that such a powerful, transformative feat of faith and levitation in which we were both encompassed existed as a viable reality for a finite span in our lives, like the freakish flight of a recalcitrant, mutant mayfly, lasting against all expectations well beyond its allotted ephemeral day—and

231

that in the particular form and intensity in which we knew it, exists no more.

In the beginning, Dani said to me, "I love you every way I know, and if there is another way, I will learn it." Fortunately for her, she has learned another way. It's not the way I would have chosen, but it's her way. And I'm glad for Dani's sake she's found a peace I haven't been able to find. I'd be a hypocrite if I could leave it at that, because, selfishly, I want her to miss me as I miss her. But if I truly love her, I wouldn't want her to know that much sorrow, such endless regret that things didn't turn out differently.

We seldom see each other anymore because of my own difficulty in accepting the compromises Dani has made with life as she feels she needs to live it. In her present circumstances, I find no place for myself as someone who loved her, in my flawed way, more than I could have envisioned loving anyone, despite the blind cruelties and blunders on both sides. It's inconceivable that I would be able to suppress the lifespring of joy and desire she aroused in me in order to become the dispassionate friend. How can I settle for a seat in the planetarium after having touched the stars?

Accordingly, we rarely speak to one another on the telephone, unless one of us, urged by some echo from that deep, shared well of yearning, needs to manufacture a flimsy excuse to call. Our mutual restraint is in the nature of respect, complicated by frustration with a solution that satisfies neither of us. In one of our last conversations, Dani said to me, "You were the high of my life." And she was, will always be, mine.

Another Side of Things
(for Susan)

Beth Karbe

I.

at parties, in support groups, during meetings
and potlucks and fundraisers and dances
it's been said to me   casually
over and over and over again
about men
"You're so lucky, you avoided all that," by lesbians
who weren't always
lesbians,
women who lived months or years
or half their lives
with men
sleeping, eating, having sex
with men
at their sides, across their tables,
these lesbians who are now
lesbians,   casual and smiling
say to me about my always having been
"You're so lucky, you avoided all that."
but until now I haven't had the courage
to answer those who weren't always
lesbians—

"*Don't* tell a lesbian
who always has been
she's lucky,
as if you *know*
what you're talking about."

II.

at 10 and 11 I knew
something terrible
was terribly wrong
I knew
when I wished I was a boy
and when in my dreams I *was* one.
waking, I would dress in T-shirts and jeans
try out for little league and football club
and try to fit in
and try and try
and not.

at 12 and 13 I was sexual with girls,
making love to five or six
in those two short years,
making love as "practice for boys"
they would say,   casual and smiling
but I knew at 12 and 13
I knew
it was not for boys I practiced
but for other girls
I thought would come
and never did.

14 and 15 were hard years,
those girls having grown casual
and smiling,
making out and making love with boys,
boys they told about "practice"
and soon "queer" and "lezzie" were words I heard
every day

234

EVERY
DAY
and those girls that betrayed me
those same girls
that weren't always lesbian
are the girls that *are* now
and the girls who smile and say to me
"You're so lucky . . . "

when I was 16 and 17 my mother stopped
threatening
to take me to psychiatrists
when all around her were mothers
of other girls of 16 and 17,
girls who were getting pregnant, smoking marijuana, drinking
at secret parties 'til two or three in the morning,
sneaking into their bedroom windows and reeking
of vomit and cheap aftershave,
and all my mother had to commiserate over
was how I'd spend whole days and nights
lying flat on my bed staring up
at the ceiling,
and that I had no friends.

18 and 19 were better years, having escaped
the town that "knew" and hated
who I was.
at a university I lived
with women my age,
women I made friends with
women I loved
women I fell in love with
who kept me an arm's length away
who craved my attention and interest
until boyfriends visited from out of town
until they turned me away
casual and smiling
and I look again to lying flat
on my bed staring up.

when I was 20 and 21 there was a sexual revolution
for heterosexual un-revolutionaries
and the second wave swept c-r groups
and feminism all over the country
and I, of course, was there
among a few lesbians
who always had been
there
and we listened quietly
and we listened
endlessly
to angry heterosexual women
complain and heal and
purge and heal and
tell horror stories and heal about the men
they would often go home to
and *keep* going home to.

III.

I am a lesbian
who always has been
lesbian
but who hasn't always
felt lucky
about not having a "choice,"
having always been different
and who,
among you,
still *is*.

IV.

at parties, in support groups, during meetings
and potlucks and fundraisers and dances
you will often hear lesbians
who haven't always been
lesbians

talk among themselves about the years behind
the men or marriages or children
talk among themselves about the years behind
with the same   solid   sense
of camaraderie and sisterhood
they enjoyed back then
those men and those marriages and those children giving them places
in the world
earning approval and privilege
they carry with them still
to parties, to support groups, during meetings
and potlucks and fundraisers and dances
lesbians who haven't always been
lesbians
talk among themselves   casual
and sometimes smiling
about their men or their marriages or their children
as if theirs is the only experience there is
as if *all* lesbians
haven't always been
lesbians
as if all of us "chose"
until a single, brave one of us
rises
having *always* been different
and who,
among you,
still *is*,
and she's told
"You're so lucky . . . "

V.

until now
I haven't had the courage to answer
lesbians
who haven't always been
lesbians,
but I'm answering you now—

"*Don't* tell a lesbian
who always has been
she's lucky,
and don't *ever* say it
smiling
or casual
or as if you *know*
what you're talking
about."

New York, 1959

Catherine Odette

It seems like I've told this story a thousand times. It seems now to have a rhythm all its own, a pace at which it needs to be told and a special atmosphere that must be present before it can even be started. Yes, I've told this story before.

If the truth were really told (and so often it can't be) the story begins when I was an infant . . . maybe only a couple of one-two-or-three days into my life . . . whenever it was that I looked out, with my Lesbian-born heart, at the people around me, and found them alien. It could even have been, say, day one, hour one, minute one. I happen to know that I was hung by my ankles and had my butt slapped by a doctor about three minutes after my birth. Maybe in his patriarchal way he thought I wouldn't keep breathing on my own if he didn't slap me, but I surely knew even then that men were not my friends. I also knew right away that I preferred not to stay in that environment. Even then, in my infant's way, I tried to run away from home—tried to find the life-supporting people that I would wait many, many years to find.

I usually startle the lesbians I tell this story to. It's part of the way that I like to tell it and part of the way I, umm, well, try to charm the Lesbians who are hearing my story. I begin a little mysteriously and then I swoop right in with a punch line. I usually say something like, "Well, ya know, I ran away from home when I was nine years old. I just had to find the

Lesbians." Invariably there comes a sharp intake of breath, eyes widen in surprise and lips drop apart in pleasure. I know what they love so much about the beginning of my story. I've told the story many times, and I've learned very well the power of those short sentences. Like the bard of earlier times, I've learned to play this for all it's worth. I never launch right in from there. Oh, no no. After I begin, I pull back a bit and ask them a question or two about how they found Lesbians. I want them to anticipate my story but I want us both to be in the glow of recollection. At that instant, I want us both to feel afresh the moment of our first time with the woman, the first of the women, who would make up our preferred company, our roommates, our lovers,   our mates.

"Well," I begin, "I ran away from home when I was nine years old." I'm never able to get right past that to the next sentence. My companion always exclaims, "My g-d! Nine years old!" "Yes," I say with a smile, in the most soothing voice I can manage. "Things were really not good at home, and I needed to be with Lesbians." She wants to ask questions. She always seems fairly bursting with admiration and excitement. But always she can maintain good decorum and let me continue. Now, I can just tell my story. The dramatics are over and we can simply be together as we recall our first time finding the Lesbians, different though those stories will be.

"That morning," I begin: That morning I got ready for school as though it were any other day. Except for a few minor changes, it could have been so ordinary. That day I put on three pair of underwear, two pair of socks and layered my dress with rolled up-to-the-knee pants underneath and a bulky sweater over my chest. It was uncomfortable to move. My feet hurt in my shoes. I hated pain of any sort, and the cramped feeling in my feet was a serious misery.

I picked up my books and coat and mentally blew a quick, sardonic kiss to the bedroom I shared with my two sisters. "I won't miss them," I thought to myself. I stopped off at the kitchen, where, between the narrow metal can-goods cabinet and the refrigerator, there was a seemingly endless supply of paper and bread-wrapper bags. I took a couple of each kind: I planned to unwrap myself at the first possible moment, stuff the dress into a bag, unroll my sensible pants for the world. I had the eleven dollars and change I had saved during the interminable previous days, one lunch-quarter at a time, and was ready to take the trolley to Back Bay station where I would pick up the train to New York. It was so simple. No one stopped me. No one asked me a single question. No one questioned my right to be on my way to New York on a school day. I had the note I had prepared, asking that the ticket agent sell me a one-way ticket to New York, Grand Central Station, please, and that the conductor keep an eye on me. I thought that was a really nice touch—making them think that they were in charge of me.

The train ride was probably the most fun I had ever had! No one at home would worry or know anything was wrong for about seven hours or so. I wasn't absent often enough for the principal to call home, and I always dawdled on my walk home, enough to make me late. The five-hour train ride into New York was nothing short of heaven. I felt absolutely definitely confident that I would find "HER" soon.

Combined with the anxiety and fear of getting caught, the excitement made me a little nauseous. I made several trips to the train's bathroom, which swayed and made me struggle to find the tiny seat. After changing out of my extra clothes in the bathroom, I found the water dispenser outside the door and had terrific fun with the flat paper cups that I spread open with my finger. The water dispenser had a push-button that released a tiny trickle at a time and the sound of the water dribbling into the cup made me have to 'go' all over again. I was embarrassed by needing at least five cups to satisfy my thirst but was having too good a time to worry about people noticing me. Every few minutes, I felt the thrill of what I was doing; it affected my heart and every so often gave me a giant rush of beats before settling back again. It was all right. I allowed myself to create "HER" face in my mind. I remember the rituals I had developed for dreaming this special dream. Each time a little different, but each time I came closer and closer to seeing myself in the room with her, just living our lives but really, really happy. It was my kid version of what I do today. Years later I learned that my vision was startlingly accurate.

The train ride was five hours long. I remember passing through New London, and thinking it was a beautiful sounding name for a city. I remember being hungry but not wanting to spend my money for a sandwich on the train. Something told me their prices would be high compared to the cost on the street. I remember telling myself to remember all the details so that I would remember this later.

When I arrived at Grand Central Station, I was elated by all of it. I couldn't take it, this mammoth excitement, this coming-true-of-the-dream; the excitement was too much. I headed immediately for a bathroom and let go of my breakfast.

The station, Grand Central Station, was immense, unlike any place I had ever been in. I think I believed it was itself, a city, because everything was right there to be had, and there were just so many people. They were rushing madly in all directions, the level of noise doing injury and the feeling of danger crushing. I was clinging fiercely to my mission but felt, for the first time, as though I had maybe picked the wrong place.

I found a place on a long bench, one like a church pew, with the beautiful wooden armrest at each end and that's where I plunked myself. I needed to think through this twist in my plan. I knew what "SHE" looked like, sort of, kind of, and I knew that if I went home now, even if I had the money (which I didn't), having run away, I would be dead meat. After only a moment's pause, my resolve was strong again and I began an "active" search right from my seat near the armrest on the wooden bench. I didn't have a watch so I'm not sure how long I waited.

It couldn't have been that long—I only went to the bathroom twice—when I saw "HER." She passed within a couple of feet of where I sat. She walked briskly, her head low, her eyes looking all over at the same time, her hands deep in her jacket pocket. Her expression was tight, closed in a study of determination. In my confidence, I didn't doubt I was wrong. I left my books on the bench and hurried after her, my heart booming again with excitement. We hadn't gone far at all. We had just passed the four-sided clock and were heading through the huge door-way arch into the next room.

Maybe I gave it away somehow. Maybe I had jinxed it all. Maybe she wasn't "HER." She suddenly turned full around and looked me right in

242

the eye. I stopped dead in my tracks and waited a split second for her to do or say something. I was horribly upset by the trapped or maybe angry look on her face. I was smiling at her, I think. I tried to look friendly. She quickly pulled out a pack of cigarettes and threw them at me. I raised my arms in front of my face in some instinctive protection and felt the dull smack of the cigarettes as they hit my arm. I knew it was all over. I couldn't look; I just couldn't watch her walk away from me, and so kept my arms up at least a minute too long and when I uncovered my eyes she was gone.

As simply as that, it was all over. I felt dreadful. How could I have failed so completely to show her I was like her. It seemed impossible that she could misunderstand. I sat back down at my bench to sort out the feelings that rushed through my youth's heart. I had found her but hadn't found "HER" yet, I reasoned, and I was alone in this massive city. If anything good came of it, it was that I saw the doors to the outside for the first time then. It was getting dark and I had no place to go. I stepped out into my first solo night in New York City. I felt very brave and decided this adventure was just what I needed to perk my spirits up. I had lost "HER" and wasn't about to go home, so I was now in charge of my life, big-time.

First things first! Food was easy. I decided to eat well the first meal, so subsequent meals could be smaller. I had two New York hot dogs with everything including the sauerkraut. In fact, I now have big buildings and hot dogs inextricably joined in my mind: I downed one and looked up at the other.

I also learned that New York doesn't close like Boston, where I had come from. People were out all night; some stores were open all night. It wasn't too safe to just go behind a building and sleep, because people were all over the place. Anyway, excitement kept me awake so I chose to go into the subway station and ride the trains. By morning I had caught a few hours sleep and had been around the city a couple of times and had mentally aged quite a bit. Sometimes the train was up in the air, high above the city and sometimes it was in long tunnels, but I enjoyed it best when we seemed almost in the country, what I know today as the neighborhoods of Queens, Flushing, Brooklyn and others. It was this ride that showed me how dangerous the city would be for me if I didn't learn to take care of myself immediately fast.

I rode close to one set of the train's sliding doors because that's where the map of the transit system was posted and, although now forgotten, I was fascinated by the names of the stops which I guessed were related to the towns and neighborhoods we passed through. Together, the hours, the city and the night rushed past me, while I allowed feelings of elation to build.

At some point, while I held the grab bar below the map, a man came silently up behind me and pressed himself into my body. He pushed against me very hard and forced me to choose to push backward against him, or let myself be smothered into the wall below the map where I would be trapped, unable to escape. The people on the train did not care enough to be involved. No one tried to stop him or to help me. I was obviously a child—and he was obviously molesting me, but I was entirely alone in the situation. It was many excruciating minutes before the next stop. All that time I had to press back against him or I would not be able to get away at all. At the very next stop, when the doors slid open, I jumped away from him right out the door of the train onto the platform. He must have thought I was going to let him do that to me forever, because when I jumped out he almost fell out also. I ran the length of the platform until I found stairs to take me down to the street. I don't know to this day where I was but from there I ran behind a building and hid myself for a long, long while.

My third day was not so disastrous as my first or second and, in fact, looms large in my personal history. After another short train ride, I responded to a whim and descended to the street. In the place I now know to be the Christopher Street area of "The Village" I found a stoop in what seemed a safe area. I sat there and began what was to be a very short vigil. I simply went behind the building when I needed relief, and bought inexpensive junk food when I was hungry enough. The weather was brisk, the passers-by were pleasant, if not overtly friendly, and there seemed to be few kids—at least none who objected to my sitting on their stoop. I was feeling optimistic again, my resolve a steel stubbornness in my mind.

I sat with my left side against the grille work of the fence adjoining the stoop, and looking through the bars, I saw her coming. Short black hair, combed sharply back. Head low, eyes taking it all in. A brown leather jacket, her hands jammed into the pockets, ending in a wide-brown elastic at the waist and wrist cuffs. Brown loafers with a dull silver dime in each coin slot were highly polished, well cared for, but clearly longtime footgear. Her slacks were blazing-white chino with a razor precise crease, the line barely disturbed by her quick pace. Her movements conveyed a firm determination. It was "HER."

This time my heart was moderate in response. How quickly we learn the dangers and pain of rejection. For a moment I saw both "HER" and myself and I was confused. She was almost in front of me, I would have to move quickly. I smiled at her. She caught my eye but didn't respond—not with a smile—but not with hostility either. That was good enough for me.

Paper bag smashed into the smallest possible package and tucked under my right arm, I shot off the stoop a few paces behind, my shoe steps giving me away. She had to know I was behind her, but her pace didn't change. My own steps were rushed to keep up and within two blocks I was breathless. I don't know how far we walked to get to the inner city trains. The neighborhood had changed and night drew close around us. The people became rougher and louder and I worked to stay close, my fear making shadows jump before they fell harmlessly away. Finally, we reached a part of town which looked more closed than any I'd seen so far. Street alcoholics lay in doorways and beside buildings. Some men were openly drinking, some looking already passed out. People didn't just loll in the street around here.

If I hadn't paid close attention just then, I might not have seen her go in. She knocked, paused a moment, then went on in. There was music coming from inside and once the door opened I could hear lots of women's voices talking and laughing. Oh, no. It was a bar! I thought. "She's going to get drunk! She's in there getting drunk and I'm out here and now she'll come out a mess and throw things at me."

I waited through the arrival of seemingly hundreds of mostly women visitors just off to the side of the building. Some wore suits, dark blues and browns with hats tilted to one side, their hair and eyes barely visible. Their attire was a statement, their look a look of take-charge. Often, the women with them wore their hair piled high in a flawless beehive. Others were more everyday, chino pants or dresses, their attire a statement I understood too. I was invisible, I think to the new arrivals, but not too far into the deep shadows. As my fear leveled off, my curiosity was just about intolerable. I didn't bother myself with questions about being at the right place or about the women I saw going in. The Lesbians-decoder instinct in my soul was at full tilt and I was desperate to be inside. Sometime in the dark of night, I pulled my courage tight around me and went up to the door. I knocked a few sharp raps—I wanted to sound authentic. A square porthole opened just over my head, just like at the castle of the wizard of oz. I stepped back so I could be seen. When she looked out, I just smiled at her. It was "HER," another one, one among the many "hers" that I saw that night. She laughed when she saw me and began to taunt me a little. "Hey, is your mama in here? Whatcha doing out after your bedtime? Hey, your mama know where you are?" Her laughter softened and she asked again, "Hey, your mama in here?" Not one to miss a chance, I nodded yes, expecting the bouncer to open the door and let me in. No such luck. She told me to run along home and wait there for my mama. I ducked back into the dark beside the building and waited. It could be a very long wait and I didn't want to fall asleep so I began pitching beer bottles against the side of the building next door. It was noisy and very satisfying and, I shortly discovered, made everyone who came out look into the alley. Lots of the women were drunk, but they were laughing and I felt so happy, just so very happy, to be with them for a moment.

I guess I could have chosen almost any of the women leaving the bar. Most of those coming out would have fulfilled my idea of "HER," although an awful lot of them looked like regular women and seemed a little risky.

II.

It was so late. I was dog-tired and nearly asleep, having wearied of my beer bottle toss. I had given up for the night now, and didn't want to move. Not until I had a glimpse of those blazing blue-white chinos. The knees bagged a little, the crease evident but no longer razor sharp. But the step was still resolute and firm. I moved on the edge of my second

246

wind and trotted off after "HER," remembering it would be a long walk. Again, I know she heard my footfall behind her. I made no attempt to hide or cover the fact that I was following her. She never acknowledged me at all that night. Not by a word, not by a gesture. I admired her cool and bravery. I aspired to look like her in those chinos. I loved her a lot.

For two more days, I walked 20 to 50 paces behind her. I studied her walk until I thought I could pick her out of a crowd. I made up stories about her life and decided maybe she needed someone to take care of her. She was always alone . . . and so was I. I was a woman now, and I would take care of her. I walked her to the trains when she went to work, but decided to wait at the station for her to come back instead of traveling around the city and spending my money. I was there at the station when she climbed into the twilight along with hundreds of travelers. I followed her to the grocery store, and on the second day dared to go inside while she bought a few things. She smoked Pall Mall and Chesterfield cigarettes, although I had never actually seen her light up. I bet she would look cool smoking a cigarette.

I stole a package of snowball cupcakes that day. You know them, they were covered with coconut sprinkles on the thick marshmallow layer. Chocolate cupcakes with creme in the middle. They were a treat but were full of sugar so they were filling too. It was kind of thrilling even though it made me sick, too. I was outside waiting when she left the store. I was so happy.

She took maybe fifteen steps before she turned around to face me. I almost cried, the panic rose so fast. An unsuppressible yelp escaped from my throat. I didn't want her to be angry or to tell me to get lost. No word from either of us. She started to say something, her eyes working to tell me quick, without preface or explanation, something I should already know. But . . . nothing. Not a word. She turned away, leaving me desolate, certain it was all over. No real change in her walk, only slower maybe, and straight home as usual. She went up the six steps to unlock the front door, leaving me sitting on the bottom stair while night closed in.

I chose the white snowball first, kind of in her honor. Then I ate the pink one, sad but not quite sure what our brief encounter meant. I guessed that she had considered me, maybe like an intriguing book cover, but I had been rejected, sort of thrown away.

From Her stoop, I watched some old man walking his dog, a spotted dog, sniffing everywhere along the sidewalk. I concentrated on the dog, trying with my mind's sheer will to make her stop in place or do some funny trick. They walked on by, passing from my right to my left. I concentrated hard and didn't hear the door open behind me. It seemed that suddenly She was there but I didn't think She was trying to be quiet.

She just said "C'mon. Food upstairs." As though I cared. As though I would live to eat a meal being that close to Her. As though anything else could matter. As though the rushing noise in my ears wasn't a faint about to happen. Up we went, me following Her, up four flights, up through unreality and amazement.

She led me through the front door into the livingroom where two more women were waiting. Both of them were beaming smiles at me as though I had just won something and they were really proud of me. A tray had been set up with two sandwiches and a tall glass of orange juice . . . clearly, they had talked about this for a while and had prepared for me to be there.

Epilogue

I lived with these women for nearly two years. Life was a "snowball cupcake," sweet and filling. We shared a great life, where I learned old-fashioned butch ways from S. and learned how to properly put out the trash from L. and J. J. taught me to smoke Chesterfields, and L. often left extra Pall Mall cigarettes in my shirt pocket. S. told me to treat all women well, to respect the varied opinions of women and to put Lesbians first in my life. We lived in a four-story walk up. We all worked because money was tight. L. was a waitress, S. worked in a factory, J. worked at a Woolworths and I did what I could. I never did dishes.

I was forcibly sent back to my parents when the truant officer caught me stacking beer bottles behind the bar when I should have been learning how to sit still for hours at a time. I wouldn't give him the names of the Lesbians I lived with because I knew they would be punished for "harboring me." Later, I tried unsuccessfully to find them. I still want very much to thank them.

Not too many years later, I fell in "love" with feminism. Putting aside the old butch lifestyle with a bit of difficulty, I now treat women better by being an equal. I have taken the advice to "respect the opinions of all women" under advisement. I would do it all over again if I had the chance.

Contributors' Notes

ADRIENNE LAUBY: I am a disabled lesbian with a history in the anti-war, feminist, and gay rights movements. My involvement with punk is a fairly recent development. I am working on a novel about the characters in "Last Night at The Core." Two of my other short stories can be found in *With Wings,* an anthology of writing about disability by women, published by The Feminist Press, and the book, *Memories and Visions, Women's Fantasy and Science* from Crossing Press.

ALISON J. LAURIE was born in Aotearoa/New Zealand in 1941 of mostly pakeha and some Maori ancestry. She presently teaches Women's Studies at Victoria University of Wellington, including a course on lesbian identity, and lives in a house by the sea with numerous poodles, cats and a goat.

ALIX DOBKIN: I was born and raised in New York City (and Philadelphia) in a culturally rich and politically aware, active, and loving family. At 16, I became a part-time professional folksinger until I graduated from The Tyler School of Fine Arts at Temple University with a BFA in 1962. After that, I worked full-time as an entertainer, which I do to this day in addition to my work as a mother, writer and lecturer/educator.

In 1973, Kay Gardner and I produced the first widely-distributed Lesbian record album, *Lavender Jane Loves Women.* Ever since I came out with Liza Cowan in 1972, my major work has been focused on the creation and development of international Lesbian Networks and the establishment of a viable Women's Cultural Industry. When I tour internationally, the enthusiastic response to my Lesbian-identified show and music thrills me. I love thrills.

My home is in Woodstock, NY with Liza.

ANNA LIVIA was born in Dublin in 1955, spent her childhood in Africa, adolescence in London; mother and sisters live in Australia. She is the author of *Relatively Norma, Accommodation Offered, Incidents Involving Warmth,* and *Bulldozer Rising*; currently working on *Minimax* (sequel to *Relatively Norma*) and *Saccharine Cyanide* (a new collection of short stories). She has also published a number of articles on: gossip, roles, presumption, sex, politics and fiction.

BERTA R. FREISTADT is a typical Londoner—born of Austro-Hungarian, Irish-Scottish parents, half Jewish and 47 years old. She has poetry and stories published in Britain by Chatto, Metheun, Prism Press, Sheba and The Women's Press. She teaches creative writing and poetry performance. A lapsed playwright soon to return to that vice again: She is not writing a novel.

BETH KARBE: I've been a lesbian as far back as I can remember, and I continue to feel deeply grateful to and inspired by those who, against impossible odds, courageously came before me.

BEV JO: I'm a working-class, disabled Dyke of Irish, English, German and French ancestry. I'm just finishing a book about Dyke Separatism called *Dykes-Loving-Dykes*, with my dear friends Linda Strega and Ruston. We're working on building an international Dyke Separatist community and love to meet other Separatists.

CANDIS J. GRAHAM: I was born on February 14, 1949 in Kincardine (Ontario) of Scottish and British ancestors. Although I dream of being a citizen of the world, I am Canadian by birth and residence. I have skin the color of aging, unfinished pine and lots of white hair. After coming out in 1974 and discovering conscious feminism at the same time, I started writing (again, as an adult, after giving it up when I was in my teens) in 1976. I have been looking for, and often finding, dykes ever since. My stories have appeared in periodicals such as *Common Lives/Lesbian Lives* and *Fireweed*, and a few anthologies including *By Word of Mouth* and *Dykeversions*. I am a contributing editor to a newsletter of innovative feminist writing, *(f.)Lip*. I support myself and my writing by doing part-time office work for a national child care advocacy association. "Baby Fingers" is dedicated to Lise Corbeil-Vincent.

CATHERINE ODETTE: I own so many labels I don't know where to begin. I am a lifelong Lesbian Separatist man-hater, a disabled, Jewish daughter of Holocaust Survivors, an anti-psychiatry survivor of much of their abuse, a shit-kickin', raised-poor dyke who thinks pain is painful, and love is lovely. I have the perfect partner, Sara, and together she and I want to be part of making a better world for dykes. I am the publisher-member of a six-women collective which puts out a radical disability rag called *Dykes, Disability & Stuff*, which can be found at P.O. Box 6194, Boston, MA 02114. 'Nuff said? Yeah.

CATHY AVILA: I came to separatism soon after my brief involvement with NOW. I still live in southern California, but my desire and need to connect with other Lesbians and work on building strong Lesbian community has me actively working on moving out of this wasteland. It never ceases to amaze me what a different woman I am and how much my life has changed since I came out as a Lesbian.

DONNA ALLEGRA: I write and dance in New York City. I have published poems and short stories in *Sinister Wisdom, Conditions, Common Lives/ Lesbian Lives*, and *Azalea*; essays in *Heresies* and *Lesbian Ethics*. I have essays in *Out the Other Side: Contemporary Lesbian Writing*, edited by Christian McEwen and Sue O'Sullivan, and *The Original Coming Out Stories*, edited by Julia Penelope and Susan J. Wolfe. And then, there are the works I've lost track of. I am working myself up to self-publishing my poems and stories.

ELENI PRINEAS lives in Sydney, playing soccer with other Lesbians as often as possible.

J. L. WILLIAMS: I am a white, working class woman with four sisters who grew up in central Arizona. My mother supported us, from the time I was seven, on a secretary's salary. Watching her, I learned the miracles sheer determination can create. I also learned the tragedy of loyalty and energy misdirected. She never wanted to be a mother, but a teacher and writer. I moved to Canada in 1975 after serving in the U.S. Navy for three years as a photographer. My first novel, *Skuttlebutt*, will be published in 1990.

JANELLE M. LAVELLE is a 37-year-old "professional queer" in Greensboro, North Carolina who is associate editor of the state's gay and lesbian newspaper, *The Front Page*, co-chair of the N.C. Human Rights Fund, and administrator of a state grant targeting AIDS risk reduction (Jesse Helms won't let her call it "safe sex") for gay men. She is a regular writer for a variety of Southern and lesbian publications, and was a contributor to the second edition of *The Original Coming Out Stories*. All of her editors complain about her paragraph transitions. She and her long-time Significant Other, AIDS worker Patricia Crocker, are seriously outnumbered by their pets.

JANET E. AALFS: I was a shy child. Now it has become difficult to shut me up. I have been writing, seriously, since I discovered pencil and paper and fighting, seriously, all my life. I live and work in the Pioneer Valley of Western Massachusetts. Lawrence College. I am a black belt in karate and arnis (Filipino Stickfighting) and am one of the head instructors of Valley Women's Martial Arts, a school for women and children. I will graduate in the Spring of 1990 from the MFA Program in Writing at Sarah Lawrence College. My writing has appeared in *Sinister Wisdom, Womanspirit, Sojourner, Lady-Unique-Inclination-of-the-Night, Praxis, Lesbian Bedtime Stories, Red Flower, Touching Fire, Common Lives/Lesbian Lives, The Evergreen Chronicles*, and *Valley Women's Voice*.

All six feet and one inch of my white, middle-class, Lesbian body that appeared on this earth (in smaller form) in 1956 is proud to be part of a family of blood relatives that includes other Lesbians, as well as to have created for myself a chosen family of loving, diverse, and rebellious women. I hope to continue sharing my life with such feisty folks and to grow ever more exuberant each glorious day.

JAY REED: Have juggled jobs as teacher, secretary, mother, office manager, campus housing inspector & conference coordinator and free-lance legal courier, mainly in the Berkeley-San Francisco Bay Area. Published a book of poems, *Infinitude* (Page/Wand Press, 1986). My poetry and short stories have appeared in *Sagewoman, Common Lives/Lesbian Lives, Forum, Wyoming, Hub of the Wheel, The Berkeley Review of Books, We Are Everywhere,* and *The Original Coming Out Stories* (Expanded Edition).

JILL FLYE: I am a 28-year-old boat-dyke from the north of England. In 1987 I joined a lesbian writers' group while living in London. "Soap" was a homework project. Since then I have travelled the English canals in my narrowboat home, working on a children's book and a lesbian novel. I'm now living on the Rochdale Canal, with dog and two cats, and I work on trip-boats.

JULIE REIDY is a Sagittarian Tiger of '62 vintage—a combination that behaves like a volvo in need of a tune-up. Spurt, splutter, spurt . . . Set out on the road from Aotearoa in 1987, temporarily broke down in London in '88 and am now recharging the batteries in a country cottage with my lover and Ludwig, the mouse catcher. Found enough ego somewhere between India and Hong Kong to want to be a writer as well as a letter writer. While most of my stories to date (all four!) have been in the lands of exotic travels I am now beginning to travel inwards and discover as yet untold stories. I have previously had travel and music articles, poems and essays published in various newspapers and magazines. This is my first venture into more permanent print.

LAURA DAVIS is the co-author of *The Courage to Heal: A Guide for Women Survivors of Child Sexual Abuse,* and author of *The Courage to Heal Workbook,* and a closet fiction writer in her spare time. When she was twenty-five she spent two years as a news reporter and talk show host in Alaska.

LINDA M. PETERSON: I live in Tokyo, Japan, with Amanda Hayman, an English Lesbian writer, and Blackberry, a Japanese cat familiar. I wish Lesbians valued their own ideas, lives and history, as much as Mormons do. Anyway, it fascinates me that I can write my ideas about my life and suddenly it's history—or, should I say?—herstory.

MARILYN MURPHY: I am an Irish/Italian, Catholic-raised, upwardly mobile, working-class, fifty-seven-year-old, radical feminist writer, organizer, political activist, Lesbian-Come-Lately and the eldest of five sisters. Two of my four sisters and one of my three daughters are also Lesbians-Come-Lately. I recently moved, with my Lifelong Lesbian Companion Lover, Irene Weiss, from Los Angeles to St. Augustine, Florida. Now, when we are not on the road looking for Lesbians, we live in a cottage on the beach at the Pagoda where we enjoy meeting all the different kinds of Lesbians who visit this Lesbian village/ resort.

MERRIL MUSHROOM: Penny is now Julia, I am still Merril, we are still friends, and my life has not been the same since we two Lesbians found each other.

ROSEMARY REEVES: It has been eleven years since my London adventure. I ended up in California, where I met nudists, pagans, communists, roller-skating women in bikinis, and people who ate watercress sandwiches. I now live in New Jersey with my lover of three years. We work in a factory and have a cat named Sappho.

SHEILA ANNE: I am a Lesbian Separatist of six years who is a second generation swedish and first generation irish-american Dyke, raised catholic in a white working-class, urban community. Having learned the pleasure of Lesbian space at the Saint's Bar, I create Lesbian and Separatist space wherever I can. Cecilia, my partner of seven-and-a-half years, and I put out *S.E.P.S.*, a newsletter for Lesbian Separatists which begins her fourth year of distribution. I look forward to a world where all my work supports only what I believe in. I hope to see you there.

SHELLEY ANDERSON was born and raised in Florida. She escaped becoming a Southern lady by joining the U.S. Army. She escaped the Army by becoming a conscientious objector. She then fled to The Netherlands, where she works as a journalist and devotes any spare time to the International Lesbian Information Service. Any time left over from this is spent writing a novel based on her Army experiences and searching for the perfect plate of grits.

SUSAN J. WOLFE: I was born in New York City, into a Jewish working-class family who expected me to get married, and I did. I now live a middle-class life in Vermillion, South Dakota as an academic—as middle-class as one can be as an out-front lesbian in a Midwest town of under 10,000 people—with the woman I've loved deeply for years. I'd say I was a common, "garden-variety lesbian," but I've never met one of those. We all seem quite extraordinary to me.

T. LYNN is an editor and freelance writer in Boston. She is currently working on her first novel.

TERRI DE LA PEÑA is a book reviewer for *The Lesbian News* in Los Angeles, and a contributor to the second edition of *The Coming Out Stories*. Her fiction appears in *Lesbian Bedtime Stories*, *Intricate Passions*, *Finding Courage*, *The One You Call Sister*, and is forthcoming in *Word of Mouth* and *Third Woman*. Following the completion of *Margins*, her novel-in-progress, Terri plans to write more stories about "Sequences" characters Monica Tovar and Jozie Krozinski.

*The Crossing Press
publishes a full selection of
feminist titles.
To receive our current catalog,
please call —Toll Free—800/777-1048.*

© Debbie Alicen

Julia Penelope is co-editor of *The Original Coming Out Stories* with Susan J. Wolfe and co-author of *Found Goddesses: From Asphalta to Viscera* with Morgan Grey. She lives near Boston.

© Debbie Alicen

Sarah Valentine's writing has appeared in *For Lesbians Only* and *The Original Coming Out Stories*.